Under the Strain of Color

A volume in the series

Cornell Studies in the History of Psychiatry

Edited by Sander L. Gilman and George J. Makari

A list of titles in the series is available at www.cornellpress.cornell.edu.

Under the Strain of Color

Harlem's Lafargue Clinic and the Promise of an Antiracist Psychiatry

Gabriel N. Mendes

Cornell University Press

Ithaca and London

First published 2015 by Cornell University Press
First printing, Cornell Paperbacks, 2015

Library of Congress Cataloging-in-Publication Data

Mendes, Gabriel N., 1972– author.
   Under the strain of color : Harlem's Lafargue Clinic and the promise of an antiracist psychiatry / Gabriel N. Mendes.
      pages cm. — (Cornell studies in the history of psychiatry)
   Includes bibliographical references and index.
   ISBN 978-0-8014-5350-2 (cloth : alk. paper)
   1. African Americans—Mental health services—New York (State)—New York. 2. African Americans—Mental health—New York (State)—New York. 3. Social psychiatry—New York (State)—New York. 4. Community psychiatry—New York (State)—New York. 5. Lafargue Clinic (New York, N.Y.) 6. Wright, Richard, 1908–1960. 7. Wertham, Fredric, 1895–1981. 8. Harlem (New York, N.Y.) I. Title.
   RC451.5.N4M43 2015
   616.890089'96073—dc23   2015005315

Cloth printing   10 9 8 7 6 5 4 3 2 1
Paperback printing   10 9 8 7 6 5 4 3 2 1

For my father Maxwell Mendes, the Tod Cliftons,
and the Lafargue Clinic patients

In practically all its divergences, American Negro culture is not something independent of general American culture. It is a distorted development, or a pathological condition, of the general American culture.

Gunnar Myrdal, *An America Dilemma*, 1944

It does not occur to Myrdal that many of the Negro cultural manifestations which he considers merely reflective might also embody a *rejection* of what he considers "higher values.". . . It is only partially true that Negroes turn away from white patterns because they are refused participation. There is nothing like distance to create objectivity, and exclusion gives rise to counter values. . . . It will take a deeper science than Myrdal's—deep as that might be—to analyze what is happening among the masses of Negroes.

Ralph Ellison, "*An American Dilemma*: A Review," 1944

The Freudians talk about the Id
And bury it below.

But Richard Wright took off the lid
And let us see the woe.

Dr. Fredric Wertham, "Underground," 1942

Contents

ACKNOWLEDGMENTS

I have been blessed with some extraordinary guides, mentors, colleagues, friends, and, above all, family. Without those people who have both challenged me and had my back as I worked on this project, the book you are now reading would never have been possible. This book had its incubation in a set of conversations I had in graduate school with a truly remarkable group of scholars and teachers at Brown University. Foremost among them was James T. Campbell, whose model of integrity and rigorous thinking and writing remains a constant source of inspiration and guidance in every single aspect of my life as a scholar. I am especially grateful to Jim for his investment in the development of this project and for his close and illuminating readings of draft after draft of each chapter. Most of all I appreciate his contagious enthusiasm for the art of historical narrative. To this day, I walk away from conversations with Jim enlightened and enlivened, rededicated to the task at hand. I also offer my most sincere thanks to Mari Jo Buhle and B. Anthony Bogues. They modeled for me all that I aspire to be as a rigorous and responsive mentor and guide to students.

While in Providence I found an invaluable intellectual community both inside and outside the walls of Brown University. I thank Doug Brown, Liza Burbank, Marcia Chatelain, Tom Chen, Themis Chronopoulos, Joe Clark,

Moritz Ege, Gill Frank, Jim Gatewood, C. Morgan Grefe, Jonathan Hagel, Anas Hamimech, Jibade-Khalil Huffman, Sheyda Jahanbani, Katie C. Miller, S. Ani Mukherji, Jason Pontius, Kate Schapira, Kate Schatz, and Sarah Wald. I especially thank Ani, Jonathan, and Sheyda, who have been my closest intellectual companions on this journey. Thank you, Katie, for allowing me to kvetch to you over the years and for letting me bombard you with crudely written paragraphs masquerading as correspondence.

This book would not have been possible without the support of librarians and archivists at Brown University, the Schomburg Center for Research in Black Culture, Yale University, Columbia University, Johns Hopkins University, and the Library of Congress. Nor would it have been possible without fellowships from the Brown Graduate School and Emmanuel College. I would especially like to thank Emmanuel College's Nancy Northrup, Bill Leonard, and Javier Marion for their hospitality and guidance during my year at Emmanuel as a Diversity Dissertation Fellow.

I thank Samuel K. Roberts for his early encouragement of my project and for providing me with a vital forum in which to share my research. Alongside Sam, a number of other colleagues have contributed to the development and completion of this project. I thank most especially Bart Beaty, Leah Gordon, and Jay Garcia. I've been tremendously lucky as well to have a set of friends and confidants who've been there to keep me intellectually and existentially sane over the years. They have rescued me from the monotony of the solitary life of the desk on many occasions. And it has often been my nonacademic friends who have reminded me of the necessity that this book be in the world for everyday people to read. Thank you to Joe Barbour, Ben Carlin, Derek Andrew Curtis, Quentin DiDonna, Jamahl Gambler, Michael Guilbert, Kibria Sarkisian, Alyasha Owerka-Moore, Darryl A. Smith, and my Tower Bar crew.

The University of California, San Diego, has provided generous research and writing support through the Hellman Family Fellowship, the Faculty Career Development Grant, and the Academic Senate Research Grant. At UCSD, I have been fortunate to have Natalia Molina and Curtis Marez as my official faculty mentors. They are two of the most patient, generous, and engaged scholars I have ever encountered within American academia. I have also been the recipient of unstinting support and guidance from past chairs of the Ethnic Studies Department, Ross Frank and Yen Le Espiritu. Not only did they read and comment on chapter drafts of the book, but they consistently showed buoyant enthusiasm for my research. I thank as well the rest of my colleagues in Ethnic Studies, its faculty, its graduate students, and its staff, most especially Mary Polytaridis and Samira Khazai for their help in navigating the UC behemoth and for their unflagging faith that I would get this book done! I also thank the Urban Studies and Planning Department, especially its chair, Steve Erie. And I must single out two recent UCSD PhDs for being treasured inter-locutors, comrades, and constant caregivers: thank you to Jose Fuste and Jade Power Sotomayor. A quick shout to Cutler Edwards, a valued friend and a real up-and-comer. Thanks to Salvador Zarate for his assistance in the final stage of completing the book.

It is impossible to reflect in words the gratitude I have for the love and support my brother Isak and my sisters Key, Ahnya, and Cybele have shown me over the years. Each of them contributed in ways tangible and intangible to my dedication to the life of the mind, the driving force of my own way of being in the world. I thank my mother, Yvonne Marie Clark, for her unconditional love and for her enthusiasm about all I say and do—just what I always need when the going is rough.

I am so very lucky that Arlene C. Lopez came back into my life just over three years ago. I am profoundly thankful for the love, patience, hard work, and commitment I receive from her. She has seriously been this book's most consistent booster since the moment I gave her the elevator pitch on its subject and its argument.

Lastly, I thank the editors of this series, Sander L. Gilman and George J. Makari, along with my editors, John Ackerman and Michael McGandy, the assistant to the director, Michael Morris, Karen Hwa, as well as the rest of the staff at Cornell University Press responsible for publishing and marketing this book.

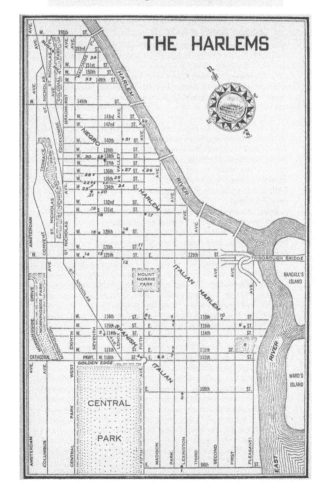

Figures 1 and 2. The Harlems. From *New York City Guide*, American Guide Series, Works Progress Administration (New York: Random House, 1939). Copyright © 1939 by the Guilds' Committee of the Federal Writers' Publications Inc.

INTRODUCTION

"A Deeper Science"

At some time or other the conscience of society will awake and remind it that
the poor man should have just as much right to assistance for his mind as
he now has to the life-saving help offered by surgery; and that the neuroses
threaten public health no less than tuberculosis, and can be left as little to
the latter to the impotent care of individual members of the community. . . .
It may be a long time before the State comes to see these duties as urgent.
Present conditions may delay its arrival even longer. Probably these
institutions will first be started by private charity. Some time or other,
however, it must come to this.

SIGMUND FREUD, "LINES OF ADVANCE IN PSYCHO-ANALYTIC THERAPY," 1918

On October 11, 1941, the *New York Amsterdam News* ran a headline: "Dick
Wright's Bigger Thomas Comes to Life in Clinton Brewer." Brewer was
a black man who had been convicted in 1923, at the age of eighteen, of
stabbing his teenage wife to death. While at the New Jersey State Prison
in Trenton, he read *Native Son*, Richard Wright's controversial novel that
told the story of Bigger Thomas, a young black Chicagoan who murders
two women, one white and one black, and is later executed. Joining many
other black male prisoners who felt that Wright had in some way told their
own story through the figure of Bigger, Brewer wrote to Wright in hopes
that the novelist might be an ally in his effort to be paroled. Impressed
by the letter—and by the fact that Brewer had taught himself music

composition—Wright visited him in prison in the winter of 1941 and soon dispatched a letter to the governor of New Jersey asking for his parole. *Time* magazine reported on Wright's successful intervention:

> The New Jersey State Court of Pardons last week paroled a lifer, Negro Clinton Brewer, because during 19 years in jail he had become a musician. He had written Stampede in G Minor, a jazz tune which sold well on an Okeh record; stood to get an orchestra arranger's job if freed. Convict Brewer, who had killed his wife during a quarrel, lost his speech because of a prison neurosis. Negro Richard Wright, author of Native Son (the story of a Negro killer), became interested in Musician Brewer. So did Jazz Pundit John Hammond and Band Leader Count Basie, who recorded Stampede and offered the prisoner a job.[1]

As Wright's biographer, Michel Fabre, later explained: "Wright . . . felt convinced, as he told the governor, that Brewer had established through his art an organic social relationship to the world, making a second offense highly unlikely."[2] He was wrong. After working with the Count Basie Orchestra for three months, Brewer killed Mrs. Wilhelmina Washington, a mother of two, because she refused to marry him. He was quickly arrested, convicted, and sentenced to death.[3]

That same October, Wright received a copy of Dr. Fredric Wertham's recently published *Dark Legend: A Study in Murder*.[4] Best remembered today as the author of the anti–comic book polemic *Seduction of the Innocent* (1954), Wertham was at the time senior psychiatrist of the New York City Department of Hospitals, as well as an increasingly prominent public voice of psychiatry.[5] He wrote to Wright at the suggestion of the radical journalist Ella Winter, an acquaintance of the novelist who happened to be Wertham's first cousin.[6] *Dark Legend* presented a psychoanalytic portrait of a young Italian immigrant, Gino, who had killed his mother, ostensibly because she had dishonored his dead father through her promiscuity. Based chiefly on a clinical examination of Gino, the book was also a work of literary analysis, with figures such as Orestes and Hamlet serving as archetypes for Wertham's exploration of the unconscious motivations that contributed to Gino's urge to commit matricide.

Wright read *Dark Legend* and immediately sent an enthusiastic letter to Wertham. "My reactions to Gino, his plight and his crime were so many and varied that it would be futile to attempt to set them down in a letter,"

Figure 3. Richard Wright (*right*) and Count Basie at a recording session in New York City on November 24, 1940. Courtesy of Bettmann / Corbis Images.

he wrote. "It is enough to say that I think it is the most comprehensive psychological statement in relation to contemporary crime that I have come across. Indeed, it is as fascinating as any novel."[7] Another letter followed, in which Wright asked Wertham to examine Brewer, whom he believed to be psychotic rather than a cold-blooded murderer. Brewer had been a guest in Wright's home, had sat with him and his wife Ellen for dinner, and news of the second murder had shaken the novelist. Wertham accepted the invitation and examined Brewer. In a later sentencing hearing, Wertham testified that Brewer exhibited a psychotic obsession with control over women and thus was "not in his right mind" at the time of the murder. His testimony was successful; Brewer was spared the death penalty.[8]

The Clinton Brewer case was for Wright and Wertham the genesis of both a personal friendship and a shared commitment to providing psychiatric care to those who had been previously excluded from it: the poor, the oppressed, and, above all, black people. Wright had been interested in the nature of madness for several years, but Brewer's second murder propelled him toward a systematic attempt to understand sources of mental stress and disorder that could lead a person to murderous violence. Wright's search for answers inspired him to participate in practical efforts to address the mental health of those he believed to be in most need of access to treatment and care: black people in the ghettos of northern U.S. cities. He was convinced that humane psychotherapy could alleviate much of the psychic strain that engendered violence against others and oneself. He joined Wertham in the belief that psychotherapy rooted in a recognition of the social realities of American life—of racism, violence, and economic exploitation—could provide a weapon in the quest for racial justice. As Wright and Wertham became closer, their relationship culminated in March 1946 with the founding of the first outpatient mental health clinic in and for the community of Harlem, New York, the Lafargue Mental Hygiene Clinic.

Under the Strain of Color tells the story of how Richard Wright and Fredric Wertham, along with an interracial group of intellectuals, doctors, clergy, and artists, attempted to establish a progressive model of mental health care as an integral part of the struggle for racial equality in the United States in the early post–World War II era. And it reveals the Lafargue Clinic to be a unique prism through which to navigate the contours of race on the unsteady terrain of the midcentury U.S. urban North.

In and for the Community

Fredric Wertham had long wanted to establish a clinic in New York City that would offer inexpensive psychotherapy to African Americans, along with anyone else who could not afford psychiatric treatment. Born in Nuremberg, Bavaria, in 1895 to a nonreligious Jewish family, Wertham attended some of the most prestigious universities in Europe, including King's College in London and the Universities of Erlangen and Munich. He received his medical degree in 1921 from the University of Würzburg, and did postgraduate work at the Universities of Paris and Vienna, becoming an assistant at Dr. Emil Kraepelin's famed German Institute for Psychiatric Research, in Munich in 1922. At the end of that year he emigrated to the United States, where he took a position at the Phipps Psychiatric Clinic at Johns Hopkins, working with Dr. Adolf Meyer, America's preeminent psychiatrist at the time. Meyer reputedly coined the term "mental hygiene" around 1910 to refer to the provision of psychiatric services outside of asylums, as a broad type of public mental health program.[9] While living in Baltimore in the late 1920s, Wertham became acquainted with the renowned lawyer Clarence Darrow. Darrow soon began referring his black clients to Dr. Wertham because he was the only psychiatrist Darrow knew who was sympathetic to examining and treating African Americans. It was then that Wertham became concerned about the lack of medical and mental health services for black Americans. When he went to work in the psychiatric clinic of New York's Court of General Sessions in 1932, he noted very early on the relationship between racism, violence, and mental disorders.[10]

There in New York City, Wertham saw repeated examples of discrimination against African Americans who either voluntarily sought psychotherapy or who were committed to institutions such as Bellevue Mental Hospital, where he directed its Mental Hygiene Clinic from 1936 to 1939.[11] If the popular 1940 book *Bellevue*, by Lorraine Maynard, is any guide, clinicians hardly regarded black patients in any ward of Bellevue as people possessing a mental makeup akin to that of any of the various "white peoples" who frequented the hospital.[12] According to Maynard, who wrote her tabloid-style, behind-the-scenes exposé with the help of a Bellevue staff doctor named Laurence Miscall,

> [Often] it is possible, with a little practice, to estimate a person's general condition by his typically racial response. . . . Most colored folk seem able to accept life as it comes and take trouble in stride. They are apt to make a fine recovery after operation because of this calm, positive flair for living in the moment. They do not get so tense and flurried as other people, and it just

doesn't occur to them to expect the worst. . . . *The average negro is often too inured to discomfort for his own good. Being less physically, mentally or aesthetically sensitive than a white*, what he will stand without a murmur is sometimes amazing to the staff.

Published in the same year as Wright's *Native Son*, this book consistently trafficked in a variety of well-worn stereotypes about how "Polacks," "Hebrews," "Slovaks," "Spaniards," "negros," and other "races" interacted with hospital staff. Perhaps unwittingly, Maynard documented how Bellevue staff used the mark of racial difference as a substitute for a truly therapeutic reckoning with the problem of diagnosis and treatment for both physical and mental traumas and diseases.[13]

Wertham's experiences at Bellevue led him to begin pushing for the establishment of a nondiscriminatory clinic that would address the mental health care needs of African Americans, and he argued that it should be housed within the black community itself, most specifically Harlem. In the late 1930s, Wertham had elicited the interest of the La Guardia administration in a plan to have New York City open and support a mental hygiene clinic in Harlem. But the city never followed through on the plan.[14] When Wertham's attempts to have a city-sponsored clinic foundered, he approached several corporations and philanthropies. He was denied by each of them.

One evening in late 1945, Wertham met for tea with Wright and Earl Brown, the first black staff writer for *Life* magazine.[15] That night, Wertham was again lamenting his inability to secure funding for a Harlem clinic project providing inexpensive psychotherapy to African Americans, along with anyone else who could not afford psychiatric treatment. Sitting in the Gramercy Park apartment in Manhattan that he shared with his wife, Florence Hesketh, Wertham jumped up from his seat and asked his guests, "Do we really need the money?" In the manner that would come to garner him both praise and scorn, allies and enemies, Wertham exclaimed, "Let's begin without money; we'll do our worrying later. All we need is talent, and I can get that. Let those of us who feel the need contribute our services and see if psychiatry cannot be given to the poor."[16]

Along with having little money, Wertham, Brown, and Wright had no space in Harlem to establish a clinic. Harlem had been a crowded and congested section of New York for many years, but the result of wartime migration was a population of about four hundred thousand African Americans living in a space designed to house seventy-five thousand people. On average there were sixteen hundred people per acre, as compared to six hundred per acre on the notoriously overcrowded Lower East Side.[17]

Wertham soon found an unlikely home for the clinic, as well as a life-long ally. In the winter of 1946, the Reverend Shelton Hale Bishop, rector of St. Philip's Episcopal Church on West 134th Street in Harlem, offered Wertham the use of two rooms in the basement of the church parish house. Bishop had learned of the clinic proposal from the writer Ralph Ellison, who had become associated with Wertham, and of the latest plan through Richard Wright. Bishop was an African American progressive Episcopal priest known for his commitment to social justice and violence-prevention programs, and one of the few prominent clergymen to embrace psychotherapy as a component of his ministry.[18]

The Lafargue Mental Hygiene Clinic opened its doors without much fanfare on March 8, 1946, and it operated every Tuesday and Friday evening until it closed in November 1958. The clinic charged its patients twenty-five cents per visit and fifty cents for testifying in court on their behalf if necessary.[19] It was free, though, for those who could pay nothing. In its first year and a half alone the clinic saw over two thousand patients, both adults and children. Some were simply in need of someone to talk to about their daily problems; some were indeed suffering from neuroses; others were diagnosed with a psychosis. Some were offered medication to alleviate the immediate tension or anxiety they were undergoing, and in some cases patients were quickly referred to hospitals that the staff deemed trustworthy. The clinic's staff was drawn from friends, colleagues, and students of Dr. Wertham, as well as members of the Harlem community. All the staff members offered their services free of charge. At its start, the clinic received only small financial contributions from individual, private donors. It would never garner the type of government or philanthropic funding it needed to develop into a full-time outpatient clinic. (In a letter to Wright, Wertham's wife, Hesketh, wrote, "There has been another rebuff from Marshall Field. I sent you the correspondence. It's really a definite class thing—no money from the rich and every day, practically, a few dollars from the poor."[20]) With the combination of Reverend Bishop's retirement from St. Philip's in 1957 and "an unforeseen accumulation of deaths and severe illnesses" among staff members in the subsequent year,

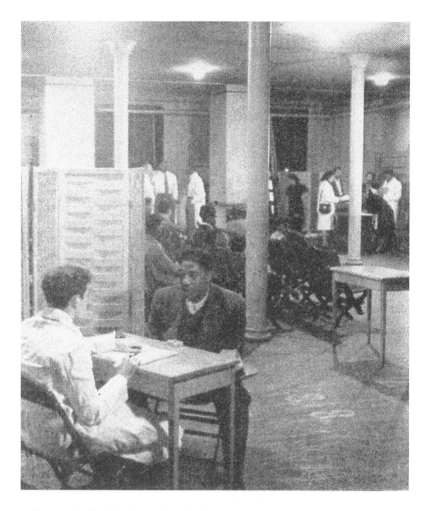

Figure 4. Inside the Lafargue Clinic, St. Philip's Episcopal Church parish house basement, February 1948. Photo by Lisa Larsen.

the Lafargue Clinic announced in December 1958 that it would have to cease operating.[21]

The clinic took its name and its animating philosophy from the Afro-Cuban French socialist Paul Lafargue. Lafargue (1842–1911) was a physician, an activist, and a social theorist, who, according to the clinic brochure, "devoted his whole life to the fight against oppression, prejudice, bigotry and false science." He also happened to have been married to Karl Marx's daughter Jenny Laura. A well-known and highly regarded public speaker, Lafargue also wrote a number of important books, articles, and pamphlets promoting revolutionary socialism. It was in the preface to his polemical book *The Right to Be Lazy* (1883) that he declared, "In the communist society of the future . . . the impulses of men will be given a free rein, for 'all these impulses are by nature good, we have nothing to avoid but their misuse and their excesses,' and they will not be avoided except by their mutual counter-balancing, by the harmonious development of the human organism." While not by any means a vehicle for bringing about the advent of communism, the clinic embodied its founders' embrace of Paul Lafargue's vision of social and psychological liberation.[22]

The Lafargue Clinic represented a landmark in both the history of African American encounters with psychiatry and the history of American psychotherapy's reckoning with the social sources of mental disorders.[23] The clinic explicitly incorporated the social experience of racial and class oppression into its diagnostic and therapeutic work. *Under the Strain of Color* shows that in doing so, the clinic was simultaneously a political and scientific gambit, challenging both a racist mental health care system and supposedly color-blind psychiatrists who failed to consider black experiences of oppression in their assessment and treatment of African American patients. The Lafargue Clinic embodied a distinctly radical confrontation of the psychic costs of antiblack oppression. In doing so, it challenged American psychiatry's fundamental orientation, directing it to the social aspects of mental disorders among the oppressed.[24]

Race, Nation, and Normality

The Lafargue Clinic emerged within a nexus of discourses and institutions in the United States that viewed the mental health of each individual citizen as a matter of grave concern for the body politic. In the wake of the Second World War, American social scientists, policy makers, and social service professionals envisioned a normal American citizen whose personality was under persistent pathogenic threats both psychic and political. This idea of normality was expressed in the psychological language of developing healthy personalities, well-adjusted individuals. A considerable number of American behavioral and social scientists, social service workers, and policy makers, particularly in the North, became concerned about whether black Americans could function as healthy American citizens.

More specifically there was an interest in understanding the cultural and personal "handicaps" blacks had internalized through years of discrimination and subjugation. Many social scientists and policy makers claimed that these impediments had generated pathologies in the mind and behavior of black Americans. Instead of viewing African Americans as inherently inferior, as prior generations had, many liberal-minded scholars and policy makers contended that years of exclusion and degradation had led to deformation in the basic personality of "the Negro." Indeed, African Americans were said to bear a "mark of oppression" that negatively shaped their very perception of self and stunted their relations with white Americans and American society in general.[25]

With the Second Great Migration of African Americans out of the South, their presence in major northern cities such as New York and Philadelphia and Detroit and Chicago, and smaller cities like Providence, led white decision makers to consider in practical terms how best to deal with this burgeoning black population.[26] The increased black presence in these cities was not just a demographic issue; many people of all races, including already established black northerners, viewed black migrants as posing social and cultural problems for their cities.[27] Politicians, philanthropists, and social scientific researchers directed their attention toward *adjusting* "the Negro" to the social norms of the urban North. Problems in areas of housing, labor, education, and corrections required both insight and programmatic thinking. The increasingly authoritative knowledge and methods of psychological science and psychiatric therapy, in coordination with the other social sciences, would not only guide the work of adjusting newly settled black migrants to their new environment, but also help adjust the remainder of the black urban population, whose cultural and family life supposedly reflected forms of pathology resulting from their marginalization from the core institutions and norms of American society.[28]

Social and behavioral scientists' focus on the pathological makeup of black people—their behavior, their culture, their social structure—was not new in the early postwar years. In the four decades prior to the Second World War, however, there had been a profound shift in the way the human sciences considered what was then named "the Negro problem." During the nineteenth century and even into the early twentieth century, the Negro problem was thought of in biological terms as the Negro's inability to adapt to the white man's superior civilization. But by the start of the twentieth century, anthropologists and sociologists such as Franz Boas and W. E. B. Du Bois began to frame supposedly racially determined, hence biologically determined, differences among human populations as the result of the contingencies of history and culture, rather than ordained by God or fixed by the hand of nature. It is difficult to overestimate the importance of this new way of thinking about human variation. By the end of World War II, social scientific thought and research on African Americans focused not on the bio-racial but on the psychological and cultural obstacles to full immersion, assimilation, and integration into American society.[29]

Race and "race relations" in general quickly came to be understood scientifically in terms of psychological difference, and psychology provided the language for understanding racism and its effects upon individual minority group members, especially black Americans.[30] Many social and behavioral scientists contended that prejudice resulted from *frustrated* intrapsychic impulses and desires that led to *aggressive* thoughts and behavior expressed as hostility and discrimination. These same scientists argued that the behavior of minority group members victimized by discrimination could be explained in terms of individuals' ability or inability to manage their responses to frustration and aggression. Many social and behavioral scientists diagnosed racial prejudice as pathological and viewed the amelioration of race relations in therapeutic terms. Advocated by a loose coalition of liberal antiracist social scientists, activists, and artists, this "psychological reworking of race" challenged and moved beyond the social ecological understandings of race expressed by Robert Ezra Park and the Chicago School of sociology, as well as the "Caste and Class" school most associated with the Yale Institute of Human Relations and social anthropologist W. Lloyd Warner of the University of Chicago and his students such as Allison Davis and the young St. Clair Drake.[31]

This psychological reworking of race represented just one part of a larger shift in the human sciences at midcentury toward a *psychodynamic* paradigm. Nowhere was this shift expressed more saliently than in the field of psychiatry. During World War II, psychiatrists were able to document and treat the effects of environmental stresses upon soldiers' personalities and behavior.[32] Extending their observations from the context of war to the rest of society, many psychiatrists contended that socio-environmental conditions were important factors in the psychological health of the American people. Psychodynamic psychiatry sought to redirect the study and treatment of mental health and illness from the primarily somatic or biological orientation that marked psychiatry as a specialty within the field of medicine. A new generation of psychiatrists, fresh from their work in the war, envisioned the psychodynamic paradigm as capable of accounting for multifarious sources of mental disorder, many of which exceeded the grasp of somatic psychiatry. Summing up the fundamental framework of psychodynamic psychiatry, the eminent psychiatrist Karl Menninger explained that "sickness and health . . . was 'a scale in the successfulness of an individual-environment adaptation.' At one end was 'health, happiness, success, achievement, and the like, and at the other end misery, failure, crime, delirium, and so forth.'"[33] This scale or continuum of adaptation on the part of the individual required psychiatrists to make use of socio-environmental research to determine the etiology—the source and point of origin—and treatment of mental disorders.

For all its promise as an innovative approach to the nature and treatment of mental illness, the new psychodynamic psychiatry largely overlooked black patients. Racism as a possible etiological source of mental disorder was largely absent from the discourse of this psychiatric movement. It was left to a small group of black psychiatrists and psychologists and their more progressive white (mostly Jewish) colleagues to highlight the relationship between racism and mental illness.

These efforts filtered into the black popular press, inspiring several articles in the *New York Amsterdam News*, the *Chicago Defender*, and the *Negro Digest*. In an article titled "Brown Breakdown," in the March 1947 issue of *Negro Digest*, journalist Kay Cremin used the recent experience of black soldiers in the Jim Crow army to draw a direct relationship between racism and mental illness among black Americans. She cited research that showed that under the conditions of segregation and the pressures of discrimination, too many African American soldiers had unnecessarily "lost their emotional equilibrium." The cause of mental illness for black soldiers was not the shock of war, as in the case of white soldiers, but the unrelenting assault of white supremacy in the military itself. Part of the problem was the inability of white psychiatrists in the military to understand the impact of antiblack racism. Military psychiatrists, the article argued, never bothered to move beyond the stereotypes of "the Negro" as lazy, criminal, or confused, and thus failed to identify racism as a primary cause of the problems some black soldiers had in "adjusting" to military life.[34]

The article extended this argument to the rest of American society. Cremin suggested that emotional and mental health problems among black Americans had to be understood as a response to the segregation and discrimination they faced in the whole of America. In a context in which the presence and authority of psychiatrists was growing and expanding into the consciousness and actual lives of Americans, this article called upon psychiatrists to take practical measures to understand racism's effects on "the Negro" and to combat them. "Failing this," Cremin warned, "white America will find itself with an ever-growing burden on its sanitariums and on its conscience: the burden of Negro mental patients whose minds have cracked under the strain of color."[35]

In the years soon after World War II, state and private foundations created new agencies and institutions to promote the mental health of the general population in the United States, but little was done to consider the specific needs of African Americans. In fact, most mental health care professionals had little to say about and little interest in the psychic health of African Americans. Even racist statements in this context were brief and dismissive. In historical studies of this moment of expansion in the provision of mental health services to the American public, black Americans' needs still rarely come under consideration.[36]

In the face of this systematic disregard, Fredric Wertham was adamant that the greatest need for mental health care existed among the most oppressed members of U.S. society, people whose psychological needs were routinely dismissed, or reduced to questions of material deprivation. "Negroes are not allowed the luxury of neuroses," he contended, adding that "the official view is that they are just unhappy, or they need housing, or they feel downtrodden."[37] Further, Wertham argued that the state's liberalizing extension of various social services failed to address the fact of unequal access to care resulting from the ingrained belief among policy makers and health care providers, not to mention many academics, that black people were simple folk whose only need was to get "fair shake" in the economy. Many whites and not a few black leaders framed "the Negro problem" as simply a matter of fairness: Negroes' lot would improve if they got a fair shot at employment and had other bread-and-butter needs met.[38] Thus, prior to the establishment of the Lafargue Clinic, most elite institutions and policy makers with power to make decisions about the distribution of material and institutional resources did not even consider that black people needed access to mental health care.

Rather than the expression of a desire "to study the Negro's personality" or a reformist political project in the vein of liberal race relations research and management, the clinic represented the more radical belief that psychotherapy could play an essential part in black New Yorkers' struggles against systemic inequality. "The Lafargue Clinic is not trying to help adjust people to a vicious environment," Dr. Wertham told one reporter a few months after the clinic's opening. "We give them the best psychiatric care to help build strong citizens, fighters against this debilitating ghetto! We want our patients to function in a changing world, and work with others to do it!"[39]

The Lafargue Clinic thus emerged at a pivotal and in some ways paradoxical moment in the history of the behavioral and medical sciences. On the one hand, the postwar years witnessed a blossoming of the fields of American psychiatry and psychology, an expansion of public and private institutions and resources dedicated to mental health care, and even a growing interest in the psychological roots of prejudice and discrimination. On the other hand, many of the same scholars, policy makers, and institutions responsible for those developments paid little practical attention to the psychological impact on African Americans of living in a racist society. Virtually no institutions dedicated to the mental health needs of African Americans, let alone any clinics offering walk-in psychotherapy in a predominantly black community, existed in the United States prior to the Lafargue Clinic's founding. It was within this paradox that the Lafargue Clinic rose and fell.[40]

Social Citizenship and Black Psychic Health

This book contributes to several long-standing and emerging conversations in contemporary African American historiography and the critical study of medicine and the human sciences. One of the most exciting areas of contemporary historical research focuses on the interlocking relationships among biomedicine, institutional racism, structural violence, and community health activism.[41] Some of the recent work in this area has drawn on British sociologist T. H. Marshall's distinction among civil rights, economic rights, and social rights to pose the question of how debates and activism focused upon physical and mental health might provide insight into the substance of citizenship for racialized and other oppressed peoples in modern liberal societies.[42] In her study of the Black Panther Party's fight against medical discrimination, Alondra Nelson refers to the distinction between civil rights and social rights and benefits as the "citizenship contradiction." She shows that the "health politics" of the Panthers sought to resolve that unique contradiction by mobilizing for access to the tangible accoutrements of social and economic citizenship for poor African Americans, in this case medical care (with dignity). Nelson's "citizenship contradiction" framework is certainly applicable to the black population of Harlem in the wake of World War II, a community whose citizenship was recognized formally in law but hardly actualized socially in their encounters with the primary institutions of both civil society or the agencies of the state.[43]

This book also joins the rich body of historical literature examining the central role that social and behavioral scientific knowledge has played in both representations of blackness and in the lives of particular black communities in the twentieth century.[44] While some of this literature has celebrated the role of social scientists and their efforts to harness their research to antiracist policy and social change, a good number of these studies present the human sciences as a primary site for the domestication of radical and/or nonnormative black intellectual and literary traditions, social movements, and modes of being in the world. In some ways taking a cue from Ralph Ellison's critical review in his *Shadow and Act* (1964) of Gunnar Myrdal's *An American Dilemma* (1944), and Albert Murray's understudied cultural criticism from the 1960s and 1970s, most importantly *The Omni-Americans* (1970), much of the historical criticism centers on how the social and behavioral sciences have used research on the cultures and psyches of racialized, particularly black, populations and community locales to portray them as "damaged" or pathological. Representations of African Americans derived from scientific research have indeed proven promiscuously manipulable in the hands of American policy makers and institutional administrators. Historian Daryl Michael Scott has gone so far as to argue that "experts who study social groups, particularly those who engage in policy debates, should place the inner lives of people off limits."[45]

I have wrestled with Scott's admonition for years as I surveyed the history of the Lafargue Clinic's efforts to link the psychological well-being of Harlem's black community to a broad campaign for social and racial justice. I have, though, come to agree with Richard Wright himself who succinctly, yet perhaps syllogistically, argued at the time of Lafargue's founding in 1946 that "oppression really does oppress." By this he meant that the targets of oppression experienced a degradation of their humanity that had to be acknowledged and combated. For Wright, since social alienation and psychic alienation went hand in glove, the battle against oppression had to be waged on the terrain of both political economy and the psyche. (Martinican psychiatrist and anticolonial theorist Frantz Fanon would soon echo Wright in a series of invaluable writings, including his 1952 study *Black Skin, White Masks*, and *The Wretched of the Earth*, nine years later.) On this score, *Under the Strain of Color* echoes Jay Garcia's recent cultural history of the psychological turn in the work of antiracist fiction and cultural criticism by people like Wright, James Baldwin, and Lillian Smith. Garcia convincingly argues that characterizing Wright as the arch-purveyor of the "psychiatric appeal" for equality founded on social science–based "damage imagery" "makes it difficult to understand the earnest disposition that led Wright and others to maintain that investigating the psychological undercurrents of the racist social order could lead to a socially viable and culturally resonant anti-racism." Both in his public advocacy and in private writing for himself, Wright held that if psychological knowledge could be harnessed to social justice within new types of institutions such as the Lafargue Clinic, the lives of the oppressed could be bettered and society on the whole transformed.[46]

Wright and Wertham embraced psychological discourse and the science of psychiatry as tools for understanding black experiences of modern American society. Yet they resisted the general aim of the behavioral sciences to help the putatively abnormal to adjust to the norms of society. Instead, they sought to develop psychiatric knowledge and therapy that might aid everyday people in confronting the social order of white supremacy and capitalist exploitation. To do so, Wertham developed a distinctive version of "social psychiatry," an orientation to psychiatric diagnosis and psychotherapy that incorporated the social world of the patient into the overall picture of mental health. Wertham did not coin the term "social psychiatry," but in his writings and public appearances, he consistently trumpeted his particular brand of conjoining the social sciences and psychiatry as a unique advance

in understanding the sources and in the treatment of personality problems and mental disorders. Social psychiatry was an attempt to reorient
the field of mental health care toward a "progressive social point of view."
Acknowledging the political nature of his efforts, Wertham explained that
social psychiatry "does not introduce social partisanship into psychiatry.
[Social psychiatry] uncovers scientifically its unconscious or conscious presence in every form of psychiatry that has ever existed. There is no science
dealing with human beings that is completely unpolitical." Psychiatry as
practiced at midcentury was sadly on the wrong side of history, according
to Wertham, becoming more reactionary and authoritarian as the great cry
for democracy went out from everyday people all over the world. "Social
psychiatry," Wertham declared, "affirms that in the historical development
of society and its use or abuse of science, periods may occur where seeming
adaptation becomes maladaptation; adjustment, maladjustment; normality, a burden; vaunted health, insidious disease. In short, where the physician may be sicker than his patient."[47]

The Lafargue Clinic became the institutional embodiment of Wright's
and Wertham's effort to align a truly *social* science with the progressive
politics of radical social change. The story of that project forms the core
thrust of this book. *Under the Strain of Color* positions the Lafargue Clinic
at the center of debates over race relations, mass culture, and the mental
and cultural health of the American citizenry at midcentury. The chapters
that follow present the intellectual biographies, and in some sense, geog-
raphies, of Wright and Wertham, exploring their encounters with ideas,
individuals, and institutions that propelled them toward that moment in
1945 when they sat in Wertham's Gramercy Park apartment and decided
to open a clinic in Harlem with or without the money to do so.

The first chapter charts how Richard Wright came to be one of the
founders of the Lafargue Mental Hygiene Clinic, exploring his early intellectual biography to analyze the increasing permeation of psychological
discourse into the science and management of race relations. Born in Jim
Crow Mississippi in 1908, Wright became part of that stream of human
movement in the early twentieth century that came to be known even at
the time as the Great Migration. Settling in Chicago on the eve of the Great
Depression, Wright soon embraced the tenets of Marxism and even joined
the Communist Party (CP) in 1932. At the same time that he encountered
Marx and the CP, he began to incorporate new theories of modern human
social structures and culture being produced by the famed Chicago School

of sociology, in particular the work of Robert Ezra Park and Louis Wirth. This chapter shows that, during his time in Chicago, Wright synthesized habits of mind, writing, and action that would lay the foundations for his later work supporting and establishing institutions dedicated to the psychological and social well-being of the poor, the neglected, and the stigmatized, most especially black recent migrants to New York City.

Chapter 1 also presents a major component of Wright's life and work that has been overshadowed by a focus on the role of the Communist Party in his formative years, along with often tortuous explications, later, of his European expatriation and embrace of Sartrean existentialism as his governing philosophy. Not only does this book chart Wright's engagement with psychoanalysis and psychological theories in general, but it presents a portrait of his practical efforts to establish an institutional structure for enacting his emergent project of transforming the way Americans discussed and approached relations between white and black people both collectively and "inter-personally." He termed his new project the "Conquest of Ourselves," and it required a form of radical introspection that he argued was the first step toward both psychological and political liberation from the constraints of white supremacy for blacks and whites alike.

While Fredric Wertham is best known for his 1954 anti–comic book polemic *Seduction of the Innocent*, very little scholarship has been published that situates *Seduction* or any of his other work within a thorough intellectual biography or within an examination of his relationship to the discourses, institutions, or practices of twentieth-century European and American psychiatry.[48] Chapter 2 not only contributes to the biographical literature on one of the mid-twentieth century's most controversial public intellectuals, but also shows Wertham to be at the center of major developments in psychiatric knowledge and therapeutic techniques. This chapter makes ample use of sources drawn from Wertham's recently opened archive of collected papers, as well as heretofore untapped material from his mentors and colleagues. Of particular interest to students of the history of medicine is the role Wertham played in navigating among German somatic psychiatry, Freudian psychoanalysis, and Adolf Meyer's eclectic, pragmatist-inspired model of psychobiology. This chapter also shows Wertham to be instrumental in the development of the study and treatment of criminal psychopathology—a specialty that became the site at which Wertham and Wright converged in the 1940s. Chapter 2 reveals much as well about Wertham's personality that sowed the seeds of his paradoxical position as simultaneously prominent yet marginal in American psychiatry.

Drawing on a diverse set of sources, including oral histories and patient files, chapter 3 presents a comprehensive exploration of the intellectual, social, and political context from which the Lafargue Clinic emerged and offers a critical analysis of the clinic's therapeutic techniques and practices, which focused on the social bases of psychic trauma, in light of the dearth of humane mental health care services for African Americans in New York City at the time. This chapter demonstrates that Wertham and his colleagues were engaging in a radical effort to link individual psychic well-being to the project of social justice and transformation. And it situates the clinic within the social, and thus racial, geography of New York City in the 1940s and '50s, as well as the institutional politics of psychiatry and psychology.

The Lafargue Clinic played a crucial yet unheralded role in the school desegregation cases that culminated in *Brown v. Board of Education*. Chapter 4 examines Wertham's October 1951 testimony to the Delaware Court of Chancery in two such cases, in conjunction with the underexamined antiracist foundations of his now infamous 1954 anti–comic book treatise *Seduction of the Innocent*. Both his testimony and *Seduction* were based on clinical psychiatric examinations of interracial groups of children conducted at Lafargue. When read together, *Seduction* and Wertham's court testimony reveal a provocative, singularly original set of arguments about racism as a public health threat to children of all races. Chapter 4 is followed by a brief epilogue.

The structure of this book has two primary rationales: first is to provide an intellectual genealogy of how the Lafargue Clinic came into being, revealed through the stories of its two primary founders, Wright and Wertham. Second, it aims to go beyond the extant historiography and critical literature emphasizing the sheer novelty and import of Lafargue's founding moment, to analyze the work of the clinic as a pivotal institution in the unfolding epochal shifts in America's simultaneous reckoning with *race* and *mental health*. What binds each chapter together with the others is a narrative exploration of the scales of historical action and change, of how biography and geography—people, ideas, and places—interact to produce the conditions of possibility for knowledge discovery and new modes of confronting impediments to living human lives with health and dignity in the modern era.

"This Burden of Consciousness"

Richard Wright and the Psychology of Race Relations, 1927–1947

With the publication of *Native Son* in March 1940 and its wide circulation through the Book-of-the-Month Club, Richard Wright became the most widely known black writer in the United States.[1] But in his everyday life and in his relations with the central institutions of American society he remained just another Jim Crowed black man. It did not help that he was also a member of the Communist Party USA. With the onset of World War II, Wright's complicated status as a black man and a Communist and yet an American citizen placed him in a peculiar position in relation to state and nation. At every turn, he faced unyielding challenges to his political and personal status and identity—almost all of which played out in public.

On January 15, 1944, the Selective Service Local Draft Board 178 in Brooklyn, New York, rejected Wright for service in the armed forces. Initially classified 1A in July 1942, thus ripe for being drafted into the Jim Crow army, by October he was granted 3A status, a designation for men who were married with children. Knowing that he still might be called to serve, Wright applied for a commission in the Office of War Information "to work in public relations or on the staff of an army newspaper." He was denied the post. Nevertheless he received another draft notice in January 1944, to which he replied with a long, emphatic letter of protest against serving in a segregated military. Within days the Brooklyn draft board reclassified Wright as 4F, unfit for service. The reason for rejection was "psychoneurosis, severe, psychiatric rejection; referred to Local Board for further psychiatric and social investigation." A report by the Federal Bureau of Investigation stated, "It appeared from the Subject's contacts with his Local Board that his interest in the problem of the Negro has become almost an obsession and it was said that he apparently overlooks the fact that his own rise to success refutes many of his own statements regarding the impossibility of the Negro's improving his personal position."[2]

It is perhaps strange now to consider how an agent of the U.S. state could conceive of Wright's efforts to combat antiblack racism in terms of mental disorder. It requires imagining a juncture in U.S. history in which psychological discourses individuated human thought and action to such a degree that the category of the political was erased. In this moment one's refusal to comply with the systematic oppression of black Americans could only register as an individual's inability to recognize the rewards of living in a purportedly liberal society and his failure to reconcile and adjust himself to his place in the social order. To consider this reign of the psychological is to imagine the restricted ambit for expressions of dissent and desire for change governing discourse on the position of "the Negro" in American society in the mid-1940s.

The irony of this moment was that Richard Wright and a number of his fellow antiracist writers, intellectuals, and activists framed their struggles against various forms of oppression in psychological terms as well. In the 1940s, Wright was particularly determined to reveal the psychic dimensions of black-white race relations as a way of highlighting the mutability of human thought and behavior.[3] He sought to denaturalize race relations by introducing the contingent dimension of the psyche. He believed that racism and its effects were not determined by nature, not fixed in the minds and bodies of different American people(s), but rather the result of socially created divisions that came to be expressed in psychic manifestations of fear and hatred. Yet the difference between Wright's vision of the psychological and the hegemonic uses of the psychological as expressed in the state's devaluing of the political was that Wright harnessed the psychological to the work of radical social and political change.

Psychology, both as science and everyday discourse, may have been the frame in which various state and civil society agencies, actors, and institutions determined the intelligibility or legitimacy, normality or pathology of U.S. citizen-subjects' utterances and behavior. But there were individuals and groups who emerged in the 1940s speaking the language of psychology with distinctly different aims, aims that might even be called counter-hegemonic.[4]

This chapter traces Richard Wright's intellectual and geographical migrations from Chicago, sociology, and communism to New York, psychoanalysis, and a broad-ranging nondenominational radicalism. He did not simply jettison one set of intellectual and political frames of thinking for another as he moved through these different spheres; the Chicago-based frames structuring his early social, political, and aesthetic thought would remain relevant and instructive for the whole of his life.[5] But, in New York during the 1940s, Wright came to foreground the psychological dimension of racial oppression in his writing and public statements. The psychic effects of black Americans' encounters with modern forms of oppression, he argued, had been ignored by both whites and blacks for far too long. "I'm convinced," Wright noted in his 1945 diary, "that the next great area of discovery in the Negro will be the dark, landscape of his own mind, what living in white America has done to him. Boy, what that search will reveal! There's enough there to find to use in transforming the basis of human life on earth."[6]

Chicago: The City and the School

Richard Wright had lived in cities before—Jackson, Mississippi, and Memphis, Tennessee—but nothing in his previous experience prepared him for the scale of modern industrial, urban anonymity and social anomie of Chicago in the late 1920s.[7] In the opening sentences of *American Hunger*, the second part of his autobiography originally combined with *Black Boy* (1945), Wright recalled that "my first glimpse of the flat black stretches of

Chicago depressed and dismayed me, mocked all my fantasies. Chicago seemed an unreal city whose mythical houses were built of slabs of black coal wreathed in palls of gray smoke, houses whose foundations were sinking slowly into the dank prairie. . . . The din of the city entered my consciousness, entered to remain for years to come. The year was 1927."[8]

At the time he came to Chicago, soon to be twenty, Wright possessed, in his words, "a vague yearning to write." He knew that in order to write he needed a more systematic understanding of his environment and the personalities of the people around him. "Something was missing in my imaginative efforts: my flights of imagination were too subjective, too lacking in reference to social action," he later recalled. "I hungered for a grasp of the framework of contemporary living, for a knowledge of the forms of life about me, for eyes to see the bony structure of personality, for theories to light up the shadows of conduct."[9] In the early 1930s, as the Great Depression descended over the United States, Wright discovered a map for his attempts to understand his world and the people in it through his encounter with the research and faculty from the University of Chicago's Department of Sociology.

The Chicago School of sociology fashioned a paradigm for urban sociology that focused on explaining the metropolis through methods gleaned from the natural sciences.[10] Founded in 1892 by Albion W. Small, the Chicago sociology department became in the first half of the twentieth century the most prominent center for research into the nature of cities and the groups and individuals they encompassed. Led by Robert E. Park, who had come to the University of Chicago in 1913 after serving as a ghostwriter and public relations agent for Booker T. Washington, the Department of Sociology developed a scientific approach to the study of how cities came into being, how they were structured, and how different social groups interacted. The Chicago School also sought to explain the impact of cities on the personalities of modern men and women. Park charged his students with approaching sociology with "the same objectivity and detachment with which the zoologist dissects a potato bug."[11] There was in the city an ecology, a natural relationship between its people and institutions, which could be studied in the way a system of plants and animals was studied. Park explained, "There are forces at work within the limits of the urban community . . . which tend to bring about an orderly and typical grouping of its population and institutions. The science which seeks to isolate these factors and to describe the typical constellations of persons and institutions which the co-operation of these forces produce is what we call human . . . ecology."[12]

Through a set of coincidences that almost seem scripted, Wright soon came into personal contact with the Chicago School of sociology. Mary Wirth, the social worker assigned to Wright's family by the Cook County Welfare Department when his family sought relief during the Depression, was married to Professor Louis Wirth, one of the most prolific members of the Chicago School. And Wright had recently attended a lecture by Professor Wirth given at a symposium organized by a writers' group he had just joined. One day in 1934, Wright walked into Wirth's office at the University of Chicago and was greeted by Horace Cayton Jr., a graduate student in sociology at the time. Cayton, coauthor of *Black Metropolis* (1945), the classic study of black Chicago, recalled the meeting:

> One day there came a tapping on the door of [Wirth's] office. I opened the door and there was a short brown-skinned Negro, and I said, "Hello. What do you want?" He looked like an undergraduate, so I was perhaps condescending in a polite fashion, and, of course, he *was* also colored. He said, "My name is Richard Wright. Mrs. Mary Wirth made an appointment for me to see Dr. Wirth." That made me a little more respectful. I told him to come in. "Mrs. Wirth said her husband might help me. I want to be a writer."[13]

By the time he had come to Wirth's office, Wright had already begun reading in the social sciences. But his venture into the halls of the University of Chicago brought him into direct contact with the era's most formidable science of modern society.

The Chicago School's research into the nature of human personality in an urban context not only influenced Wright's understanding of black experiences of migration and city life, but also shaped the form in which he would express the meaning of those experiences. He found in Chicago School sociology both a paradigm for understanding the process of modernization through urbanization and a valuable narrative model in ethnographic life histories. In W. I. Thomas and Florian Zianecki's *The Polish Peasant* (1917), one of the first comprehensive studies in U.S. urban sociology, the authors demonstrated the scientific utility of the life histories of Polish immigrants to Chicago. At the time the primary method of social investigation was the broad social survey, but Thomas and Zianecki emphasized that the life history was a valid piece of evidence from which to draw generalizations about the impact of migration and urbanization on the lives of a previously rural people.[14]

Wright wanted to convey the meaning of African Americans' experiences of the transition from small, rural community to vast, urban society. In broad social terms, black migrants' experiences of mass migration from rural to city life paralleled those of other racial and ethnic groups. Yet Wright was interested in the particular implications of blacks' migration and urbanization. He began to write of the personalities of black men and women who had succumbed to the pressures of city life: "My reading in sociology had enabled me to discern many strange types of Negro characters, to identify many modes of Negro behavior; and what moved me above all was the frequency of mental illness, that tragic toll that the urban environment exacted of the black peasant."[15] What was initially a personal concern with the relation between migration and urbanization and their effects on black personality proved, in retrospect, to be the seed of Wright's interest in establishing a clinic in the capital of black America: Harlem, New York.

For Wright, black life in the city was characterized by a tension-filled proximity to the most vaunted aspects of modern Western civilization—industry, commerce, skyscrapers, and most of all a sense of possibility. This proximity inspired the same impulses for acquisition and status shared by whites in American society. But denied the opportunity to act on these impulses, blacks on the whole were forced into a relationship to the rest of society characterized by Wright as "teasing torture."[16] This experience of modern society warped how black people related to one another and to themselves. Wright thus sought to use his writing to change how African Americans saw themselves, to show them that there were broad social and historical reasons for why they lived in poverty and disfranchisement, to show them that their personalities were negatively conditioned under the regime of white supremacy, that they were not born weak or fearful or angry, but made so by American society.

Wright saw "the Negro" as both a universal and exaggerated version of all oppressed groups in American society. (He would later discover that this sentiment was shared by his friend and Lafargue Clinic cofounder Dr. Fredric Wertham.) As he would later note regarding *12 Million Black*

Voices (1941), his study of black migration: "I want to show in foreshort-
ened form that the development of Negro life in America parallels the
development of all people everywhere."[17] For Wright the plight of
"the Negro" was bound up with the plight of all oppressed people, and the
fight for black liberation could mesh with the struggle of others for radical change. Wright explained, "I felt certain that the Negro could never
solve his problem until the deeper problem of American civilization had
been faced and solved. And because the Negro was the most cast out of
all the outcast people in America, I felt no other group in America could
tackle this problem of what our American lives meant so well as the Negro
could."[18] Perhaps the Depression brought these insights to full consciousness in Wright, and maybe they were present since he began to put the history of "the Negro" in the broader social context presented by the Chicago
School. Either way there is no question that Wright's growing radicalism
derived from his own experience, and it developed through a perceptive
reading of the bases of oppression in American society.[19]

Richard Wright and the Chicago Communist Party

At the very same moment he encountered the Chicago School's science of
modern society, Wright immersed himself in the world of radical politics
as a member of the Chicago Communist Party. Wright later claimed to
have felt no attraction to the Communist Party initially, but his work in
the cultural wing of the revolutionary workers' struggle in the early 1930s
brought him into direct contact with the party, and he soon joined. He
later suggested that when he joined his friend Abe Aaron at the John Reed
Club in Chicago in the summer of 1933, he was simply seeking a place to
come and discuss his own writing and the process of literary creation itself.
The John Reed Club was an organization devoted to incorporating writers
and visual artists into the larger project of proletarian cultural creation that
was part of the Communist Party's program during the late 1920s into the
1930s. In the John Reed Club and in the Communist Party, Wright found
his first sustained friendships with white people, men and women who
took his mind and his writing seriously. The party became the primary
avenue for Wright's contact with the broader world of politics and culture,
a world beyond the South Side ghetto.[20]

It is easy to see why Wright would be attracted to a political party that was explicitly challenging white supremacy and seeking rights for "the Negro." In the 1930s, the Communist Party appealed to "the black masses" to join it in revolutionary struggle. "Here at last in the realm of revolutionary expression," declared Wright, "was where Negro experience could find a home, a functioning value and role."[21] The party linked the black struggle for freedom with the aims of the proletarian revolution. Though the Communists' association with the black civil rights struggle had begun years earlier, the worldwide economic and social crisis of the Great Depression gave new weight to the need for a vision of society that dissolved the old order built on racial and class differences and oppression. According to one contemporary of Wright, the Communists worked harder than any other political party in America to challenge white supremacy. The Communists "pushed Blacks into Party work . . . they nominated Negroes for political office, dramatized the Black man's problem, risked social ostracism and even physical violence in behalf of Black people. No political party since the Abolitionists challenged American racial hypocrisy so zealously."[22]

Wright claimed, however, that the Communist Party had failed to articulate its vision and program in ways that could appeal more widely to black Americans, especially those who had migrated from the South into cities like Chicago. When Wright's mother came upon him reading *The Masses* and *Anvil*, she looked at the images of bulging-eyed workers clothed in ragged overalls, holding red banners and "waving clubs, stones, and pitchforks," and asked him, "What do Communists think people are?" If the message was not clear to his mother, then the Communists were indeed going to have real trouble attracting the black masses.

Wright envisioned a unique role for himself in the party as a conduit between the Communists and the masses of common black people like his mother: "I would address my words to two groups: I would tell Communists how common people felt, and I would tell common people of the self-sacrifice of Communists who strove for unity among them." He decided that his contribution to the translation of Communist ideology and black experience would be to write a series of life histories of black Communists, men who had taken the leap and joined with the revolutionary workers of the world.[23]

Wright encountered his first major conflict within the Communist Party when he set out on his new project. As a member of the party, he was assigned to a unit on the South Side of Chicago, the "Black Belt." A unit was the basic mode of organization for the party, and a unit leader directed each member into activities promoting the policies and programs ordered by the Communist International in its seat in Moscow. Wright's goal of being a writer contrasted with the vision of most of the black Communists he encountered in the South Side unit. They held intellectuals in suspicion of being class traitors or, even worse, Trotsky-ite apostates. Wright was questioned about the books he read and the ideas he held. Some of his comrades suggested he was a "smuggler of reaction," because he read bourgeois books. One fellow black Com-munist flatly informed him, "Intellectuals don't fit well into the party, Wright." He was stunned. How, he asked, could a man who swept streets for a living be branded an intellectual? Wright had come up against a deep-seated mistrust of people who asked too many questions, not to mention men who wrote "bourgeois" novels.[24] While the party may have supported the idea of creating proletarian literature, offi-cials in the Chicago Communist Party questioned his aims as a writer and asserted that it might be impossible to reconcile the desire to be a creative writer with the duties of community organizing and political agitation.[25]

Wright remained determined, though, to write the life histories of several black Communists. By capturing their stories he would be able to explain African American experiences of becoming modern men—through migration and urbanization—and describe the process by which "the Negro" became a self-conscious participant in the revolution-ary proletarian struggle. The life histories were to form a series of bio-graphical sketches titled "Heroes, Red and Black." There was, according to one Wright biographer, "ample precedent for this literary genre in pro-letarian literature, but Wright also had a personal reason for choosing this mode of expression": it was a way to reflect his own experience of emer-gent self-consciousness without writing explicitly about himself.[26]

The first story he wished to tell was that of a man he later called Ross, whom Wright saw as a representative type: "Distrustful but aggressive, he was a bundle of the weaknesses and virtues of a man struggling blindly between two societies, of a man living on the margin of a culture."[27] Ross was in fact a man named David Poindexter, whom Wright had met in 1934. At the time, Poindexter was on trial for "incitement to riot." Wright was fascinated by Poindexter, a gifted storyteller, who often recounted his experiences of being a stevedore on the Mississippi River and the many tricks he had used to outsmart southern white men.

Wright viewed Poindexter not as just one man on the move, but as a sociological type, a representative of a vast social and historical process. For Wright, Poindexter embodied Robert Park's theory of the marginal man. Marginal men represented social hybrids who lived in constant negotiation of the culture of the tribe and that of the new environment in which they found themselves. Wright wanted to tell the story of the marginal man in the figure of Poindexter: "I felt that if I could get his story I would make known some of the difficulties inherent in the adjustment of a folk people to an urban environment; I would make his life more intelligible to others than it was to himself. I would reclaim his disordered days and cast them into a form that people could grasp, see, understand, and accept." "Heroes, Red and Black" represented Wright's earliest attempt to study human personality and behavior systematically, and it laid the foundation for Wright's later use of life histories and character studies for his writing.[28]

Unfortunately for Wright, the party viewed his life history project with suspicion. Perhaps he picked the wrong life story; not only was Poindexter under indictment for incitement to riot, but he was also in trouble with the Central Committee of the Chicago Communist Party. According to Wright, Harry Haywood, member of the Communist International Committee and newly installed South Side unit leader, let him know that Poindexter had gone down an incorrect path, veered from the party line, and flirted with nationalism. Wright simply wanted to tell Poindexter's story because of his "typicality" as a black migrant whose marginality had planted the seeds of a radical, rapidly modernized consciousness—a consciousness materialized through revolutionary political action.

If Wright's depiction of this scenario is to be believed, then it is doubtful whether the party unit on the Black Belt would have supported his aim to write these short biographies of any of Chicago's black Communists. Wright's comrades were invariably suspicious and distrustful of his intellectualism and his aspiration to become a writer. By 1936, Wright was at odds with the Communist Party. At the time of his conflicts within the party, Wright was being forced to choose between his writing and organizing a committee within the black community against the high cost of living (something Wright claimed to know nothing about). When Wright pleaded to Haywood that he was in the middle of writing a novel, while working full time to support his family, the South Side unit leader replied, "The party can't wait. . . . You'll find time to write." "But I work during the day," Wright pleaded to no avail.

Wright found "relief from these shadowy political bouts" in one of his jobs secured through his social worker Mary Wirth's help. At the South Side Boys' Club, Wright supervised recreation for boys and young men. His relief must have come in listening to these black young men, watching and recording their behavior, not for science but for his own writing. "I kept pencil and paper in my pocket to jot down their word-rhythms and reactions." Wright later explained that it was his time working at the Boys' Club that enabled him to sit down at his typewriter and begin to draft *Native Son.*[29]

The South Side Boys' Club was founded in 1925 by utility tycoon Samuel Insull and a group of like-minded men in order to do something for the "underprivileged boys who were a constant source of trouble" along the eastern border of the Black Belt. Wright clearly was aware that two of the backers of the South Side Boys' Club also headed the Chicago Real Estate Board, a group responsible for implementing restrictive covenants to keep white neighborhoods in the city white and thus maintain the settlement of African Americans only within the Black Belt. Located closer to the heart of "the colored district," the club aimed to "instruct 'colored boys' in 'citizenship and respect for the law'" and "to create in the minds of young boys right attitudes and sounder thinking on the various problems they will face at a later time."[30]

Wright was ambivalent about his role in an institution designed to redirect the energies of "misbegotten delinquents in training." While happy to have a job in the midst of the Depression, he had serious doubts about what good he was doing and what an institution like the Boys' Club could do to address the real, human needs of the floating, dislocated boys who came to the club. Wright described the boys as "a wild and homeless lot, culturally lost, spiritually disinherited, candidates for the clinics, morgues, prisons, reformatories, and electric chair of the state's death house."[31]

Wright saw in these boys the embodiment of a figure he had been consciously trying to imagine and put into words: Bigger Thomas, the young black man who would become the protagonist of *Native Son*, the book that propelled Wright to literary stardom. At the Boys' Club he would "work hard with these Biggers, and when it would come time for me to go home I'd say to myself, under my breath so that no one could hear: 'Go to it, boys! Prove to the bastards that gave you these games that life is stronger than ping-pong. . . . Show them that full-blooded life is harder and hotter than they suspect, even though that life is draped in a black skin which at heart they despise." Wright took a perverse sort of comfort in how the Boys' Club youths could not be contained by "ping pong tables" and the like. Their energies, desires, and frustrations couldn't simply be neutralized by a place to come for several hours to "blow off steam."[32] (These boys would also be those whom the Lafargue Clinic might reach and provide alternative modes of navigating and maybe even changing the ghetto.)

In a memorable scene at the end of *Native Son* the mother and father of Mary Dalton come to visit Bigger Thomas in jail in order to persuade him to reveal who else had a hand in murdering their beloved daughter. Bigger refuses to speak with the Daltons, but his lawyer, Boris Max, uses the occasion to impress upon Mr. Dalton the nature of Bigger's case. In response to Mrs. Dalton's claim to have tried to help Bigger and send him to school, Max explains that "those things don't touch the fundamental problem involved here. This boy comes from an oppressed people. Even if he's done wrong, we must take that into consideration." Mr. Dalton says that no matter what this young black man has done to his family, "I want you to know that my heart is not bitter. . . . What this boy has done will not influence my relations with the Negro people. Why, only today I sent a dozen ping-pong tables to the South Side Boys' Club." In response, Bigger's lawyer exclaims, "My God, man! Will ping-pong keep men from murdering? Can't you *see?* Even after losing your daughter, you're going to keep going in the same direction? . . . This boy and millions like him want a meaningful life, not ping-pong."[33]

Wright's experiences at the Boys' Club led him to question the purpose and utility of recreational and social agencies for African Americans. He later mused that "only a revolution could solve [the] problem" of the emotional and social dislocation of black boys like those of the South Side Boys' Club.[34] Despite their falling far short of a societal revolution he believed necessary, by the mid-1940s Wright would lend his name and energy to institutions devoted to the emotional and mental health of just this same type of boy. His experience at the South Side Boys' Club enabled him to discern what truly helped boys in need and what was merely a diversion.

On May Day 1937, Richard Wright was physically tossed from the ranks of the Communist Party's public parade through the streets of Chicago. Wright had naively expected to participate as normal in May Day festivities. But he had been branded an enemy of the party for his associations with Poindexter and for his unwillingness to give up writing fiction. Wrestling briefly with the idea of going back to the parade and forcing himself back into the ranks, he returned home instead. But soon he stepped back outside, determined to visit friends, anyone he could talk to about the exclusion and desperation he felt.

> I rose . . . and went out into the streets. Halfway down the block I stopped, undecided. Go back. . . . I returned to my room and sat again, determined to look squarely at my life. What had I got out of living in the city? What had I got out of living in the South? What had I got out of living in America? I paced the floor, knowing that all I possessed were words and dim knowledge that my country had shown me no examples of how to live a human life. All of my life I had been full of a hunger for a new way to live.[35]

Just weeks later, Wright placed first in all Chicago for the postal exam, but turned down a permanent job at the Post Office. Instead he decided to move to New York City. He was going to become a full-time writer.[36]

Richard Wright in New York

Despite his trials with the Chicago Communists, Wright made his way in New York through his connection to the Communist Party. As he settled in New York, Wright became an active member of the Harlem branch of the party, which had been established the year before. The Harlem branch was headed by Benjamin Davis, a black Harvard Law School graduate who had made his name defending Angelo Herndon, a black Communist sentenced to a chain gang for leading a peaceful protest in Georgia. Wright became Harlem editor for the *Daily Worker*, the national newspaper of the Communist Party. Over the course of his first year, he wrote hundreds of articles. Initially enjoying his work within the party, as well as his writing and editing duties, Wright soon felt constrained by having to "toe the Party line." He hated having to write propaganda and began referring to the *Daily Worker* as "Stalin's newspaper." According to one Wright biographer, "By December [1937] Wright was restless. He was a prisoner of the Party; he was living in Harlem, yet another black ghetto; and he was wasting more time on drudgery and earning less than he had at any time in the last two and a half years." In a letter to Ralph Ellison, another aspiring writer who had become his closest friend in New York, Wright declared, "It was not for this that I came to NYC. I'm working from 9 a.m. to 9 and 10 p.m. and it's a hard, hard grind. Can't do any work, haven't the time. I am thinking definitely in terms of leaving here, but I don't know when. I seem to be turning my life into newspaper copy from day to day; and when I look into the future it looks no better. I don't want to go back to Chicago, but where else is there?"[37]

In 1938, Wright decided to stay in New York because he began to achieve much of what he set out to do when he left Chicago. Early in the year he joined the Federal Writers' Project, writing the "Harlem" chapter of *New York Panorama*, an encyclopedic work on the history and culture of each major section of the city. Wright then entered the mind of the American reading public that year through winning *Story* magazine's national writing competition, one of the most prestigious awards a young writer could achieve. Not only did Wright win the cash prize of $500, but his collection of short stories was published by Harper & Brothers under the title *Uncle Tom's Children*. On the strength of this work, Wright was able to secure a Guggenheim fellowship, which paid $2,500, a sum greater than the yearly salary he would have earned at the Chicago Post Office.

During this time, Wright was completing a new novel about one of those boys who had frequented the South Side Boys' Club.[38] He wished to use one character to portray the full texture of these black boys' lives, the conditions they lived under and the anger and fear that governed their own perceptions of the wider world. Most importantly, Wright wanted to tell the story of how one young black man becomes so conditioned by the fear white society has instilled in him that in a moment of crisis he can only respond out of fear.

Bigger Thomas and the Sources of Literary Creation

In *Native Son* Wright told the story of Bigger Thomas and changed the way millions of white Americans saw the black men in their midst. Bigger is a young product of urbanization, resulting from the Great Migration of African Americans from the South to the cities of the North. An aimless, poor, petty criminal, he takes a job as a chauffeur for one of the wealthiest families in Chicago, the Dalton family. One night Bigger must guide his boss's drunken daughter, Mary, to her bedroom. When Mary's blind mother appears in the bedroom, Bigger becomes so fearful of being caught in the white girl's bedroom that he accidentally smothers Mary to death to stifle her possible screams. To dispose of Mary's body, Bigger cuts her to pieces and burns her up in the Daltons' furnace. On the lam, Bigger later kills his black girlfriend Bessie Mears, deliberately, because he fears she will turn on him. Fear had created Bigger, and fear was the emotion that governed Bigger's actions under trying conditions. Wright's portrait of Bigger and the environment that created him through marginalizing and stultifying him challenged whites to see their culpability, their own participation in the violence of antiblack racism and capitalist exploitation.

On March 12, 1940, less than two weeks after *Native Son* was published, Richard Wright gave a lecture at Columbia University titled "How Bigger Was Born." Wright's lecture was both an explanation and defense of his novel and its main character. Wright aimed, as well, to prepare readers for a new type of figure in American literature: a young black man who was simultaneously enmeshed in American civilization while being closed out from any true identification or participation in the institutional and cultural life of that society. Wright posed the question of how a young black man who knows nothing but oppression makes sense of American ideals of liberty, justice, and industry. Bigger, Wright explained, was the literary manifestation of the modern black individual, who, bereft of the cultural armament of his forebears, thrashes about in the hard, cold city, bumping against all the codes and mores erected to keep the unruly in place.

Bigger Thomas and *Native Son* represented revolts against the constricted ambit allowed for modern black humanity. In his lecture, Wright gestured toward something often denied in the average American Negro of the day—psychological complexity. Wright explained that he "felt bound to account for and render" the substratum of Bigger's thoughts and behavior, "a level as elusive to discuss as it was to grasp in writing." "I had to deal with Bigger's dreams, his fleeting, momentary sensations, his yearning visions, his deep emotional responses. . . . I had to fall back upon my own feelings as a guide," said Wright, "for Bigger did not offer in his life any articulate verbal explanations."[39]

In the years immediately following *Native Son*, Wright further embraced psychoanalysis and other psychological sciences as guides to understanding his own thinking and for plumbing the "inner landscapes" of his fictional characters. Dr. Fredric Wertham, who in the years since the Clinton Brewer murder case through which they forged their initial collaboration had become one of Wright's most valued mentors and friends, shared with Wright the belief that psychoanalysis and literature were naturally aligned. By exploring the unconscious—that reservoir of primal fears, hopes, and desires animating human behavior—artists, analysts, and critics could gain access to a significant determining source of creativity. Moreover, the unconscious was where the mind directed its repressed energies, memories, and experiences, which in rare circumstances could be sublimated into great art.

Thus, soon after Wright and Wertham became close friends in the early 1940s, Wertham proposed an experiment, a psychoanalytic exploration of the unconscious sources of some of the most important themes and scenes in *Native Son*. Wertham wished to demonstrate that "unconscious material enters definitely into a work of art and can be recovered by analytic study."[40] Referring to "How Bigger Was Born," Wertham explained that Wright's "conscious account" of the creation of the novel and its main character, while "sincere," was partly an "unconscious rationalization."[41]

Published in a 1944 article titled "An Unconscious Determinant in *Native Son*," Wertham's reading of Bigger Thomas's murder of Mary Dalton (while her blind mother was in the room) was the result of Wright's assent to undergo psychoanalysis. Wertham began with the basic question: "Had the author [Wright] any knowledge or remembrance of a situation where a boy like Bigger worked in a white household, where there was a tense emotional atmosphere between the *dramatis personae*?" In his teens, Wright had been a handyman in the home of a white family known for being liberal toward Negroes, relative to other whites in Mississippi in the 1920s. Through a stream of associations, Wertham was able to conjure from Wright a memory of being fifteen years old and walking in on the adult daughter of his white employer while she was undressing. Mirroring Bigger Thomas in the home of the Daltons, Wright was consumed with shame and fear over his transgressive proximity to this young white woman. But unlike Bigger, who of course kills Mary Dalton, Wright had repressed his emotions and his memory.[42] And unlike Bigger, Wertham contended, Wright's experiences unconsciously fed his creativity. Further, Wright was also able to draw an association between the name Dalton and something he had learned while working in a medical lab: Daltonism is a form of blindness—a technical term for color blindness. This experiment offered further evidence to both Wertham and Wright that psychoanalysis—and psychotherapy in general—could yield insights into the unconscious motivations that guide one's personality and actions, especially in areas of creativity. More specifically, psychoanalysis could offer Wright a map for freeing those repressed bits of his past so that they might serve as a basis for literary creation.[43]

Despite Wertham's argument that psychoanalysis revealed more about the novel than the author's rational explanation, Wright was not fully convinced. Reflecting on the experiment with Wertham, he noted in his journal that "what was uncovered was vital and interesting but sadly incomplete." The unconscious was indeed essential to literary creation. But, for Wright, psychoanalytic theory was not dynamic enough to account for "why a man wants to create anyhow." Wertham had shown how certain repressed experiences in Wright's past found their way into *Native Son*, but, Wright noted, "he did not tell how I had come to use them," which to Wright was the key question, akin to the issue of how unconscious thoughts and impulses are translated into action, or in this case literary representation. Wright concluded that "there's a lot here which psycho-analysts do not know. Psychoanalysis is still a science in its enfancy [*sic*]."[44]

Wertham's experiment with Wright exemplified, though, the growing currency of psychoanalysis as it permeated many areas of American culture.[45] Their collaboration and friendship indicated, as well, the increasing collaboration of black and white progressive intellectuals in which aesthetic, political, and scientific concerns bled together, blended, and often created unexpected conduits, circuits, and avenues for the creation of art, ideas, and ultimately institutions. In the case of Wright and Wertham, they shared a peculiar and paradoxical mix of prominence and marginality, which created the conditions of possibility for them not only to experiment with the borders of science and art by applying psychoanalysis to the creation of a living writer, but soon to experiment with institution building.

"Towards the Conquest of Ourselves"

Wright remained a member of the Communist Party even after he had become the most famous black American writer in the world through the notoriety of *Native Son*, but that would change soon. Wright's increasing attention to the world-historical conflicts of the Second World War, and a deeply personal exploration of the meaning of black experiences within the war era's tumult, led him in new political and intellectual directions in the early 1940s. In the winter of 1942, Richard and his wife Ellen left the Communist Party, convinced it no longer spoke to the concerns of African Americans. The Communist Party's Popular Front policy of unconditional support of the Roosevelt administration's battle against fascism had placed Wright in the untenable position of having to remain silent on racist state policies. Because the United States was now an ally of Soviet Russia, the Communist Party USA tamped down its crusade for black civil rights during the war and required all party members to avoid criticizing America's adherence to Jim Crow policies. When the party refused to support calls to end discrimination in the military industries and to desegregate the U.S. armed forces, the Wrights simply stopped participating in all party activity.[46]

Wright's break with the party was not public, though, and it did not become so until Wright published "I Tried to Be a Communist" in two installments of the *Atlantic Monthly* in 1944. Wright later reflected privately on the meaning of his departure from the party:

> As anyone with common sense could guess, I was a Communist because I was Negro. Indeed the Communist Party had been the only road out of the Black Belt for me. Hence Communism had not been for me simply a fad, a hobby; it had deep functional meaning for my life. Therefore when I left the Communist Party, I no longer had a protective barrier, no defenses between me and a hostile racial environment that absorbed all of my time, emotions, and attention. To me the racial situation was a far harder matter than the Communist one and it was one that I could not solve alone.[47]

Several friends close to Wright at the time suggested that he did indeed feel alone in his radicalism—alone on the left fighting for black rights while also fighting to find new ways of expressing the meaning of African American experience.[48] There is no question that despite his prominence as a public spokesman, Wright experienced a particular marginalization, in many ways the result of that very prominence. Privately, Wright once cried out to himself, "Oh, God, how lonely I am with this burden of consciousness!"[49] This could be read in universalistic terms—as a cry of human existence. Yet Wright's self-described "apartness" also provided him with the space to examine the meaning of American life, especially along the color line. As emotionally painful as his departure from the Communist Party was, Wright continued searching for answers about what it meant to be black in America, what it meant to be modern, and what was the best way to struggle against oppression.

In the early 1940s, Wright repeatedly declared *fear* to be the fundamental emotion guiding black personality and behavior. And he sought to tap into the meaning of that fear as a source of insight and creativity. Wright contended that "none of us want to believe that fear—a fear that lies so deep within us that we are unaware of it—is the most dominate [*sic*] emotion of the Negro in America." He continued, "But what if we are afraid and know it and know what caused it, could we not contain it and convert it into useful knowledge? But we are afraid and we do not want to tell ourselves that we are afraid; it wounds if we do; so we hug it, thinking that we have killed it. But it still lives, creeping out in a disguise that is called Negro laughter." Wright called upon his fellow African Americans to face the fear of exploring the psychological and emotional effects of racist oppression. He called this process "the Conquest of Ourselves."[50]

Wright presented the challenge of self-conquest as a new and most important front in "the Negro's struggle for freedom." By delving into the "dark byways of the Negro heart," both blacks and whites would be able to face the deep, inner meaning of black oppression. In an unpublished lecture written during the Second World War, he defined this conquest as a form of "supreme self-consciousness" about who black Americans were and why they reacted as they did to the conditions of their environment. He declared, "I maintain that we need a hardness of heart and mind toward ourselves, in our efforts to look at ourselves; perhaps after all, we may find there, over and above the shameful fear, other emotions which, in the light of world conditions, will redeem the initial shame."

Black Americans' psychological introspection could serve themselves and be a guide to the subjugated peoples of the world. "By comparing our reactions with the reactions of other submerged groups," Wright explained, "we can see that our reactions are but a part of a common pattern of living in the world today. If we can do this, our shame vanishes; we assume a responsible, human attitude toward what we are and, in turn, we get a glimpse of what is likely to happen to the rest of the world. . . . Ultimately, we shall discover we are merely human, despite all our strangeness." Wright claimed that he was trying to get his fellow Negroes to see that the struggle for rights and freedom should begin with knowing who they are and "knowing our needs in their deepest sense."[51]

Through "the Conquest of Ourselves," Wright sought to shake up his audience, to have them think of black identity and black liberation in radically expansive terms. Wright's views here were emblematic of his quest for a new framework for approaching America's race problem in the 1940s. He was fashioning a language for both blacks and whites to look deep within for the fundamental reasons why they feared and hated not only each other, but themselves. Wright was not alone in this quest.

Toward a "Psychological Approach to Race Relations"

Between 1941 and 1946, there was no man closer to Richard Wright than Horace R. Cayton Jr., coauthor of *Black Metropolis: A Study of Negro Life in a Northern City* (1945). Wright produced some of his most gratifying writing in collaboration or conversation with Cayton, namely *12 Million Black Voices* and *Black Boy / American Hunger*. Cayton sought to join with Wright in shepherding a new black intellectual movement in which psychological knowledge would inform and guide the exploration of modern American culture and lead to new modes of creativity in Negro literature. "You could lead this thing, Dick," Cayton wrote. "I don't mean a formal movement or anything like that, but you could nurture it, encourage it."[52] Cayton and Wright also planned a magazine to be named "American Pages" that would "psychoanalyze" the white reading public, as well as an anthology of black scholarship on the race problem to be titled "The Negro

Speaks." However, neither project ever materialized. The two men may have met years before in Louis Wirth's office at the University of Chicago, but it was not until 1940 that they actually came to be close friends and collaborators.[53]

Wright's attraction to Cayton as a friend derived from Cayton's honesty about how racism had affected him personally. Wright once noted to himself: "I like Horace because he's scared and admits it, as I do." Their relationship was characterized by an intense interest in the theoretical insights of psychoanalysis for the Negro, as well as practical aims for aiding "the Negro" in managing the damaging effects of racism on *his* personality.[54] "About the whole problem of psychoanalysis," Cayton wrote to Wright, "I would like to talk to you at length. Especially would I like to discuss the question of what constitutes the rock bottom of the Negro's existence & personality structure—his earlier psychological conditioning in the family or his reaction to his subjugation. My notion is that they are curiously blended—one reinforcing the other to produce the most devastating results. However, I would have to talk to you about this at length. It is not in the literature and we could make a real contribution if we could express it."[55]

Both Wright and Cayton were in the process of articulating a view of America's race problem that emphasized the psychological, particularly psychoanalytic, aspects of race relations. Neither of the two men, however, disputed the social, systemic nature of race relations—instead they shared the view that a deep "substructural" understanding of what motivates behavior at the level of race and racial difference could contribute to the vast body of knowledge on "the Negro problem."

In April 1943, Wright took a trip with Cayton that would change both men's lives and careers. Charles Johnson, the eminent Chicago-trained sociologist and chairman of Fisk University's Social Sciences Department, had been trying to get Wright to visit the campus in Nashville. After declining Johnson's requests for two years, Wright accepted Cayton's request to accompany him to Fisk to present a lecture. Prior to the Fisk visit, he met Cayton in Chicago, where Cayton arranged for Wright to give a lecture at the Chicago Institute for Psychoanalysis on the utility of psychoanalysis for understanding fear and hate in the American Negro. At the institute, Wright met Dr. Helen V. McLean, who had recently begun analyzing Cayton. Through her association with Cayton, who introduced her to Charles Johnson and his Race Relations Institute, McLean would emerge as a prominent advocate for the inclusion of psychoanalysis in discussions of American race relations. Wright's lecture at the Institute for Psychoanalysis inspired him to look into his own past to explain why he and other blacks reacted as they did to the anxiety engendered by white racism.[56]

When Wright got to Fisk, he did something no other black man had done prior to his visit: he told a southern interracial audience the truth about the deep emotional pain inflicted on black people by whites in the Jim Crow South and how blacks, unable to retaliate, unleashed physical and psychological violence on one another. Wright told these truths through direct reference to his own experiences and thoughts of growing up in Mississippi and Memphis. This talk sowed the seeds of his desire to draft a full-scale autobiography, later published as *Black Boy*. And as soon as he returned to New York, Wright began writing in earnest; in seven months he completed the manuscript that told the story of his life up to his departure from Chicago in 1937.[57]

The version of *Black Boy* first published in 1945 was an unflinching portrait of Wright's experiences growing up in extreme poverty in Mississippi. Revealing the psychological costs of growing up black in the Deep South, *Black Boy* depicted Wright's story of surviving the bleak and oppressive smothering of life under Jim Crow and within a vicious family of black men and women broken by white supremacy and self-loathing. Portraying Wright's youth from his childhood in Jackson, Mississippi, and Helena, Arkansas, to his adolescence in Memphis, Tennessee, from where he left for Chicago at the age of eighteen, *Black Boy* emphasized the harm a racist society does to its most vulnerable members. It told of young Richard's survival and his finding refuge in the magic of words, of reading and writing. It charted his attempts to find a viable identity apart from the one imposed on him by white racism, and it depicted his own struggle for a form of existential, if not social, freedom. Most controversial of the book's themes was that black people themselves were the most ardent agents of the wounds and hurt of this violent society; that within black families and black institutions such as the church and school, the fear and anger of black adults was recycled and unleashed upon black children.[58]

Wright's insights into the motivating forces of fear and hate in both the formal and intimate relations between whites and blacks had a direct influence on Cayton's experience of psychoanalysis, as well as the career of Cayton's analyst Helen McLean. Wright's autobiographical and explicitly psychoanalytic arguments about the conditioning sources of "Negro personality" formed the basis of several articles and conference papers written separately by Cayton and McLean. Wright's views also influenced McLean's treatment of Cayton. Cayton revealed that

> together Dr. McLean and I fought through layer after layer of resistances, which I had erected in an attempt to protect my tender ego from the healing effects of ventilation. In the early stages of the game, race was a convenient catchall for everything that happened to me; often I used it as a rationalization for personal inadequacies or as a means of preventing deeper probing into my own personality. But to the end race remained one of the most important factors in my existence: it ran to the core of my personality; it formed the central focus for my insecurity; I must have drunk it in with my frightened mother's milk.[59]

Cayton used the occasion of reviewing *Black Boy* to enunciate a new psychoanalytically based theory of black identity. He argued that

> the central theme of *Black Boy* can be summed up in the *fear-hate-fear complex of Negroes*. The fears and insecurities and above all the feeling of guilt and the fear of punishment for that guilt, which all men have to some extent, according to the psychoanalysts, is different for the Negro. In the white man this feeling can often be shown to be false, a figment of his imagination, a holdover from early childhood experiences. It can more easily be resolved by treatment by the psychiatrist or even by rational cogitation. But the Negro living in our society cannot so easily be convinced of the irrational nature of his feelings of fear and guilt. . . . The Negro's personality is brutalized by an unfriendly environment. . . . Such attacks on his personality lead to resentment and hatred of the white man. Fear leads to hate; but the personality recoils with an intensified and compounded fear. . . . It is this vicious cycle [of hate-fear-hate and back to fear] in which the American Negro is caught and in which his personality is pulverized by an ever mounting, self-propelling rocket of emotional conflict. . . . This complex of emotion is the heritage of the race.[60]

To support his argument, Cayton cited none other than Dr. McLean. McLean herself was citing Richard Wright when she wrote, "Fear is probably the predominating feeling of any persecuted minority toward the strong dominating group. In the winter of 1943, Richard Wright . . . gave us at the *Institute for Psychoanalysis* a tragically beautiful analysis of how this fear, with its concomitant reactive hostility, affects the entire life of the Negro."[61]

Through this circuit of citation, Cayton concluded that the admission of fear provided the foundation for an honest examination of the effects of oppression on black Americans. One concern for Cayton was that Jim Crow's effects reached far beyond the Mississippi plantations of Wright's youth. Cayton soon argued that the movement of African Americans north and west during the Second World War had changed "the Negro problem" from a sectional to a national problem. Even more, "the Negro problem" had become in recent years part of the worldwide issue of "color and democracy" and the global war against fascism. These trends meant that the problems of Jim Crow oppression had traveled as "the Negro problem" traveled "because the Negro's position in the social structure of the South molds the type of personalities which migrate to the North. Further, the attitude of the dominant group in the North [whites] is influenced by the history of the nation, and the past and present attitude of white southerners."[62]

For Cayton, a social scientist, the problem of race hate, as he termed it, begged for a psychological analysis that went to its root causes and addressed its effects. And while initially using the language of morality, following Swedish economist Gunnar Myrdal's pronouncement of the race problem as a moral dilemma in the white man, Cayton soon drew on the deep, psychological bases for race thinking and race relations. Building on his arguments in his review of *Black Boy*, Cayton made his strongest case for "a psychological approach to race relations" in a 1946 article bearing that title. "Without under-evaluating the necessity to know and be familiar with the system of race relations and its objective manifestations in our culture, I believe that it is time to devote some of our attention to the deeper, more elusive and irrational elements which make the perpetration of these phenomena possible and make it so difficult even for men of good will to effect a change."[63]

In "A Psychological Approach to Race Relations," Cayton supplemented his analysis of the fundamental problem of fear in Negroes with a reading of the white Americans' "guilt-hate-fear complex." He contended that "the white man suffers then from an oppressor's psychosis—the fear that there will be retribution from those he has humiliated and tortured."[64] Cayton sought a deeper understanding of the motives and forces in both races that proved to be obstacles to any substantive advances in relations between individuals or groups of different races. Drawing on psychoanalysis, Cayton argued that conscious rationalizations for why whites attempted to dehumanize blacks—"the Negro is a primitive, dangerous person who must be kept in subordination. Negroes do not have the same high sensibilities as do whites and do not mind exploitation and rejection. Negroes are passive children of nature and are incapable of participating in and enjoying the higher aspects of general American culture"—were, in reality, screens, shrouds for the unconscious guilt, hate, and fear residing in the deep substructures of the white psyche.

Cayton wrote to Wright often during the time he was formulating his new vision for race relations. And he sought reassurances and support from Wright that this was the correct direction for his research on the race problem, as well as his career as a race relations expert. Cayton was buoyed by the revelations coming out of his psychoanalysis with McLean and hoped his new insights would prove to be a real contribution to knowledge and action in the field of race relations. Moreover, Cayton hoped to establish a common thread between his own analysis of the race problem and the revelatory insights of Wright's *Black Boy*.[65]

Some critics praised the writing in *Black Boy* but doubted whether Wright's unique story held psychological or even political implications for the rest of black America held in the yoke of Jim Crow. In his review of *Black Boy*, published in 1945, Fredric Wertham chided critics of the autobiography for complaining that it was not a typical story. He explained that as a "psychiatrist who has especially studied the lives of Negroes from the point of view of psychotherapy, I must record the opposite opinion. While this is the story of an individual, it is at the same time a highly typical story." Writing for a medical audience, Wertham argued that this climate of fear and cycle of hurt had clinical significance for his colleagues.

An understanding of the type of experience so forcibly described in this book is not just an addition, but is an essential foundation of knowledge for the psychiatrist who wants to understand the Negro child or adult. A white man, no matter how well-disposed[,] believes that by treating a

Negro kindly he should elicit a like response. That is because he does not understand the context of what Negro experience springs from and does not give full value to the whole environment, which is usually hostile. It is this hostility of the environment which reinforces the old childish anxieties in a continuous stream.

Wertham was on the verge of a *sociogenic* argument for explaining mental disorders in black Americans, which meant the source of mental illness might be located in the social order rather than the individual's psyche or his inherited constitution.[66]

Concluding the review, Wertham wrote, "It would seem to me as a psychiatrist that most of the literary critics, much as they have praised the book, have missed a salient point. Perhaps it is a point of which the author himself is unaware. This is not a book about racial intolerance. It is a book about American civilization, about modern civilization in general. The material of this book approximates the experience of too many people all over the world." As specific as the book's story was, specific to Wright and to the generalized black experience of Jim Crow oppression, Wertham's insight was that there was a struggle going on in the modern world being played out in the individual lives of billions of people. That struggle was for the will to survive in a hostile world.

In actuality, Wright was very much aware of the universality of his story. On the radio show *The Author Meets the Critics*, Wright explained that "one of the things that makes me write is that I realize that I'm a very average Negro. . . . Maybe that's what makes me extraordinary." His self-awareness that his own experience represented something universal in modern black experiences of American civilization was indeed that which made him exceptional. Or rather it was his capacity to communicate the meaning of these experiences that distinguished him. Wright's claims about the broader significance of his own story were founded on a wide-ranging argument that black Americans' experiences of modernity were concentrated, exaggerated versions of all peoples' lives within the modern world, most especially the oppressed. Wright saw "the Negro's" experience of modernity as symbolic and representative of everyone's human struggle for survival and humanity in a machine age. Wright explained that "Negro life in the U.S.A. dramatically symbolizes the struggle of a people whose forefathers lived in a warm, simple culture and who are now trying to live the new way of life that dominates our time: machine-civilization and all the consequences flowing from it. It must be understood that when I talk of American Negroes, I am talking about everybody."[67] Wright was then committed to what we may call a radical universalist humanism while being committed to exploring the uniqueness of "the consequences flowing from" black American encounters with modernity—white supremacy and capitalist exploitation being the most significant components of this encounter. Wright consistently argued that his task and, by extension, that of all black intellectuals was to expose and publicize the truth of black experiences of living in America. Moreover, the meaning of this experience was his quarry.

At the center of Wright's overall vocation was a practical commitment to providing African Americans with the institutional means for making sense of their experience. While Wright had been at odds with the central institutions of black American life, its schools, churches, and families, because they had meted out much of the constraints upon his own personal development—and they offered, in Wright's eyes, a restricted vision of what a human being could become—Wright was most critical of the exclusion of black Americans from the institutional life of American society. It was not that he deemed black institutions inferior to white; it was that the whole nature of African Americans' relationship to the anchors of society, the sites in which the individual develops an image of himself and the world in which he lives, was distorted by racism. For Wright, segregation was fundamentally violent, blacks were to be contained, limited in their movement and presence in institutions both public and private. New types of institutions were needed to counteract the violence of segregation.

Race Relations, Philanthropy, and the Children of Harlem

By the mid-1940s, Wright was no longer a formal member of any political party or antiracist organization. He was, however, part of a loosely knit group of white and black intellectuals, physicians, and activists on the left who were committed to fighting fascism abroad, while also confronting racial and class oppression in the United States. Alongside his black colleagues who had coalesced around "The Negro Speaks" project, Wright found friendship, intellectual stimulation, and a shared commitment to activism with such figures as Fredric Wertham, filmmakers Willard Maas and Marie Menken, and music producer John Hammond. In 1944, Wright established a friendship with Dorothy Norman, a wealthy Jewish intellectual, who wrote a weekly column for the *New York Post* and published the journal *Twice a Year*. Like Wright, Norman was a noncommunist progressive who was committed to exploring the deeper bases of race relations, while also engaging in practical projects to address the needs of black New Yorkers. Norman often entertained international political and intellectual figures while they visited New York. It was at her home that Wright met the French existentialists Jean-Paul Sartre, Simone de Beauvoir, and Albert Camus.[68]

In the 1940s, Wright and his fellow progressives became increasingly concerned over the breakout of racial hostilities. They were not alone in worrying about the specter of racial violence. Race riots had erupted in such cities as Detroit, Los Angeles, and New York, crucial sites mobilized for the war effort. Tensions between blacks migrating for jobs created by the war and the already-settled whites in cities across the United States became palpable for many Americans. The possibility of race war in the United States was on the minds of many Americans at this moment.[69]

As early as 1941, Anna Kross, a court magistrate in Harlem, urged "the leading citizens of the white and Negro community" to form the City-Wide Citizens' Committee on Harlem to address the escalating tensions. The aim of the Citizens' Committee was "to relieve the suffering and the tensions, to fulfill the promise of equality of opportunity and true democracy for the Negro people; to try to make up for the neglects and mistakes of the past in the relations between Negro and white communities; and to contribute toward a morale based upon a real stake for the Negro people in the democracy and in the victory of the United Nations." Dorothy Norman was on the board of directors of the Citizens' Committee, along with prominent New York City clergymen, activists, politicians, judges, and physicians, including the Reverend Adam Clayton Powell Sr. of the Abyssinian Baptist Church and the Reverend Shelton Hale Bishop of St. Philip's Episcopal; A. Philip Randolph; Robert F. Wagner Jr., who later became mayor of New York; Judges Hubert Delaney and Justine Wise Polier of the City's Domestic Relations Court; and the psychiatrist Dr. Viola W. Bernard of Columbia University Medical School. Several of these figures would soon play prominent parts in the story of the Lafargue

Clinic. Wright was not a member, but through his acquaintance with a number of people on the Citizens' Committee he became a part of the larger push to help the community of Harlem.[70]

One of the main contributions of the Citizens' Committee was its call for measures to provide delinquent and neglected black boys with more caring and therapeutic institutions. In New York City during the late 1930s and early 1940s the New York Children's Court and city social agencies tended to blur the lines between neglected black children and those who were deemed delinquent. In many cases, judges designated black children who needed foster care as delinquent because there was no place apart from correctional institutions to send them.[71] During this period most foster care facilities and group homes for dependent and neglected children were run by private agencies, mostly by churches. Despite funding from the city and state, these private agencies maintained strict control over their provision of services, thus enabling them to exclude Negro children from their foster care and child guidance facilities. An exception was Catholic Charities, which closed its institution for dependent Negro boys in the fall of 1940 and integrated black children in its already existing institutional and foster-care system. But Protestant agencies, to which the vast majority of black children would have been referred, refused to accept black children within their established facilities and foster-care programs. Members of the Subcommittee on Crime and Delinquency of the Citizens' Committee on Harlem soon coalesced around a project that would ensure that black boys had a caring place to go if declared delinquent by the New York City Domestic Relations Court.[72]

Several members of the Citizens' Committee on Harlem came together in 1942 to save the Wiltwyck School for Boys. Wright would soon join them to champion the work of the school. Founded in 1937 by the Protestant Episcopal Mission Society and located ninety miles north of Manhattan in Esopus, New York, the Wiltwyck School provided physical and psychological care for black boys eight to twelve years old, but by 1942 it stood at the brink of closure. A nonsectarian interracial committee was formed to see if it was not possible to find the funds to keep the school running. First Lady Eleanor Roosevelt was among the noteworthy roster of Wiltwyck's board of governors. An august list of social reformers and activists joined her: politicians, ministers, jurists, doctors, and psychiatrists. One of the board members was Rev. Shelton Hale Bishop of the St. Philip's Episcopal Church, future home of the Lafargue Clinic. What really enabled Wiltwyck to stay open was not the prominence of its board, though, but the funding it received from donors such as Marshall Field III, the department store heir and newspaper magnate, and Marion Ascoli, the daughter of Julius Rosenwald, founder of Sears, Roebuck.

When asked to help publicize the work done at Wiltwyck, Wright immediately signed on, but not without reservations. The whole framework of philanthropy and race troubled him. He noted in his journal, "I am convinced that Wiltwyck is a damn good cause for it is trying to rehabilitate broken boys, emotionally damaged boys who need a chance." Nonetheless, he had misgivings about the efficacy of such a small institution. "I could not but keep thinking that the school can take care of but a few of the many who need attention, and that it would not in the long run solve anything." Wright was also skeptical of some of the women on the board of directors. After attending a cocktail party at the home of Mrs. Trude W. Lash, secretary of the Wiltwyck board, Wright described in his journal feeling puzzled by rich white people who gave their time and money to aid underprivileged black people. "Really, now, why," he asked:

> Why do they take up their time? Only a revolution can solve that problem, but they like to sit and give money. What do they get out of this giving? I cannot but think that there's a delicate element of sadism in it all. And it is good to play the lady to helpless boys. Has not American nobility assumed the guise of giving money to the helpless? Is not that one of the ways in which Americans who are rich can feel good? And is it not really a counterpart, the opposite, of the white man who stomps a Negro?[73]

Wright's cynicism about these philanthropic white women was matched by his skepticism of white men like Marshall Field III and Edwin Embree of the Rosenwald Fund. After a meeting at Field's Manhattan apartment on January 12, 1945, Wright declared to himself,

> Yes, I'm now more convinced than ever that we Americans have subtly evolved a magic, a folklore of race relations in these United States. . . . In this year 1945 race tensions, as they call them, [are] rising and these wealthy, responsible men know it; so they want honestly to do something about it,

but never the right thing. They call folks together to see what can be done; they form councils, committees, etc.; and then they proceed to say that their hearts are in the right places, that it must be hell to be a Negro, that this and that ought to be done. . . . And they wind up with nothing concretely done. The main problem of shunting Negroes into a separate life is not really touched; it is skirted, always, in thought and feeling.[74]

Wright was the most prominent black writer of the day and a vocal spokesman for African American rights, so there was no way that he would refrain from working with the race relations experts and liberal philanthropists.[75] But he was also determined to change the terms of the field of race relations.

Wright placed emotional and psychological health at the center of race relations discourse. He identified "emotional deprivation" as a problem just as grave as the material and social deprivation that came from segregation in ghettos like Harlem. In 1945, he drafted a long article titled "The Children of Harlem," about the conditions of life that had produced the boys sent to the Wiltwyck School. Eventually condensed into a shorter article published as "Juvenile Delinquency in Harlem" for Dorothy Norman's *Twice a Year*, the essay exemplified his emphasis on the psychological consequences of racism, as well as his interest in institutions devoted to countering those consequences.

According to Wright, black juvenile delinquents were most often the children of recent migrants to the city. He claimed that more often than not, these boys came from families whose roots were in the South and whose family structure reflected the disorganization and disruption of urban poverty resulting from New York City's version of Jim Crow. He wrote, "One can say that these boys are neglected, that they are delinquents, that they are problems; but the real name for their ailment is that they are emotionally deprived, that they have had no chance to reach out and attach their feelings to those things in our world that we deem right and necessary . . . they have had to carry their burdens of fear and anxiety each day and each hour." Wright wanted to show how black migrants' daily struggle to survive in the city directed their energies away from their children's emotional needs and how this neglect contributed to juvenile delinquency.[76]

In his essay, Wright made dramatic claims about the larger significance of the lives of boys like those of the Wiltwyck School. "When the American environment touches the Negro boy," argued Wright,

> the glaring defects of that environment become known. The emotional deprivation that is found among the black boys of the huge cities is but a reflection of the emotional deprivation that stalks the homes of black boys, that exists in the parents of the boys; and the emotional deprivation that grips black life in America is but a reflection of that which grips the white population in different ways and in various guises. Human beings cannot grow out of bleak stony soil. There has not yet been enough real living in our land, living that in its richness can reach out and embrace not merely eighty boys, but millions of them.

Wright claimed that if "we can save these boys, we can save America. For what is wrong with these boys, what is lacking in them, is, in varying degrees, wrong and lacking in our whole culture." It was a claim that echoed his contention in "Towards the Conquest of Ourselves" that blacks were "exaggerated Americans," a notion also held by Fredric Wertham and fellow black writers like Ralph Ellison and Horace Cayton.[77]

Much of Wright's writing in this period was geared toward addressing the conditions in cities that created the boys who ended up in Wiltwyck. But his broader aim remained illuminating "the naked experience of Negro life." In his journal in the winter of 1945, Wright meditated on the importance of this project: "When the feeling and fact of being a Negro is accepted fully into the consciousness of a Negro there's something universal about it and something that lifts it above being a Negro in America. Oh, will I ever have the strength and courage to tell what I feel and think; and do I know it well enough to tell it?"[78]

Over the course of ten years, Richard Wright assimilated a vast body of scientific knowledge regarding modern society and the psychological roots of human behavior. He used this knowledge for a form of radical introspection that culminated in *Black Boy (American Hunger)*. Beginning in the early 1940s, Wright asked black and white Americans to engage in the same type of introspection, to look deep within themselves to understand the fundamental sources of their thoughts, feelings, and behavior on matters of race. This introspection, he believed, would provide a new footing for race relations in America. Wright's new vision for race relations found expression in both his writing and in new institutions devoted to helping black New Yorkers explore and counter the effects of living in a hostile, racist society. It is in the context of Wright's unflinching confrontation with the policies and practices of white supremacy in American society and his call for introspection among whites and blacks that we can understand the significance of his involvement with projects like the Wiltwyck School and soon the Lafargue Mental Hygiene Clinic.

2

"Intangible Difficulties"

Dr. Fredric Wertham and the Politics of Psychiatry in the Interwar Years

In May 1928, Dr. Friedrich Ignanz Wertheimer sent out greeting cards to his friends and colleagues notifying them that on the occasion of his naturalization as a U.S. citizen he had changed his name to Frederick Wertham.[1] Born in March 1895 in Nuremberg, Bavaria, Wertham, after receiving an MD and becoming a psychiatrist in 1921, sailed to the United States in 1922 to join the staff of Baltimore's Phipps Psychiatric Clinic at Johns Hopkins University. Wertham was one of the many European Jewish scientists, scholars, and artists who immigrated to the United States between the two world wars. Attracted to the Phipps Clinic because of the innovative clinical psychiatry of its director, Dr. Adolf Meyer, Wertham brought with him a wide training in somatic psychiatry with its emphasis on the organic basis of mental illness, as well as training in psychoanalysis with its opposing emphasis on the relation between instinctual drives, repression, and intrapsychic sources of mental disorder. "With the long distance between psychoanalysts and those who would rather solve the problems of psychiatry without psychiatry," Adolf Meyer himself once wrote, "Wertham is apt to be the best prepared person . . . to find and establish sound relations."[2] He arrived prepared to make his mark in the burgeoning field of psychiatry in America, both as a clinician and as researcher. Yet at the very moment he committed himself to being an American citizen, Wertham's position both at Phipps and within American psychiatry as a whole was in jeopardy.

Wertham may have embraced formal American citizenship through naturalization, but the young doctor apparently had failed to adapt culturally to American norms of collegial exchange and identification with the group. At least that was how his supervisors and colleagues perceived him. Adolf Meyer later explained to Wertham the core of his problems fitting in at Phipps in terms of assimilation: "One simply has got to surrender all concern of priorities and a lot of those appertinences [*sic*] that go with European grades and positions. This is the critical point and question everywhere—an issue of vital importance in matters of Americanization." Meyer explained that publications alone would not "make superfluous a sense of the dependability and spontaneity of give and take and having things to offer and a tendency to share and stimulate that mean a lot to the whole group one wants to join. Just what it is that makes a man wanted is probably less dependent on formal status and record here than anywhere in the world."[3] Wertham's early problems at the Phipps Clinic would have a lasting effect on his relationship to American psychiatry. Wertham quickly earned a reputation for being a troublemaking outsider, which became common knowledge throughout American psychiatry.[4]

Wertham desired nothing more at this time of his life than to become a leading figure in the field of psychiatry. Perspicacious, energetic, and rigorous, he seemed destined to assume a leading role in the expanding field of American psychiatry after World War I. Yet throughout his career in psychiatry Wertham would continuously fail to observe the codes of professionalism that marked one as a candidate for elite institutional leadership and unimpeachable prestige in the wider field. And he compounded this with a strident advocacy for linking psychiatry to social justice. His seeming lack of collegiality, along with his politicizing of psychiatry, repeatedly alienated the very people and institutions upon which he might have had the greatest influence. For that failure, Wertham became a marginal figure within psychiatry, irrespective of his many contributions to the field—from original studies of the human brain to studies in the psychopathology of violence.[5]

Wertham's relation to American psychiatry mirrored Richard Wright's outsider relationship to the main social and cultural institutions of segregated black society, as well as Wright's critical distance from the mainstream of white American culture. Like Wright's experiences with black churches, schools, and politicians, as well as white philanthropists and cultural brokers, Wertham's contact with the central institutions of American psychiatry enabled him to grasp the habits of mind that governed the field's inner workings. Wertham developed, though, a critical perspective on psychiatry's fundamental claims to scientific truth and institutional power. And, mirroring Wright's role in the official work of race relations in the years surrounding World War II, Wertham inhabited a paradoxically prominent though marginal place within psychiatry.

This chapter argues that Wertham's marginal position in American psychiatry created a space for him to develop a radical critique of the science of medical psychology.[6] In that space he fashioned a philosophy and practice of psychiatry he termed *social psychiatry* that culminated in the establishment of the Lafargue Clinic.

Wertham and Wright were in many ways deracinated from the traditions and disconnected from the institutions that gave sustenance to the vast majority of the peoples from which they came. Wright famously dislodged himself from the bounds of traditional black American Christianity and from established black political discourses, namely liberal integrationism and black nationalism. Most of all Wright used both fiction and autobiography to challenge traditional representations of black consciousness and black cultural life. Wertham was Jewish by birth, but there is no indication from any of his writings or public statements that Judaism held any place or meaning in his personal or cultural life. Early in his life Wertham committed himself to the study of medicine, and this embrace of science propelled him on a quest for associations with the best representatives of medical knowledge wherever they might be found. In the process he left behind any meaningful identification with Bavaria, the land of his birth, or the small Jewish community of Nuremberg from which he came.

Both Wertham and Wright became marginal men in the sense that the Chicago School's Robert Park had described, men uniquely positioned to negotiate between the identities ascribed to them through social categorization and their own self-chosen identifications with the modern, cosmopolitan consciousness of the polyglot social world of the metropolis.[7] They both possessed a relentless hunger for truth that militated against any form of mystification or soft-pedaling. Behind each man's hunger was a very mundane expectation of social justice born of a desire to eradicate the sources of social misery for all people. Wright's questioning of the strictures of his family and community, and his fight against discrimination and oppression, are well known—as are the violent repercussions unleashed upon him by those closest to him and by white authorities, including the U.S. government.[8] The story of Wertham's quest, his struggle, his failures and successes, is not as well known.

There are three major phases of Wertham's life that shed light on how he came to cofound the Lafargue Clinic. The first phase centers on his youth and education in Germany and England before and after the Great War; the second encompasses his experiences in Adolf Meyer's Phipps Psychiatric Clinic in Baltimore and his sojourn back to Germany in 1930–32, the very moment of the Nazi Party's ascendance; and the third phase revolves around Wertham's time in New York City, as he entered the fields of criminal psychopathology and forensic psychiatry and developed his own brand of social psychiatry while working in the psychiatric clinic of the Court of General Sessions (renamed the New York City Supreme Court), the Bellevue Hospital Psychiatric Department, and the Queens General Hospital Psychiatric Division. It was in these phases of his life that Wertham encountered the institutions, discourses, and personalities with which he would wrestle to find a place, in the end opting for a place on the margin.

Wertham's path to founding the Lafargue Clinic with Wright in 1946 was a circuitous journey filled with mishaps, accidents, and unpredictable consequences of even the best intentions. Yet his story parallels Wright's in that both men were migrants, displaced initially by far-reaching, world-historical events—in Wright's case the Great Migration of blacks into the metropolises of the North, and in Wertham's the Great War and the troubled peace in Europe. These displacements ignited in each man a particular type of restless search to understand the new contexts they had entered, as well as the social forces that shaped the people they encountered in such places as Chicago, Baltimore, New York, and for Wright ultimately the whole world.

The Education of Fredric Wertham

Wertham was born at the beginning of Wilhelm II's tumultuous reign as kaiser of Imperial Germany. He was one of five children born to Sigmund and Mathilde Wertheimer, nonreligious Jews whose families had resided in Bavaria for several generations. At the time of his birth, Jews were a very small percentage of the total population of Nuremberg.[9] Little is known about Wertham's parents or their influence on the person Fredric became later in life; they scarcely figure in their son's memoirs. Wertham once described his father to a friend as a prosperous businessman. Yet the year before Fredric was born, his father Sigmund and his uncle Adolphe lost the family business, a firm that distributed hops to beer makers in Central and Eastern Europe. (Adolphe later referred to Sigmund as "dear, but unsuccessful.") In "Episodes: From the Life of a Psychiatrist," an unpublished collection of reminiscences, Wertham made no reference to his family or his youth growing up in Nuremberg. According to one biographer, Wertham would remain detached from his family throughout his life, maintaining a "studied distance" even from his two brothers and two sisters, one of whom, Ida, became a prominent medical historian.[10]

Wertham's most important familial connection was to his uncle's family in London, a relationship that would have a profound influence on his orientation toward social justice. The year before Fredric was born, his uncle Adolphe had moved his family from Nuremberg to Melbourne, Australia. Baptized as Christians in Melbourne, Adolphe and his wife Frieda changed their surname to Winter. They moved back to Europe in 1910, settling just outside London. The Winters were responsible in large part for Fredric coming into contact with English literature and culture, and in many ways for him becoming an Anglophile. Over several summer visits to the Winters, he became enamored with the English language, its literature and modern ideas emerging in pre–World War I Britain. It was in the Winters' home that Fredric first read Charles Dickens and heard discussions on Fabian socialism, which foresaw the transition from capitalism to socialism through enlightened reform rather than proletarian revolution. Accompanied by his cousin Ella, who would soon be attending the London School of Economics, Fredric heard Sidney and Beatrice Webb speak on Fabianism, and with Ella he read and debated Marx and Engels's *Communist Manifesto*. It must have been a liberating and enlivening experience for Wertham on these summer trips, because after one year at the University of Munich, where he began his studies in medicine, he left Germany to enroll in King's College at the University of London.[11]

Wertham's university education was interrupted by the beginning of World War I in August 1914. Under Britain's Aliens Restriction Act, Wertham was required to report to the British War Office in June 1915 for internment. He was sent to Lofthouse Park, near Wakefield, Yorkshire, in north central England. A former amusement park, Lofthouse Park was divided into three smaller camps, one of them designated as a "gentlemen's camp," for those "prepared to pay ten shillings a week for the privilege of being there."[12] Wertham paid the fee and lived in the gentlemen's camp for a short while before being relocated to another camp on the Isle of Man.

Wertham never discussed publicly the emotional impact of being held in an internment camp, but his time at the Isle of Man camp had a clear influence on the direction of his broader intellectual development, especially deepening his interest in medical psychology. During his interment he worked with several doctors, especially with an interned doctor who was formerly with the Pasteur Institute in France. He also gained practical experience working in the camp hospital. During this time, Wertham immersed himself in reading psychology, "particularly medical psychology," including psychoanalysis. But for his internment, Wertham might never have developed a professional interest in medical psychology.[13]

At the end of the war, Wertham was released from the Isle of Man camp and returned to Germany, where he continued his medical studies. His foray into medical psychology attracted him to a career in psychiatric medicine. After attending the University of Erlangen for a brief period, he enrolled at the University of Würzburg in Bavaria, receiving his medical degree in 1921. Soon after, he served as an intern in a series of psychiatric clinics on the road to being certified as a psychiatrist.

It is worth stopping to consider why Wertham decided to return to Germany after the war. His rationale remains unclear, given his love for British intellectual culture, as well as his connection to the Winters. Perhaps it was to be closer to his family in Nuremberg. Perhaps he wished to join in the rebuilding of his homeland—by treating the war-fractured veterans and civilians.[14] Whatever his motives may have been, his decision to continue his studies in Germany rather than England would engender a quest to democratize the practice of psychiatry.

The Growth of Clinical Psychiatry in Europe

In the early 1920s, Wertham encountered a version of clinical psychiatry that would influence his approach to the science of human thought and behavior throughout his life. Over the previous quarter century, psychiatrists working primarily in Switzerland and Germany had begun to develop a science of medical psychology devoted to explaining how mental disorders related to the biology of the human organism, most especially the workings of the brain and nervous system.[15] The new psychiatry aimed to medicalize the study and treatment of madness. Beginning in the late nineteenth century, mental disease was increasingly seen as an illness—it could be diagnosed, and a prognosis could be pronounced, just as with any other medical disorder. A mental disorder had a history—onset, course, outcome, and a variety of possible interventions and therapies.

By the time of Wertham's medical education in Germany, much of psychiatry conceived of mental diseases in terms of discrete clinical entities that required distinct protocols for treatment. Confinement in asylums decreased, and more inpatient and outpatient hospital clinics were established. This change in Germany had begun before the Great War but accelerated rapidly in the postwar years, primarily because of the need for such clinics in industrial centers. Urban clinics affiliated with universities such as Berlin, Heidelberg, Leipzig, and Munich proliferated as the population of cities increased. "These clinics," writes historian Eric Engstrom, "became loci about which the nascent discipline increasingly congealed and expanded and on which the prestige and influence of late nineteenth and twentieth-century psychiatry came to rest."[16]

Upon completing his degree, Wertham served as an intern in Emil Kraepelin's Munich Institute (the German Research Institute for Psychiatry), one of the premier psychiatric research institutes in Europe.[17] Though brief, Wertham's time under Kraepelin's guidance would provide him with a model of scientific rigor as well as a cautionary tale regarding the use of psychiatry toward reactionary political ends.

Kraepelin dominated the field of German medical psychology. Born in 1856, the same year as Sigmund Freud, he received his medical degree in 1878 at the University of Würzburg. He was instrumental in directing psychiatry toward the university and developing psychiatry as a clinical science and subspecialty within medicine. He worked to identify and study discrete disease entities, to classify and understand the different forms of chronic mental disorders in the same way that a general physician dealt with organic diseases. Kraepelin devised the fundamental framework for classifying mental illness (nosology) and was the first to discover, study, and treat systematically what he named *dementia praecox* (premature dementia, later termed schizophrenia) and manic-depressive disorder (later bipolar disorder).[18] In the process, Kraepelin established clinical psychiatry as a viable branch of medicine. Prior to the wide acceptance of Kraepelin's diagnostic and classification system, general physicians and biological scientists had tended to view alienism, as psychiatry was termed at the time, as unscientific and nonrational, more bound by custodial care than scientific methods of diagnosis and treatment. Kraepelin changed that.[19]

The Kraepelinian model, part of a broad medicalization of psychiatry in post–Great War Germany, influenced profoundly Wertham's early career. "Working in his clinic in Munich was an important part of my psychiatric education," Wertham later remarked.[20] The clinic was designed for "the study of the essence and origination of the mental diseases." It included a "clinical-experimental department with a small ward and serological, chemical, and psychological laboratories, an anatomic-histological department and a demographic-statistical department for the study of degeneration." During his time at the clinic, Wertham's research interests moved toward questions of the somatic, or physical, sources of mental disease. He indeed learned a great deal at the clinic in Munich, as several of his first publications in the United States consisted of studies in the relationship between histopathology of the brain (organic problems) and mental disorders among adult men and women.[21]

"This Haven of German Science"

The years immediately following the end of World War I were among the most chaotic in modern German history. There was considerable strife between old and new political parties vying for rule in postwar Germany. The region of Bavaria, particularly Munich, was the theater in which battles raged between the majority Social Democrats and new, radicalized Independent Social Democrats (USPD) led by the Jewish journalist Kurt Eisner.[22] All the while, right-wing groups were trying to counter both parties' versions of social democracy. In the wake of the briefly successful leftist revolution in Bavaria and the short-lived Bavarian Soviet, "the obsessive fear of a new Bolshevik rising led the military and civilian authorities to encourage political movements of a nationalist character." In an effort to subdue dissent and establish order in the land, a newly installed conservative government in Bavaria declared "a state of emergency to restrict socialist parties and encourage 'anti-Marxist' ones."[23]

In the midst of German political turmoil, the language of psychiatry gained significant explanatory power. Apprehension about the collapse of German society and the collapse of individual psychic health pervaded the psychiatric profession and suffused public discussions of the nation's future. "The great majority of our people have suffered an enormous loss of nervous strength and resistance through the frightful excitements and deprivations of the long war," wrote one prominent psychiatrist, "with the result that they are far more susceptible to incitements and provocations than in times of good health, and lend an open ear to wild rumors and agitation which, if nervously strong, they would reject. Thus the sickly mental state of the individual as well as the masses has contributed to the upheavals in which Germany now finds itself."[24]

Some German psychiatrists restricted their concerns about German psychic health to the revolutionary German Left, especially its "Jewish element." Emil Kraepelin was particularly instrumental in pathologizing left-wing activists and inciting suspicions of Jewish radicals in particular. Writing in 1919, Kraepelin used the language of social Darwinism to argue that "in every mass movement we encounter traits which clearly indicate a deep affinity with hysterical symptoms. Above all, we assume that the actual leaders of such movements, the greater part of the mentally deficient comrades, are unsuited for the intuitive, instinctual resolution of the struggle for existence." One historian notes, further, that Kraepelin argued that the Jewish race "showed an abnormally high disposition toward psychopathology, as revealed by their 'talent in languages and in acting,' their ambition, and their skill as 'piercing critics.'"[25]

Kraepelin aligned his psychiatric research and clinical practice with reactionary political forces, including groups advocating eugenics and restrictions on social welfare programs.[26] He was one of the most ardent opponents of the Bavarian Soviet and the traditional Social Democratic Party. He was suspicious of the idea of democracy in general; life's experiences, explained Kraepelin, "had made me doubt whether rule by the people with its vulnerability towards merciless social climbers, screamers, and demagogues could bring happiness to humanity." Kraepelin was also a strong German nationalist and conservative who linked his scientific pursuits to the strengthening of the nation-state and the Teutonic race in the wake of its defeat in the Great War. Concluding his memoirs in 1919, Kraepelin wrote of the importance of his clinic: "We hope that the intended further development of this haven of German science will help reconstruct our national integrity effectively."[27]

The unseemly marriage of reactionary politics and science in Germany in the wake of the Great War left a mark on Wertham. His recollection of one particular case at Kraepelin's clinic in Munich provides some sense of his perspective at the time. "The case discussed that of a youth who had killed an old man in a cellar for a gold watch," wrote Wertham. "This took place in the Germany after World War I, with its poverty, unemployment, unrest, and bloody struggle between the democratic forces of the people and the well-organized political reaction." Without so much as "studying the young man's inner life history," Kraepelin pronounced him a "common murderer."[28] This unscientific indifference to the question of this young man's mental state must have grated on young Wertham. Perhaps witnessing the alignment of psychiatry with rearguard politics in Kraepelin's clinic propelled Wertham toward a deeper embrace of progressive politics. Perhaps he began then to imagine a place away from Germany, where he could practice psychiatry and conduct research in a more hospitable atmosphere. Maybe there was a place where psychiatry and progressive politics met, where the science of mental health was integrated into a broad effort at social betterment.

Spurred by such experiences in Munich, Wertham began to inquire into prospects of immigrating to the United States, where the field of psychiatry was burgeoning. With the support of two prominent American neuropsychiatrists, whom he had met when they visited the Munich Institute, Wertham persuaded Dr. Adolf Meyer to accept him as member of the Phipps Psychiatric Clinic staff at Johns Hopkins University.[29] And so, in August 1922, at twenty-seven years old, Wertham sailed to the United States. As he embarked on his journey across the Atlantic he must have been both daunted and dazzled by the prospect of practicing his craft in a foreign land. He had by then developed into a cosmopolitan, progressive intellectual, with few links to his family or his home in Nuremberg. Unlike Richard Wright, who famously documented his mixture of hope and anxiety on the eve of leaving the known world of the Jim Crow South for Chicago, Wertham unfortunately left no record of his state of mind as he left Europe for the United States.[30]

A Pragmatist Psychiatry

American psychiatry in the early twentieth century initially embraced many aspects of German models of treating mental disorders. Dissatisfied with the custodial work of monitoring the chronically mentally ill, American psychiatrists, like their German counterparts, sought to develop the distinctly medical, particularly therapeutic, aspects of their specialty. They began to shift the locus of their profession from the "asylum . . . to the research institute and psychopathic hospital." The Phipps Psychiatric Clinic at Johns Hopkins epitomized the transformation of American psychiatry in this period. Launched in 1908 through the philanthropy of Henry Phipps, a Pennsylvania-based entrepreneur associated with Andrew Carnegie, the Phipps Clinic became the model for university-based psychiatric teaching institutions, echoing the clinic model of the German universities.[31]

Through such institutes as Phipps and the Boston Psychopathic Hospital, American psychiatry was in the process of distinguishing itself as a viable branch of medicine—most especially in contradistinction to nonscientific but widely popular forms of mental healing, including "mind cures" such as Mary Baker Eddy's Christian Science. One Boston neurologist explained the adoption of the term "psychotherapy" in this context: "Psychotherapy is a most terrifying word, but we are forced to use it because there is no other which serves to distinguish us from the Christian Scientists, the New Thought people, the faith healers, and the thousand and one schools which have in common the disregard for medical science and the accumulated knowledge of the past."[32] Responding both to nonscientific mind-cures and to general medicine's increasing effectiveness in establishing the source of disease, preventive measures, and productive therapeutic techniques, psychiatrists repositioned themselves as practitioners of a *dynamic* science.

In distinction to the general physician, psychiatrists claimed to integrate the physical and psychic dimensions of mental functioning. Dynamic psychiatry developed "a new model of psychic distress" in opposition to the sharp distinction between health and disease; the aim was now to assess why and how an individual with a unique physical and psychic history had developed a disordered mental state. Rather than employ a dichotomy between fixed states of normality and abnormality, the new psychiatry imagined a continuum of order and disorder. The result of this new orientation in psychiatry was an eclectic blend of somatic, psychogenic, and environmental or sociocultural explanations for mental health and illness.[33]

No figure was more instrumental in developing and promoting the new dynamic psychiatry than the Swiss-born Adolf Meyer. From the time he arrived at Chicago in 1892 until his death in 1950, Meyer changed the scope and practice of psychiatry in America. In successive positions at Kankakee Hospital in Illinois, Worcester Sate Hospital in Massachusetts, the Pathological Institute of New York State Hospitals, and finally as director of the Phipps Psychiatric Clinic at Johns Hopkins, Meyer systematized the treatment of mental patients through a strict method of integrating information from life histories with the results of psychological and physiological tests. He was one of the first psychiatrists in the United States to incorporate Kraepelin's system of classifying the major mental disorders, including dementia praecox and manic-depressive psychosis.[34] Though he maintained a lifelong skepticism about the practical utility of psychoanalysis as therapy, Meyer was also one of the first in the United States to incorporate psychoanalytic principles into psychiatric education.[35]

But what distinguished Meyer most, and what must have appealed to young Wertham, was that he went beyond his Swiss training as a neurologist and beyond Kraepelin, both scientifically and politically. He crafted a uniquely American brand of psychiatry he termed "psychobiology," and he became a founding participant in the mental hygiene movement of the Progressive era. Meyer's science and his politics went hand in glove and had a profound influence on Wertham's development as a psychiatrist and as a politically engaged intellectual.

Mental hygiene meant the application of a public health approach to the study, prevention, and treatment of mental "defectiveness" and disorder. Both a medical and political project, the mental hygiene movement was part of a broader political and social struggle on the part of early twentieth-century Progressives to bring scientific knowledge to bear on the order and regulation of American society.[36] In 1909, the National Committee for Mental Hygiene (NCMH) was founded by a small group of former mental patients and by a "cadre of 'psychiatric progressives,'" including Meyer. The movement's rank and file were men and women swept up in the Progressive moment of reform. The NCMH used publicity and education to convince Americans that human personality was malleable and not fixed through heredity, and that practical measures, especially education, could be taken to prevent and alleviate mental disease. The mental hygiene movement was the primary force behind the establishment of new types of institutions that brought psychiatrists out of asylums and into the broader community, particularly into urban America. Hoping to bring a rational system to bear on the provision of mental health care, mental hygienists used both scientific and moralistic language to argue that the best care for the clinically ill required a preventive approach rather than treating the already far gone. In all, historian Sol Cohen notes, "Hygienists set out to accomplish in the battle against mental illness what medicine had accomplished in the campaign against tuberculosis."[37]

Through his development of psychobiology as the paradigm for mental hygiene efforts, Meyer laid the scientific basis for the whole movement. Meyer's approach to mental disorder, as a component of the general "organismal" life of human beings, was that of unity, of unification of each part of man's being. His psychobiology rejected the dualism of mind and body, as well as the division of psychology and biology, often called psychophysical parallelism.[38] The body, the mind, and the individual's experience were to be approached unitarily. As Meyer explained, "My work, and indeed my whole philosophy, makes for as much unification and condensation as possible, but with a very clear right to define units and to choose them so as to satisfy my need of consistency and comprehensiveness. The person and the group being my problem, I have to take the person as one of the units and I do so without dividing it into a biological and a psychological body."[39] For psychobiology to make sense in practice, the doctor had to be trained in various physical and natural sciences, as well as what Meyer termed the nonnatural sciences of philosophy and sociology. Meyer's orientation was founded on a grasp of what he called *ergasia*, "mentally integrated activity," and looked at how the individual as a whole organism reacted to life situations. Abnormal or dysfunctional reactions were called, in Meyer's obscure terminology, *pathergasia*.[40]

Kraepelinian classification of mental disorders as disease entities was less important in Meyer's psychobiology than assessing the functional health of the patient as "an organismal unit."[41] Meyer and his students spoke of "reaction types" rather than mental diseases: dementia praecox or schizophrenia became schizophrenic-reaction. Such disorders represented *types* of response to one's objective and subjective situation as a psychobiological unit, manifestations of "habitually inadequate adjustment to the environment." As one biographer notes, Meyer "inaugurated a search for the specific dynamic factors that led to the schizophrenic reaction and introduced a practical emphasis on the possibility of preventing the disease by the timely adjustment of life habits. . . . As a result of Meyer's dynamic approach to schizophrenia, American psychiatrists experienced a new wave of therapeutic optimism in their treatment of this formidable disease."[42] Meyer's approach to schizophrenia exemplified his pragmatic philosophical orientation to the problem of the psychobiological life-world of the human being.

Meyer's pragmatism emerged from direct contact with its chief philosophical architects. Upon his arrival in Illinois in the early 1890s, Meyer became acquainted with the preeminent pragmatist John Dewey and "the newly emerging Chicago school of functionalism." Along with Dewey, Meyer developed intellectual relationships with other pragmatists, including Harvard's William James and historian James Harvey Robinson of Columbia University. Convinced that experience superseded the abstract and deductive categories and methods of reasoning derived from Continental philosophy and science, pragmatism represented what philosopher Morton White termed a revolt against formalism.[43]

Following James's and Dewey's rejection of the Cartesian division between mind and body—function and structure—Meyer embraced the functionalism inherent to pragmatist philosophy. The focus of psychological investigation "was no longer . . . to be abstract mental elements . . . but rather the *situation*, defined as that which combined the human organism and its environment in one analytic scheme and in relation to which neither the organism nor the environment could be considered separately or independently."[44] For Meyer, the philosophical orientation of pragmatism could be applied almost seamlessly to the problem of diagnosing and treating mental disorders. With its emphasis on the "fundamental heterogeneity of factors that affect mental life," including the organic, psychic, and social, Meyer's psychobiology would frame Wertham's own pragmatic social psychiatry.[45]

Wertham claimed psychobiology's pragmatic orientation to be the most dynamic force in contemporary American psychiatry. In 1925, he wrote a long review of contemporary research in American psychiatry for a German journal. "A fundamental trait of American psychiatry seems to me to be a consciously pragmatical attitude," he observed. "It is . . . not content either with sharply defined diseases and fixed fatalistic constitutions as entities, or with the static . . . concepts of descriptive psychology. Modern American psychiatry has as its basis a dynamic psychology." In order to illustrate the pragmatic tendency of American psychiatry, a stamp more significant in this branch of medicine than others, Wertham pointed to Meyerian psychobiology. Praising psychobiology, he emphasized its focus on the reaction of the "organism as a whole" to its total situation. Expanding his survey of the American scene, Wertham noted that the "pragmatic-dynamic conception of psychopathological phenomena favored the 'infiltration' of American psychiatry with ideas and formulations of suggestive psychotherapy and psychoanalysis." Many American psychiatrists in the 1920s exhibited a general scientific and therapeutic openness to ideas and techniques that addressed the nature, source, and treatment of various mental disorders, including both neuroses and severe chronic psychoses.[46]

Physique and Character

Wertham's first monograph, *The Significance of the Physical Constitution in Mental Disease*, represented a probing engagement with a central problem in both German and American psychiatry, conducted within the psychobiological frame. He began with the human body and asked whether it was possible to identify any correlation between differences in constitutional type and manifestations of particular mental disorders. Using a combination of visual observation, anthropometric measurement, and clinical diagnosis, he sought to provide precision to the definition of constitutional types and to establish any correlation with psychopathology. The 1925 publication of an English translation of Ernst Kretschmer's *Physique and Character* was the obvious prompt for Wertham's investigations. In this influential work, Kretschmer had correlated distinctive body types with schizophrenia and manic-depressive psychosis, producing a typology that quickly became the standard in both European and American psychiatry. Unfortunately, noted Wertham, "The constitutional types of Kretschmer have already led with some authors to a terminology in which morphological and psychiatric expressions are mixed." "Although we must assume that structure and function have a definite relationship . . . in the sphere of psychobiological integration," Wertham explained, "both the extent and nature of this relationship are as yet unknown and a field for investigation." Thus, "to use morphological constitutional signs for psychiatric diagnosis or prognosis is premature."[47]

Wertham's exploration of the relationship between physical constitution and mental disease led him directly to the central question in the social and medical sciences in the early twentieth century: What role did heredity play in determining the normal or abnormal functioning of the human organism? The concept of human constitution reflected new scientific conceptions of heredity. Refusing a "theoretically binding" definition of the human constitution, Wertham provisionally referred to those psychophysical elements in the individual "which are definitely more influenced by heredity than by environment." In order to investigate the possible psychobiological import of the human constitution in the study and treatment of psychopathology, he began with an internal critique of modern psychiatric studies, questioning the utility of "heredo-biological" determinism. He noted, for example, that "knowledge of even a complete family history does not give a clue to the pathogenetic factors of psychoses." He argued that the modern dynamic and analytic orientation in psychiatry had proven to be most effective in diagnosing and treating mental disorders.[48]

The dynamic orientation led Wertham to reconsider the question of normality and abnormality in human psychology. Wertham noted from the outset of his study that through anthropometric quantification, physical anthropologists had achieved effective classification of normality and abnormality in the human species.[49] "It is, however, exceedingly difficult in psychopathology to make a generic distinction between abnormal and normal," he continued. The new dynamic study of psychopathology, derived largely from Freudian analysis, had demonstrated, according to Wertham, "that elements of certain psychopathological reactions reach far into the sphere" of not only those persons whose constitutions may have predisposed them to abnormal functioning, but "even into the group of normal people."

The implication was that constitution, or biological inheritance, did not necessarily determine an individual's reactions to experience, or his or her relative normality or abnormality. While entertaining the possibility of hereditary determinants of psychopathology, Wertham remained suspicious of theories of mental disease that did not account for the individual's life experience. Wertham's scientific orientation at this time thus reflected Meyer's tutelage and influence: he expressed an openness to the integration of somatic and dynamic approaches to the mental functioning of the human organism.[50]

"Intangible Difficulties"

For his first five years at Johns Hopkins, Wertham seemed to have settled well into the clinical structure of the Phipps Clinic. But a professional dispute over his role at the clinic erupted in late 1927, permanently affecting the direction of his career. As a resident psychiatrist and later associate in psychiatry, Wertham initially served as a clinician and medical instructor within the inpatient division. It was through this clinical work that he was able to accumulate research subjects for his study of constitution and mental disease. Because it was a research and teaching department of Johns Hopkins Hospital, the Phipps Psychiatric Clinic primarily offered inpatient treatment to men and women who exhibited early signs of mental disorder, patients who might be both "diagnostically complicated and therapeutically promising."[51] There was also a dispensary, or outpatient treatment division, attached to the clinic. The dispensary reflected the preventive orientation that had emerged from the mental hygiene movement.[52] Beginning in the fall of 1927, Dr. Meyer placed Wertham in a supervisory and teaching role in the dispensary.

Wertham was now to share duties in both the main hospital and the dispensary. He and Dr. Esther Richards, the resident in charge of the dispensary, had previously worked together on a number of cases in the hospital, but the new dispensary arrangement provoked considerable tension and disagreement over the division of labor. Though Dr. Richards was the supervising staff member, she was expected to share the clinical and instructional administration of the dispensary with Wertham. According to Wertham, she refused to do so, assigning him the least interesting patients and making him more of a babysitter to the Hopkins medical students and interns than the instructor he wished to be. Conversations gave way to a series of letters, with Wertham initially requesting clarification of his responsibilities and later accusing Richards of marginalizing him. "The work I have a chance to do in the dispensary at present is really only the least important odds and ends which do not leave me a chance to satisfy my desire for real responsible work," he complained. "As far as my present work in the dispensary goes, I could be easily replaced by someone—be it said in all modesty—with much less experience than I have had. If you feel that you cannot turn over to me some definite and circumscribed part of the dispensary work (either with patients or teaching or both) then my present function could be easily turned over to one of the house staff on one of the days he is in the dispensary." Richards, stung by Wertham's reproachful tone, dismissed him as a malcontent, a view that Meyer apparently came to share.[53]

The conflict at Phipps coincided with a pivotal point in Wertham's life. In 1928, he was naturalized as an American citizen, an event he marked by changing his name to Frederick Wertham. At about the same time, he married Florence Hesketh, a young artist from Maine who had contributed figurative drawings to his study of human constitution. But the dramatic changes in his life did little to temper Wertham's problems at Phipps, where he faced a swarm of hostile colleagues. According to Meyer, Wertham exhibited a number of "intangible difficulties" working with his fellow staff members, exemplified not only in the row with Dr. Richards but also in personal antagonism with another German expatriate psychiatrist, Oskar Diethelm. In the case of Dr. Diethelm, Wertham was forced to write a formal explanation to Meyer after Diethelm accused him of deliberately countermanding the treatment plan for a particular patient. Wertham denied the charge: "Dr. Diethelm used as usual a trivial incident to stir up feeling against me." He added, "What I cannot explain is Dr. Diethelm's continued only badly-concealed hostility against me, since I have done very much to help him in his early and later adjustments."[54] The dispute culminated in Meyer's suggestion that Wertham seek a position away from Johns Hopkins. As he had with Dr. Richards, Meyer sided with Wertham's opponents. In later recommendation letters for Wertham, he made specific reference to the circumstances of Wertham's problems fitting in at Phipps.

The Americanization of Fredric Wertham

Wertham's departure from Phipps coincided with the opening up of the field of neurology and psychiatry. And he sought a place for himself in the revision and reorganization of programs and facilities at major universities, including the University of Chicago, where he visited soon after leaving Johns Hopkins. In the spring of 1929, Dr. Franklin C. McLean wrote to Adolf Meyer inquiring about whether Wertham was qualified to head the psychiatric division of Chicago's Department of Medicine. The university as yet had no department of psychiatry, nor had it established a psychiatric clinic akin to the Phipps Clinic at Hopkins. "Our problem at present is a double or perhaps a triple one," wrote McLean. "We want immediately a man who can take charge of the work in psychiatry with students. . . . At the same time we want an individual who can be appointed in the Department of Medicine and who can assist us with psychiatric problems arising in the hospital and out-patient department." This same man would be in line for the chairmanship of a new Department of Psychiatry at Chicago. "I have outlined our needs in detail in the hope that you could tell me quite candidly your opinion as to how Dr. Werthan [*sic*] might fit into the picture." Another University of Chicago administrator, who had met Wertham at Phipps, had expressed concern to McLean over Wertham being German and whether students would be receptive to him. "While I have not seen Dr. Reed since he talked with Dr. Werthan," McLean continued, "I suspect that his doubts with regard to Dr. Werthan are based on the question of personality rather than of nationality."[55]

In a long and remarkably revelatory reply to Dr. McLean, Meyer presented a portrait of a complicated and troubled figure, brilliant but failing. Declaring that Wertham's German background had not elicited any prejudice among the Hopkins medical students, Meyer went on to praise his intellectual acuity and his ability to translate a command of the current medical and psychological literature into his practical work at Phipps. But he also conceded Wertham's difficulties working with colleagues. "You are quite right in surmising that the questionable part of his psychiatric equipment lies in the personality ingredient," he wrote. "In temperament he is shy, reserved, and shows an embarrassment in group discussions which puts him at a disadvantage in expressing the contribution which he has to offer. I have felt that these characteristics were accentuated by the fact that he has while here with us been in a psychiatric environment where the opinion of myself and other seniors on the Staff unconsciously inhibited him in an expression of himself." Despite his reservations, Meyer concluded his assessment of Wertham with a tentative gesture of support for his candidacy for the Chicago position.[56]

Without knowing about Meyer's account of his personality to McLean, Wertham wrote a memorandum to Meyer assuring him that he had learned from his time at Phipps and that he had "sufficiently adjusted to American conditions." Wertham reminded Meyer that "you said of me more than once: that I take criticism much more easily than other people." "I believe," he surmised, "that Dr. McLean keenly feels the responsibility of introducing a psychiatrist into his clinics, and that if I do not receive from you the highest recommendation, or if the slightest qualifications about my character are made, he will drop his plans." Wertham was clearly worried that Meyer's doubts about him would doom his chances of being hired by McLean. He pleaded to Meyer, "My feeling is that Dr. McLean is a very cautious man (especially with regard to psychiatry) and that this whole matter is entirely in your hands. Please do the best for me you can." Unfortunately for Wertham, Meyer's letter was in the mail two days before this note. After receiving Meyer's qualified endorsement of Wertham, McLean decided ultimately not to hire the young doctor.[57]

In the summer of 1929, Wertham faced the prospect that he would not secure a position commensurate with his qualifications as a clinical psychiatrist, researcher in neurology, and instructor in psychiatry. Such was his reputation that neither Chicago nor any other prominent institution was willing to gamble on hiring him. Following a letter in which Meyer frankly explained to Wertham why he had not been promoted and rehired at Phipps, and why he could not offer his highest recommendation, Wertham decided to look for opportunities outside of clinical psychiatry.

In the fall of 1929, after a rejection for the directorship of the Psychopathic Hospital in Iowa City, Iowa, Wertham applied for a fellowship from the National Research Council (NRC) in Washington, D.C. He proposed a year of study in the laboratory of Dr. Walther Spielmeyer at the German Research Institute for Psychiatry in Munich. After the NRC's initial denial of Wertham's application, Meyer wrote follow-up letters to each member of the fellowship committee. It was a strong display of support, in stark contrast to his other Wertham reference letters. He stressed the importance of Wertham's plan for research into the fundamental structure of the brain that makes it an organ with functions akin to other organs in the human body. "I have been greatly distressed about the fact that Dr. Wertham's application for a fellowship created the impression that he was not applying for an important lift in the fundamental sciences. . . . I find that the basic interest in structural neurology has greatly lagged during the last twenty years. . . . The National Committee for Mental Hygiene is training hordes of psychiatrists and psychologists who have not a ghost of an idea of the nervous system. I consider this a misfortune. Wertham should help in creating a sense of the importance of the basic necessities." Concluding this appeal in a manner that only "the dean of American psychiatry" could get away with, Meyer wrote, "There is no personal favoritism involved. It is a

really important question concerning the soundness of psychiatric foundations. Don't you agree with me?" Just over a month later the chairman of
the NRC Medical Fellowship Board wrote to Meyer announcing that on
reconsideration of Wertham's application he was to be granted a one-year
fellowship for study in the histopathology laboratory of Dr. Walther Spielmeyer at the Munich Institute.[58]

Of all his professional choices, Wertham's decision to return to Munich in
1930 is the most difficult to understand. Perhaps it was professional desperation, or maybe he just dissociated his personal aims from the political climate
of Germany at the time. While his research project would be conducted
solely in the neurological laboratories of the Munich Institute, he must have
been aware of the overarching program of the institute, which aligned psychiatric research with the broad project of German racial hygiene.

A bastard child of social Darwinism, German racial hygiene combined
the ideological fear of racial degeneracy with scientific research sanction-
ing the promotion of biological purity through the elimination of diseased
stocks. Emil Kraepelin, who had overseen the establishment of the Munich
Institute, and his student Ernst Rudin, director of the Department of Gene-
alogical Demographics, were central to the infusion of eugenic thought into
German psychiatric research. Rudin was the key figure in establishing a
wide-ranging investigation of the genetic basis of psychiatric diseases. "The
results of [Rudin's] psychiatric genetics," explain two German medical historians, "would provide knowledge and techniques with the help of which
Nature's 'remorseless weeding out' could be replaced by a policy of preventive selection, carried out by scientifically-based political measures directed
against the transmission of defective hereditary dispositions."[59] "Preventive
selection" would provide the scientific sanction for Nazi eugenic campaigns.

In the years between the end of World War I and the Nazis' coming to
power in 1933, eugenics and racial hygiene were so ingrained within the
mainstream of German psychiatry that perhaps Wertham simply regarded
their ubiquity in the way that a progressive white person studying at Duke
or Emory may have looked upon the pervasive white supremacy of the
Jim Crow South. The difference, however, was that by 1930 being a Jewish medical scientist in Munich, irrespective of name changes and Americanization, could prove quite dangerous for Wertham, as the "positive"
eugenics program of improving the populace had turned toward targeting
Jews as the greatest stain on the purity of the "Aryan" race.[60]

Wertham appears to have been more concerned with the mundane issue of his own professional survival. In May 1931, away in Germany, Wertham saw no real prospects for a neuropsychiatric position in the United States. "I am afraid my future is still painfully doubtful," he wrote to Meyer. During his time in Munich, Wertham corresponded regularly with Meyer, using the guise of updating him on his work in the Munich Institute's laboratories. The real purpose of the letters was to glean from Meyer any leads for work back in America.

Wertham continued, however, to make it difficult for Meyer to support his candidacy for important clinical and administrative positions without qualification or reservation. Throughout 1930, Dr. Spielmeyer wrote to his old friend and colleague Meyer explaining that he had come to see Wertham as unreliable and untrustworthy. According to Spielmeyer, Wertham had misrepresented his status at Hopkins to his German colleagues, claiming that he was to return to Phipps with a promotion in the coming fall. Wertham also made it known that in the event he was not returning to Phipps, he had a great many positions to choose from in America, thanks to Meyer, who had allegedly called him America's best psychiatrist. More troubling than the disingenuous talk was that Wertham exploited the laboratory's technical assistants for his own purposes. When Spielmeyer pointed out these and other problems to Wertham, the latter reacted very unpleasantly, compelling Spielmeyer to take a tough stance. Spielmeyer learned also that Wertham spoke negatively in an aggressive way ("*het-zen*") about him and his department to American colleagues. But this had little effect, Spielmeyer explained to Meyer, because those colleagues did not think very highly of Wertham himself.[61]

The impact of Wertham's perceived unprofessional behavior—his duplicity, "aggressiveness," and self-deception—is crucial for understanding the path he followed in his professional and intellectual life in the 1930s and 1940s. Contrary to what he told his German colleagues, the only prospect he had back in the States was a position at Worcester State Hospital in Massachusetts, with a possible teaching appointment at Clark University. Wertham suggested to Meyer that accepting a mid-level position at a second-tier institution would be a "step down" for him, adding that "the situation has very much changed since the time when you were in Worcester [at the turn of the century]." Meyer protested that rather than something to be despised, the Worcester-Clark position offered Wertham the critical test of directing "a large staff and variety of interests and a danger for you to get into difficulties in matters of sharing the opportunities and duties." In the tone of one émigré to another, Meyer instructed Wertham that "any suggestion that a real opportunity to do good work is not satisfying one's dignity gets a strong reaction" in America.[62]

Perhaps Meyer was more sensitive to issues of status and rank than some. He had experienced his own Americanization and was surely attuned to the nativist tenor of American cultural politics since the Great War. In the mental sciences, with so many contacts between native-born Americans and immigrant experts (like Meyer and Wertham), in collaboration and competition, professional assimilation often must have meant learning to be "more American." Wertham's reputation for being a troublemaking (foreign) outsider was now common knowledge throughout American psychiatry, placing his professional future in palpable jeopardy. What remains unclear is whether Wertham's foreignness derived from his being German or Jewish, as there were prejudices against both groups within different sectors of American society in the 1920s and early 1930s. Perhaps at different times and in different circumstances either mark of difference intensified the feeling of his colleagues and prospective employers that he bore the stamp of the "aggressive Teuton" or the "pushy Jew." Either way, the conflation of his personality with his race was inescapable for Wertham.[63]

Toward a Science of Criminal Psychopathology

Without any definite prospects for employment and without a home of his own, Wertham returned with his wife to the United States in October 1931 in the midst of the worldwide economic depression. He and Hesketh settled for the remainder of the fall in Hillsdale, New York, a small town near the southwestern corner of Massachusetts. Wertham left little record of this period in his life. It is quite likely that the Werthams were houseguests of Dr. Horace Westlake Frink, a psychiatrist whom Freud himself called America's best psychoanalyst. Understanding the difficulties his friend faced, Frink must have offered the Werthams a haven at a troubled time. It is also likely that Frink not only discussed psychiatric theory and therapy with his guests during their fall 1931 stay in Hillsdale; he appears to have psychoanalyzed Fredric Wertham at this time.[64]

Frink had a brilliant start to his career, publishing one of the first important works in psychoanalysis by an American, *Morbid Fears and*

Compulsion: Their Psychology and Psychoanalytic Treatment (1918). At Freud's insistence, the New York Psychoanalytic Society had unanimously elected Frink president first in 1913 and later in 1923. But Frink suffered from periodic bouts of severe depression that led to suicide attempts and hospitalization. During Freud's training analysis of Frink in 1923, the master meddled in his student's personal and romantic life, suggesting he divorce his wife and marry another woman, who Freud argued was a more suitable match for Frink. After following Freud's advice, Frink returned from Vienna very depressed and promptly committed himself to the care of Adolf Meyer at Phipps in May 1924. Perhaps that is when Wertham and Frink became close friends.[65]

The period soon after his stay with Frink marked another key turning point in Wertham's career. Wertham shifted his research and therapeutic focus from the somatic neuropsychiatry of his constitution and brain studies to criminal psychopathology and forensic psychiatry. Perhaps his time with Frink helped Wertham to re-envision his role in psychiatry. Or, quite likely, the Depression forced him to adapt to the exigencies of the psychiatric job market.

In December 1931, Wertham accepted a position as "junior alienist" at Bellevue Hospital, where he helped to organize and run a psychiatric clinic for the New York Court of General Sessions. Prior to the court clinic's founding, a single physician at the infamous Tombs jail who had no training in psychiatry might examine a problematic prisoner. And if the "patient" had any luck he might be referred to the prison ward at Bellevue. At the beginning of the 1930s, however, a number of important committees composed of jurists, criminologists, and psychiatrists, including the National Commission on Law Observance and Law Enforcement, recommended that "the larger courts [should] be encouraged to establish their own psychiatric clinic."[66] Through the collaboration of Bellevue Hospital's Dr. Menas Gregory and Judge Cornelius F. Collins, and with the support of New York's Mayor Jimmy Walker, the Court of General Sessions, the country's oldest and largest criminal court, began to require a routine psychiatric examination of all convicted felons both prior to sentencing and probation decisions. Not only did the court clinic offer Wertham a foothold in psychiatry after years of uncertainty; the clinical work with the convicts also became the foundation for one of the most fruitful phases of Wertham's career.

By Wertham's own account, his interest in criminology dated back "to medical school days when I used to go regularly to court proceedings in cases where psychiatric questions came up."[67] Wertham's own ideas about what was then called "medico-legal contacts" and his preparation for the work of the court clinic also developed from practical experience while in Baltimore of examining patients who had committed criminal acts and through testifying in court. What distinguished Wertham's new immersion in the fields of criminal psychopathology and forensic psychiatry was that it coincided with the very moment when American courts, prisons, and asylums were beginning to look to psychiatry for scientific explanations of criminal activity, with special attention to the personality makeup of repeat offenders.[68] As the case of Clinton Brewer would later demonstrate, it was through these scientific and juridical developments that the paths of Richard Wright and Fredric Wertham began to converge.

By the early 1930s, legions of psychiatrists, including some who were psychoanalytically oriented, began to look at psychopathology as the field in which answers to criminality would be found. In 1931, the year of Wertham's appointment to the court clinic, the American Psychiatric Association formed the Committee on Forensic Psychiatry to explore the contacts between medical psychology and criminology. In the same year, one of the most influential texts representing the new developments was published. *The Criminal, the Judge, and the Public*, by Franz Alexander and Hugo Staub, was a psychoanalytically informed study originally published in German but then translated into English, specifically for an American audience.

At the same time, competing views of crime from the field of sociology emerged emphasizing the environment, not individual psyches, as the proper unit of analysis for illegal and antisocial behavior among adults and juveniles. Major studies in this area were published in the period that Wertham was working in the court clinic, including studies on crime and juvenile delinquency by Sheldon and Eleanor Glueck in Boston and Clifford Shaw from the Chicago School of sociology. In psychiatry, a new field of criminal psychopathology emerged in the 1930s, which Fredric Wertham would contribute to and reorient toward the social.[69]

Dark Legend

Wertham's orientation toward the social bases of criminal psychopathology and human violence in general took shape in the mental hygiene institutions where he worked in the 1930s. And Wertham's career as a public advocate for social psychiatry would emerge in the 1930s, when he turned his attention to what he termed medico-legal work. Wertham claimed that the scientific work of determining facts in questions of legal responsibility was part of a fundamental reorientation of psychiatry toward the *social*. "It is the historical function of psychiatry in relation to law at the present time to introduce into criminal cases facts and interpretations of facts which psychiatry and psychoanalysis have taught us," he later explained. Such an attempt, he added, would "not only help in the proper disposition of cases but will aid in the prevention of crime and will lead more and more to adoption of the principle of safeguarding of the community. Moreover, the courageous and practical psychiatric study of criminal cases will have a healthy reverberation on psychiatry itself for the development of a long-overdue social psychiatry."[70]

Wertham believed he was ready to direct a major mental hospital in New York City or Washington, D.C., where he could best develop and apply his social psychiatry without supervision. When the superintendent position at St. Elizabeth's, the federal mental hospital in Washington, was vacant in 1937, he again wrote to Meyer, hoping to secure support for his application. He seemed to think that his reputation in the field had been rehabilitated over the last few years through his work at the Court of General Sessions clinic and as director of the Mental Hygiene Clinic at Bellevue and through his work with social agencies and the courts in New York City. Characteristically, Wertham's letter to Meyer expressed a peculiar blend of resentment, entitlement, and self-doubt. Angry that he was not getting due recognition for the advances he was making in psychiatry, he paradoxically expressed his doubts about his own qualifications for the St. Elizabeth's post. "Of course I do not know whether I would be able to do justice to such a difficult position. . . . But I cannot help taking into account some of the recent appointments in psychiatric institutions and measuring them against the standards of the 'prospect' of future psychiatric work."

For Wertham the question of his "prospects" had everything to do with the established view of what was the proper work of the head of a psychiatric hospital. "Whatever interest and ability I may have for research," he wrote, "may of course minimize my chances against somebody who was the administrator of some larger institution, since to many it seems to be so unacceptable that in psychiatry clinical research and administration are inseparable."[71] Meyer let him know that if asked he would "be glad to give expression to the appreciation with which I look back to your work as resident." But he returned to the problem of Wertham's nationality, noting that because "one had to deal directly with committees and not infrequently with commissions of investigation probably does not make it particularly easy for anyone not born American."[72] Perhaps Wertham's nationality proved to be the main obstacle to his obtaining the St. Elizabeth's position; perhaps his reputation for being difficult had reached the federal selection committee. For whatever reason, the post was given to someone else, pushing Wertham further to the margins of American psychiatry.

Disappointed and discouraged, Wertham returned to his research in criminal psychopathology and therapeutic work. As a psychiatrist for the Court of General Sessions clinic, he began testifying in a number of infamous criminal cases. Robert Irwin, for example, was a young man who committed a triple murder in 1937 using an ice pick. Prior to the murders, Irwin had been sent to Bellevue Hospital because he had attempted to castrate himself. During his stay in Bellevue, he came to Wertham's attention because of the peculiar nature of the attempt at self-harm. Wertham began prolonged psychotherapy with Irwin, claiming later that he had in fact performed the first psychoanalysis of a murderer prior to the act of killing. The hospital released him despite Wertham's warning that he would commit other acts of violence. After the murders, Wertham examined Irwin again and testified unsuccessfully that the young man suffered from a mental disorder at the time of the murders.[73]

Wertham had discovered in his work with Irwin a diagnosable disorder he termed the "catathymic crisis." In this mental disorder an individual became fixated on the commission of a violent act against himself or an *other* as "the only way out." Wertham discovered in several patients he encountered at Bellevue and the court clinic a form of disordered thinking precipitated by circumstances that were not psychogenic or organic in nature, but experiential and social, such as hardships or abuse as a child. In such cases, a crisis developed in the individual, typically through five stages:

1. Initial thinking disorders, which follow the original precipitating circumstances.
2. Crystallization of a plan, when the idea of a violent act emerges into consciousness.

3. Extreme tension, culminating in the violent crisis, in which a violent act against oneself or others is attempted or carried out.
4. Superficial normality, beginning with a period of lifting of tension and calmness immediately after the violent act.
5. Insight and recovery, with the reestablishment of an inner equilibrium.

The important factor in identifying a catathymic crisis, according to Wertham, was the "exclusion of all other mental conditions that have to be considered in differential diagnosis," namely whether the individual's symptoms and actions indicated a different mental disorder, such as schizophrenia with paranoid delusions.[74] A person experiencing a catathymic crisis might indeed suffer from other mental disorders (hence the differential diagnosis procedure), but the most salient feature of the catathymic crisis was its transitory nature; upon completing the violent act, the individual returned to a state of equilibrium or normality. Psychoanalytic psychotherapy, argued Wertham, could intervene with the catathymic patient and redirect the belief of the patient that violence was the only way out.[75]

Without any knowledge of one another's existence, Richard Wright and Fredric Wertham simultaneously began in the late 1930s to write the stories of two young men who committed murders reflecting the basic pattern of the catathymic crisis. Bigger Thomas's response to the trauma of antiblack racist oppression was a simmering hostility toward his own people and an obsessive fear and hatred of whiteness. In *Native Son*, whiteness was embodied in characters like the Dalton family, yet Wright also represented whiteness in the amorphous blur that followed Bigger as his fear overwhelmed him in moments of crisis. While Bigger never *consciously* set out to kill off the power of whiteness by murdering a white person, his accidental smothering of Mary Dalton led him to an acknowledgment that to strike against whiteness was his wish all along.[76]

In the aftermath of the murder, Bigger experienced a profound "lifting of tension and calmness" in the manner that Wertham described in the fourth stage of the catathymic crisis. "The thought of what he had done, the awful horror of it, the daring associated with such actions," Wright narrated, "formed for him for the first time in his fear-ridden life a barrier between him and a world he feared. He had murdered and had created a new life for himself. It was something that was all his own, and it was the first time in his life he had anything that others could not take from him. Yes; he could sit here calmly and eat and not be concerned about what his family" or anyone else thought or did. After being convicted and sentenced to die, Bigger attained an awareness of how the experience of oppression had shaped his relation to himself and to a racist society. He came to express a semblance of insight into the meaning of his crimes. To the dismay of his lawyer, Max, Bigger cries out, "When a man kills it's for something. . . . I didn't know I was really alive in this world until I felt things hard enough to kill for 'em. . . . It's the truth, Mr. Max. I can say it now, 'cause I'm going to die. I know what I'm saying real good and I know how it sounds. But I'm all right. I feel all right when I look at it that way." Bigger's newfound ability to rationalize his violent acts reflected what Wertham described as the final catathymic stage, in which an inner emotional equilibrium was established.[77]

Gino, the true-life subject of Wertham's 1941 book *Dark Legend: A Study in Murder*, was a young man vastly different from Bigger Thomas. Yet Bigger's and Gino's violent responses to inner conflict represented cautionary tales to a society oblivious of the suffering of its invisible youth. Sometime in the early 1930s, Gino (a pseudonym) emigrated from Italy to New York City with his mother and younger brother and sisters. By all accounts from his neighbors and family, he was happy, friendly, and a hard worker at his various jobs. But one night he waited until his mother was asleep, grabbed a common bread knife, and stabbed her thirty-two times; he then calmly walked down to the corner store and told a policeman of his crime. Gino claimed that he killed his mother because she had dishonored his family, most especially his dead father, by her promiscuity—she had had a series of lovers in the seven years since her husband's death, refusing to marry any of them.

Wertham encountered Gino in the Bellevue Hospital prison ward and soon examined him in order to form an opinion as to his mental state when he committed the murder. Testifying before the New York State Lunacy Commission, Wertham claimed that Gino was legally insane at the time of committing the crime, arguing that Gino suffered from an "almost specific disorder" in discrimination between right and wrong. "He regarded as moral, and even heroic, a deed that was most abhorrent to the conscience of normal man," wrote Wertham. Accepting Wertham's opinion, the commission declared the youth insane and committed him to a state asylum for the criminally insane.[78] But none of Wertham's questions about the heart of Gino's case had been answered. Why had a seemingly normal, hard-working immigrant young man committed the execrable act of matricide? If Gino was unable to determine right from wrong at the time of the crime, was there an underlying mental disorder that Wertham might discover through further psychiatric examination?

Anxiety about manhood was a central feature of Gino's plight. Through extensive psychoanalysis with Gino, Wertham was able to uncover a deep-seated inner conflict with roots in the social structure of patriarchy and its attendant normative expectations. The youth's matricidal impulse derived from his inability to manage the anxiety of becoming a man, and the unwieldy feelings associated with his anxiety were displaced onto his mother. At the same time, Gino built up an idealized image of his dead father, resulting in an unconscious fear of not living up to that father-ideal. Wertham referred to Gino's inner conflict as the Orestes and Hamlet complexes—the blending of a distorted, negative mother-image and an idealized father-image.

Wertham's great hope in examining the case so thoroughly was that he might identify a pattern in Gino's thinking and behavior that would provide psychiatrists and the rest of society with signposts to prevent such acts of violence. He may have identified the broad basis of Gino's morbid thinking that led him to matricide, but he had thus far not been able to diagnose a specific mental disorder that would fit the case. He ruled out schizophrenia, manic-depression, and any organic disorder of the brain or nervous system. Wertham discovered in Gino the archetypal case of the catathymic crisis. Through Gino's narrative of his life leading up to the murder and his description of his state of mind afterward, Wertham identified criteria that corresponded to his clinical description of the disorder's process. As with Bigger Thomas, and in other cases of catathymic crisis, Gino's "violent destructive act seemed to have been a rallying point for the constructive forces of his personality."[79]

In each case of the catathymic crisis, Wertham identified a social basis to the emergence of the pattern of thinking that led to a violent resolution. His patients exhibited an inability to constructively manage their feelings of powerlessness. They had no healthy outlets for expressing their fear and anger. In virtually every case of murder he encountered as a clinician, the patient had had contact with both law enforcement and social service agencies prior to committing the act of violence. If these agencies could work in concert with a new type of psychiatry that recognized the social background of the individual, the specific pressures relating to his or her position within the social order, then perhaps the individual's fear and hostility could be redirected toward developing healthy alternatives to violence.[80]

The publication of *Dark Legend* provided Wertham an unprecedented audience for his ideas about the social basis of criminal psychopathology and the study of violence in general. Well-received by critics in the national press and among artists and intellectuals, the book launched Wertham's career as a public voice of psychiatry. Soon after *Dark Legend*, Wertham became a regular book reviewer for the *New Republic* and the *Nation*.[81] Unfortunately the book had little effect on his position in American psychiatry. In the year prior to *Dark Legend*'s publication, Wertham had had another row with a supervisor while working at Bellevue. Transferred to the Queens General Hospital Mental Hygiene Clinic, he was more marginalized than ever from the centers of American psychiatry.

Demoralized and forlorn, Wertham sought guidance from his long-time mentor, Adolf Meyer. Wertham laid himself prostrate before Meyer. "I have now worked twenty years in American psychiatry, seven of them in your clinic," he wrote. "But I spend my time doing the most ordinary kind of routine work, and whatever I do in the line of research has to be carved out of my nights and Sundays and vacations. I am sure you will not blame me if I am longing for a position where I could use my gradually acquired facility for organizing, teaching and research and clinical work, and if I have to face a time when there may be no place in American psychiatry as it is developing for somebody with my earnestness and training, and give up psychiatry altogether."[82]

Nothing practical came of Wertham's entreaty to Meyer. Yet perhaps this low moment in his professional life led him again to reimagine and reinvent himself as a psychiatrist and as a burgeoning public intellectual. In the early 1940s, in the context of a world at war, Wertham recognized that his expertise on the problem of human violence and his ability to convey the lessons of medical psychology in layman's terms could offer guidance to a society in crisis. In this moment he began in earnest his quest to develop a new orientation for psychiatry that incorporated the social world of everyday people. On a practical level he came to see the need to develop his science outside the prevailing order of American psychiatry. Fredric Wertham decided at this point to move beyond the walls of established psychiatry to realize his increasingly radical scientific vision.

"Between the Sewer and the Church"

The Emergence of the Lafargue Mental Hygiene Clinic

Living in the rectory of the St. Philip's Episcopal Church during the Great Depression, Elizabeth Bishop could occasionally hear her father, Rev. Shelton Hale Bishop, the church's pastor, as he counseled his parishioners in a nearby room. While he primarily offered advice for newly married couples or those facing domestic difficulties, Elizabeth saw that he sometimes left his office knowing his pastoral counseling was insufficient. Reverend Bishop told his family that some of those whom he counseled were in real need of professional psychiatric care. He was often exasperated that there was no suitable place to refer black New Yorkers for psychotherapy. One of the oldest black congregations in New York, at West 134th Street and Seventh Avenue, St. Philip's sat at the intersection of Upper Manhattan that the U.S. Census defined as the Central Harlem district. Harlem Hospital, just a few blocks away, would have no outpatient psychiatric clinic until 1947 and no department of psychiatry until 1962. When Bishop suggested going to Harlem Hospital for emergency treatment, his parishioners usually rejected the idea: "I'm not going there; they'll strap me down on a gurney and have the police take me to Bellevue. And if I go there, they'll send me along to Manhattan State Hospital, where I'll never be heard from again."[1] When in the winter of 1946 a young Ralph Ellison asked Bishop if he would be interested in meeting with a group of men and women who wanted to open a walk-in mental health clinic for the people of Harlem, Bishop immediately embraced the idea.

Bishop had been trying for years to persuade the New York Department of Hospitals to establish a mental health center for the black community of Harlem. Appointed pastor of St. Philip's in 1933, he quickly became one of the black community's most vocal advocates for civil rights and economic opportunity. He was active in Progressive politics and social movements in the 1920s and '30s, including working with the Socialist Party on the presidential campaigns of Norman Thomas, and he participated in founding the Fellowship of Reconciliation, an ecumenical precursor to the Congress of Racial Equality. In the late 1920s, Bishop established a department of social welfare within St. Philip's, which became increasingly vital during the Great Depression, supplementing any relief benefits African Americans in Harlem may have received from the City of New York. Under his leadership, St. Philip's membership had grown, attracting not only the traditional upper crust of black Harlem's Episcopalian elite, but many of the West Indian and southern-born migrants who streamed into Harlem through the 1940s.

Saint Philip's was Bishop's base of activism.[2] From St. Philip's, he looked outward to the whole of the Harlem community and was keenly aware of the difficulties finding adequate housing and employment, especially for new migrants. But he also had a larger vision of the health of black Harlem, its emotional and psychological well-being. When Bishop once requested that the city establish a fully staffed, fully funded mental hygiene clinic, officials in the Department of Hospitals pointed to Bellevue or claimed that black people only needed life's basics; "Negroes don't need psychiatry; they simply need bread."[3]

One evening in March 1946, Reverend Bishop led a group of visitors down to the basement of the St. Philip's parish house. Richard Wright, Fredric Wertham, and Dr. Hilde L. Mosse, Wertham's Queens General Hospital colleague, followed Bishop through a maze of hallways, down a flight of stairs, and into a dirty two-room basement furnished with nothing but a wobbly red table and several unvarnished benches. There sat a

Figure 5. Fredric Wertham and Rev. Shelton Hale Bishop in front of St. Philip's Episcopal Church, February 1948. Photo by Lisa Larsen. Courtesy of the Library of Congress.

young black woman, who had heard a rumor that a free psychiatric clinic was opening in the basement of St. Philip's. "How much money are you going to take from me," she asked. None, they told her. Dr. Mosse sat down with her, and over the course of several minutes discovered that in the past few months she had spent all her savings on shock treatment for anxiety, depression, and suicidal thoughts. This woman was the Lafargue Clinic's first patient.[4]

A remarkable convergence of both history and autobiography brought Wright, Wertham, and Bishop together in 1946 to establish the Lafargue Clinic. Three distinct traditions—black intellectual radicalism, Jewish émigré scientific radicalism, and the Progressive black church—met together in the basement of a church in Harlem to address an urgent community need. Beyond the immediacy of providing inexpensive and accessible mental health care within the Harlem community, the founders of the clinic confronted one of the central problems of postwar American society: the psychic fallout of black Americans' struggles to live a human life in an antiblack social world. This world required blacks to accommodate the ideology of white supremacy, while systematically subjugating them as a source of readily exploitable labor.[5] And so Wright's writings and activism joined with Wertham's politicized medical science and Bishop's Christian social justice traditions to set in motion the creation of a new type of institution on the American scene, the Lafargue Mental Hygiene Clinic.

"Harlem: Dark Weather-Vane"

Harlem in the 1940s differed considerably from the celebrated days of the New Negro Renaissance years of the mid-1920s. In the midst of the First World War, tens of thousands of blacks from the South and from the West Indies had descended upon that six-square-mile section of Upper Manhattan, and by the start of the Great Depression the black population of Harlem had increased from nearly thirty thousand to over two hundred thousand.[6] Most of those who moved to Harlem were the second and third generation of black people born outside slavery, and many envisioned themselves as "New Negroes," casting off offending minstrel images of docile and "happy-go-lucky darkies." In Harlem, a critical mass of New Negroes worked self-consciously to forge a new assertive identity for black

Americans. The resulting community of black people established Harlem as the Mecca of "Negro culture and society."[7]

But the Great Depression hit Harlem hard, harder even than it had hit Richard Wright's Chicago. The boom years of the 1920s, when black men and women could find work in the light industries within and around New York City, turned into the depressed 1930s. Black people bore the brunt of economic catastrophe. Not only were blacks in Harlem less likely to be employed than their white fellow New Yorkers; they often had difficulty gaining access to welfare relief and the social agencies that administered New Deal programs and services. A major riot in March 1935, sparked by rumors of a department store clerk killing a young black boy, led to days of violent unrest. It also produced a good deal of liberal hand-wringing about the conditions of life for New York's black minority, segregated into a small section of the city and discriminated against in all facets of the institutional life of New York. A comprehensive report on the Harlem "disturbance," written in large part by the Chicago School–trained black sociologist E. Franklin Frazier, detailed the conditions in Harlem that led to the outbreak of mass violence and offered specific recommendations for remedy. Wary, however, of the broader New York public's response, Mayor Fiorello La Guardia shelved the report, demanding that its findings not be released to the public (though the *New York Amsterdam News* printed it serially in the following year).[8]

In the wake of the 1935 outburst, Harlem became to some observers the measure of black America's collective health and well-being. In his essay "Harlem: Dark Weather-Vane," Alain Locke, doyen of the Harlem Renaissance, contrasted the hopeful moment of the Renaissance ten years prior with the reality of Harlem's becoming an "over-expensive, disease- and crime-ridden slum." "What we face in Harlem today," wrote Locke, "is the first scene of the next act—the prosy ordeal of the reformation with its stubborn tasks of economic reconstruction and social and civic reform." No matter how one characterized the events of March 1935, the riot served a diagnostic purpose, according to Locke, making plain the significance of the Negro's oppressed condition. "As the man farthest down," wrote Locke, "[the Negro] tests the pressure and explores the depths of the social and economic problem. In that sense he is not merely the man who shouldn't be forgotten; he is the man who cannot safely be ignored." Yet Locke, like many other black and white intellectuals and civic leaders,

remained hopeful that Negroes and whites might work together to confront the social and economic ills of Harlem, particularly in areas of housing and health. Harlem, once a sign of the Negro's cultural advancement,
a self-conscious, representative community of strivers, was now the symbol
of the struggle against the dire conditions of the urban ghetto.[9]

Harlem's paradoxical status as both Mecca and ghetto intensified with
the onset of World War II. Negro migration to New York and other northern cities shot up rapidly, as industries needing labor opened their doors
to black workers.[10] As migrants streamed into New York, they encountered an entrenched, systematic residential segregation. Those who came
to Harlem were squeezed into already overcrowded tenements at a higher
rate than the notoriously densely packed Lower East Side of turn-of-
the-century Manhattan.[11] In his famous autobiography, *Manchild in the
Promised Land*, Claude Brown lamented the plight of these migrants: "It
seems that Cousin Willie, in his lying haste, had neglected to tell folks down
home about one of the most important aspects of the promised land: it was
a slum ghetto. There was a tremendous difference in the way life was lived
up North. There were too many people full of hate and bitterness crowded
into a dirty, stinky, uncared-for closet-size section of a great city."[12]

Yet even in this ghetto, a new black militancy emerged, born of a mixture of participation in and exclusion from the nation's wartime mobilization. The war forced black Americans into a peculiar position, as it asked
them to participate in the defense of the nation, but on Jim Crow terms,
with no changes in blacks' second-class status. Most whites must never
have expected that the war would provoke a widespread assertive mood
among black Americans. Harlem was ground zero for black American
democratic aspirations, and the tone of these hopes was militancy.[13]

The Harlem community reflected its new militancy in both its institutions and in a general mood. Many believed that the city, and the country,
for that matter, was on the precipice of catastrophic change.[14] Writer James
Baldwin, a Harlem resident through the Depression and war, recalled
that "all of Harlem, indeed, seemed to be infected by waiting. I had never
known it to be so violently still. Racial tensions throughout this country
were exacerbated during the early years of the war, partly because the
labor market brought together hundreds of thousands of ill-prepared people and partly because Negro soldiers, regardless of where they were born,
received their military training in the South."[15]

In response, a coalition of black and white liberal leaders organized around combating antiblack discrimination in New York City. The City-Wide Citizens' Committee on Harlem was formed in 1941 to address the same oppressive conditions that led to the paroxysm of mass violence in Harlem in 1935. Members explicitly linked its program to the broader national issue of fighting Jim Crow, while fighting the war abroad. Their work was part of the wider, national campaign, Double V, victory against fascism at home and abroad, promoted by the black press and the rest of black civil society. The Citizens' Committee, while initially dedicated to the problems that stimulated chronic juvenile delinquency among black youth, expanded its purview to address the several areas of city life that were primary sources of grievance among Harlem's residents: housing, health and hospitals, education and recreation, employment, and crime and delinquency. Hoping to stem the rising tide of hostility, yet well attuned to the militant mood of the people, the committee called for both immediate remedies—especially an end to employment discrimination and to racist policing of Harlem—and "long-range social reconstruction" of New York City in relation to its black citizens.[16]

But the Citizens' Committee's reform work was no match for what Baldwin termed Harlem's "need to smash something." As he explained, "To smash something is the ghetto's chronic need. Most of the time it is the members of the ghetto who smash each other, and themselves. But as long as the ghetto walls are standing there will always come a moment when these outlets do not work." On August 1, 1943, Harlem erupted for one night of mayhem, sparked by rumors that a police officer had murdered a black soldier who was still in uniform. After recent mass violence between whites and blacks, and whites against Latinos, most notably in Detroit and Los Angeles, there was a simmering sense that the whole of America could erupt in race war.[17]

Many contemporary observers took pains to explain that "the Harlem disturbance" was not a race riot. Unlike Detroit and other conflagrations, the violence on the streets of Harlem did not involve members of different races attacking one another. Rather, as Richard Wright told one reporter the day after the outburst, the riot seemed to be a response to the wartime "economic pinch," with the rioters turning their ire against property rather than persons. Black people had expressed a general grievance about the way they had been cooped up in Harlem and exploited by shopkeepers and excluded from the general prosperity they witnessed all about them in the United States. While the origins of the Harlem riot seemed to lie in the economic order of things, the outburst was for many a harbinger of more chaos, perhaps a race war to come.[18]

Fredric Wertham predicted that unless something was done to address the hostile atmosphere created by Jim Crow in the North, New York City might see an unprecedented explosion of violence in the streets. He argued that northern racism, "half-concealed and generally insidious," produced psychological conflicts distinct from those engendered by stark southern white supremacy.[19] He explained that African Americans uprooted from the South and encountering northern society inevitably experienced various forms of alienation. Many black patients he encountered were what he called "mental DP's (Displaced Persons)."[20] Wertham used the language in the air during the World War II years likening black migrants to the war's roaming refugees in Europe—DPs.[21] Blacks too were experiencing the traumatic effects of loss, dispossession, and instability.

Wertham was not the only person who adopted the term DP in reference to southern-born black migrants in New York City. In his essay "Harlem Is Nowhere," Ralph Ellison referred to blacks in early post–World War II America as "displaced persons of American democracy." Ellison's and Wertham's appropriation of the term represented a call to Americans to consider migrating black Americans as part of a global phenomenon unleashed by the Second World War. The notion of displaced persons resonated with many Americans aware of the predicament of refugees with no home country in which to settle. Wertham and Ellison thus made black Americans' recent experience migrating from the South to the urban northern ghetto conceptually legible, as part of the upheavals shaping the postwar world.[22]

Migration and the associated changes in work, family, and recreation produced a destabilizing effect on the psyches of some African Americans who settled in Harlem. In a 1936 study, renowned epidemiologist Benjamin Malzberg found that during June 1928 to June 1931, out of a total of 1,403 of "U.S. born Negroes admitted to all institutions for mental disease in New York State, only 130, or 9.3 per cent, were born in New York State." The other 90.7 percent, the 1,273 admitted to mental hospitals, were migrants. Malzberg argued that "it seems a justifiable conclusion, therefore, that migration is in itself and through its attendant circumstances an important contributory factor in the causation of mental disease."[23] The loss of home and place was a profoundly important variable in the psychological well-being of the black migrant. The rankest white brutality may have been absent in the North, and formal equality recognized in law, but racial discrimination confronted black northerners at every turn. Such contradictions, Ellison argued, left "even the most balanced Negro open to anxiety."[24]

Segregation and Mental Health Care in New York City

Fredric Wertham often regaled Wright with stories of the terrible treatment of the mentally ill in New York City. According to Wright, Wertham had "a dark story to tell of how hospitals are run," especially the treatment of black New Yorkers at Bellevue and other hospitals, as well as blacks' exclusion from services at centers such as the New York Psychiatric Institute attached to Columbia University. As a psychiatrist in the New York City Department of Hospitals system, Wertham came into contact with the black men, women, and children hospitalized for various mental disorders, which he identified as having their etiology in the oppressive social order of Depression- and war-era United States. He described his failure in the 1930s to get the La Guardia administration to establish an outpatient psychiatric clinic in Harlem, a time when even Harlem Hospital, the only city hospital in the area, offered no psychiatric services.[25]

The burgeoning black population of New York City faced outright exclusion from mental health care. From the late 1930s through the 1940s, residential segregation and official health care policies denied African Americans access to the increasing number of psychiatric facilities within New York City. Between 1940 and 1950, the official number of black people in New York City grew from 458,444 to 749,080. While this population increasingly settled north and east of Harlem, about 70 percent of black New Yorkers were concentrated in Harlem. Black sociologist E. Franklin Frazier noted that "although as a result of a Supreme Court decision racial restrictive covenants are no longer enforceable, residential segregation and slums remain the Negro's most important problems" in large cities of the North such as New York.[26]

Sections of the city were divided into Health Areas for census purposes, making where one resided the basis for access to hospitals and psychiatric facilities located in other districts.[27] One 1942 report on the availability of psychiatric services for black children explained that for black New Yorkers, districting was used against them when applying for help because, with characteristic circular logic, "they are out of district," making the psychiatric services offered in various Manhattan hospitals nearest to Harlem largely irrelevant. Further, this report found that two of the most prominent "in-service" psychiatric research and treatment centers, the Psychiatric Institute at the Columbia Medical Center and the Cornell Medical Center, were "essentially closed to Negroes." Thus while hospitals in different districts were establishing or expanding both inpatient and outpatient psychiatric services, black New Yorkers were both restricted from admission to facilities outside their communities, owing to residential segregation, and denied access within their own districts to adequate care and treatment, as a result of unequal provision of health care facilities and programs within sites such as Harlem Hospital.[28]

In 1942, the Sub-Committee on Health and Hospitals of the City-Wide Citizens' Committee on Harlem recommended the establishment of a mental hygiene clinic in Harlem. The committee proposed a clinic designed "to combat frustrations, behavior and personality problems, and crime incidence in the community, and a psychiatric ward in Harlem Hospital for observation and diagnostic purposes." The problem of black New Yorkers' lack of access to facilities for psychiatric treatment within their own communities was now publicly placed before city officials and private agencies and institutions whose mission was purportedly the provision of various forms of health care and welfare services to those in need.[29] However, it wasn't until the Lafargue Clinic had been up and running for several months, proving itself a vital service to the Harlem community, that city hospital officials were persuaded to establish a mental hygiene clinic within Harlem Hospital. Even then, the clinic had only one full-time psychiatrist and a total staff of six nurses and assistants.[30]

For Wertham the nature of the psychiatric treatment blacks received was just as significant as the question of access. He feared that even if African Americans did gain access to psychiatric facilities, they would be receiving forms of treatment founded on a misguided approach, an approach that failed to understand mental disorders whose etiology was to be found in the social order of an oppressive society rather than the pathology of an individual psyche. Blacks constituted a reported "50% of the [annual] intake" at the Bellevue psychiatric ward, according to one early 1940s report, which of course means that they had access to a form of psychiatric care.[31] Even so, there is no indication that blacks in New York considered Bellevue a place where they would be both respected as human beings or receive the type of care and treatment that acknowledged the socio-psychological stress of living in oppressive conditions. By most accounts, blacks at Bellevue were treated according to the reigning stereotypes of black inferiority and puerility.[32]

Philanthropy and Failure

In the spring of 1945, Wertham phoned Wright with the idea of establishing a clinic in Harlem that would provide psychotherapy at the cost of a quarter per visit. Wertham envisioned an inexpensive outpatient psychiatric clinic in Harlem, open several evenings per week, and staffed by volunteer psychiatrists, psychologists, social workers, and nurses. Wright said he would see what he could do to help him with the plan, immediately suggesting that they approach the Field Foundation to secure funding. Wright had recently attended a luncheon at Marshall Field's Manhattan home to discuss a new race relations commission. Wright generally disdained the "folklore of race relations," but he understood the practical value of proximity to men such as Marshall Field III and Edwin Embree, director of the Julius Rosenwald Fund, the philanthropic agency of the Sears, Roebuck fortune. At the Field luncheon he happened to sit next to Louis Weiss, Field's lawyer, who had made overtures of friendship. Engaging in a "long and amazing talk" about race, economics, and psychology, they agreed that "making what Negroes experience known to the American people was one of the most powerful things that could be done to help solve the race problem." Weiss was keen to support any work being done in that direction, so Wright naturally thought of him when Wertham proposed the Harlem clinic.

A mental hygiene clinic in Harlem would not only serve its patients, thought Wright; it would make public the psychological and emotional effects of antiblack discrimination and segregation.[33] In June 1945, Wright arranged a dinner at Weiss's home, where Wertham would be able to present the clinic plan in full detail. Wright and Wertham assumed that they, along with their wives, would be the sole guests of Mr. Weiss. They were surprised then when two other people joined the dinner party. Sitting with Mr. Weiss were two "consultants," one a prominent juvenile court judge and the other a psychoanalyst, both known "for their high-toned public utterances about social and philanthropic matters."[34]

What occurred was a fiasco. Immediately following Wertham's presentation of his plan and request for funding, the two consultants dismissed the plan as unrealistic. They offered several objections: black Harlemites would never come to a clinic run by a white psychiatrist; the clinic would simply be reproducing the same structure of white doctors' control that existed in psychiatric institutions throughout the city. They advised Weiss that the Field Foundation should have nothing to do with Wertham's envisaged clinic. Weiss agreed.

Decades later, Wertham would recall this meeting as one more indication of the failure of liberal philanthropy, of the inability of powerful liberals to imagine new methods of providing care and treatment for the poor and excluded.[35] "I really got a great feeling of let-down after the dinner at Mr. Weiss,'" Wertham wrote to Wright a short time after the failed meeting. "You see, I think I know even a little more about what happens to children in Harlem than you do, how they are really crushed so that they can possibly never come back again."[36] Wertham may have been exasperated by the Field Foundation's rejection of his proposal, but he remained determined to establish a clinic in Harlem that would use psychotherapy in the broader cause of helping black New Yorkers to "survive in a hostile society."

The Struggle for Mental Hygiene for Black Americans

Prior to Wertham's and Wright's efforts in the mid-1940s, professional and lay concern for the provision of mental health care to black Americans had coalesced around the founding of the Committee for Mental Hygiene for Negroes (CMHN), a short-lived project that did not last through the war. Founded in December 1939 at St. Augustine's College in Raleigh, North Carolina, the committee grew out of the experiences and advocacy of one lone African American woman named Rosa Kittrell. Kittrell had herself been hospitalized for mental illness, first in North Carolina and later in New York. As a patient she discussed with her psychiatrists "her resolve to work for better psychiatric care for her people." When she returned to her home in White Plains, New York, she organized the White Plains Mental Hygiene Group, collaborating with her psychiatrist to convene a group of mental health professionals and representatives of historically black colleges and universities, including Howard University, the Tuskegee Institute, and Meharry Medical College in Nashville, Tennessee.

The committee launched a campaign to create psychiatric hospitals at Howard and Meharry, modeled on Boston Psychopathic Hospital and the Phipps Clinic of Johns Hopkins Hospital. It also called for the development of regional mental hygiene groups to promote awareness of the psychiatric needs of Negroes, as well as the establishment of preventive public mental health clinics in Negro communities. Some on the committee were worried that the proposed hospitals would simply be another accommodation to Jim Crow segregation, arguing that efforts should be directed toward combating discrimination in already existing state and private hospitals. Others suggested it was not necessary to choose between challenging discrimination and establishing facilities for Negro patients. Given the reality of segregation, efforts on both fronts were essential.[37]

The United States' entry into World War II interrupted the work of the committee, as many of its officers and members were called upon to serve in the war effort. The primary question posed by committee chairman Dr. T. P. Brennan was, "What justification does this program have in our War?" For Brennan, the issue of addressing the mental health needs of Negroes, as the signal minority people in American society, was part of the larger politics of minority-majority relations in a democracy: "This is a subject that has a legitimate psychiatric and mental hygiene component. In it, exquisitely potent human and social processes are at work. They are processes that do things to individuals—to individuals on both sides of the relationship." Arguing that psychiatry constituted a valid tool for both the exploration and solution to the individuated effects of race relations, Brennan maintained that the work of the CMHN was vital and must continue in the midst of the war.[38]

Unfortunately, no record exists of the committee being a persistent and effective advocate for the provision of mental care for black Americans during or after the war. In the wake of an initial mobilization in the early 1940s, there is no indication that the work of the committee gained much traction within the broader campaigns to promote the expansion of mental hygiene services and facilities in the postwar era. Various members of the advisory council, including Harlem's Rev. Adam Clayton Powell Jr., seemed relatively well positioned to influence policy changes and the redirection of material resources toward Negro mental health needs. It appears that the committee simply faded away. We are left to wonder where went the concerted energy and interest of members of this organization.

Northside Center for Child Development

While efforts to organize a comprehensive system of mental health care for black Americans may have faltered as a result of wartime mobilization, concern over the emotional and mental health of black children led to the birth of a new institution that paralleled the establishment of the Lafargue Clinic. The Northside Center for Child Development opened in Harlem the very same month as Lafargue, March 1946. Northside differed, however, from Lafargue in that its founders, Drs. Kenneth and Mamie Clark, were psychologists, rather than psychiatrists. The Clarks envisioned a place for troubled children of all races to receive psychological testing and counseling, as well as remedial education. The Clarks approached children's mental health issues with a blend of Progressive-era child guidance interventions aimed toward children's basic social adjustment and novel socio-environmental behavioral sciences that used testing and therapy to diagnose and rehabilitate troubled children. In practice this approach directly confronted the Negro child's social and cultural experience of antiblack racism and the effects of societal marginalization.

In the early 1940s, the problems of black children had become a focal point for mental health professionals, juvenile court jurists, and liberal philanthropists determined to improve public and private child guidance services designed to combat juvenile delinquency and education-related maladjustment. A number of men and women who sat on various sub-committees of the City-Wide Citizens' Committee on Harlem soon became integral participants in the founding, operation, and financing of the Northside Center.

While Northside and Lafargue shared a similar orientation to addressing the psychological effects of racism, the Clarks succeeded in gaining philanthropic support where Wertham could not. The same philanthropists who rejected Wertham's plan became the primary underwriters of the Northside Center. The two Field Foundation "consultants" who counseled Louis Weiss to reject Wertham's plan appear to have been Children's Court judge Justine Wise Polier and Dr. Viola W. Bernard, a prominent New York psychoanalytic psychiatrist. These two women served on the board of directors of Northside, and it was Dr. Bernard who ultimately convinced Marion Ascoli to be chief sponsor of the Clarks' new institution. Ascoli was one of Julius Rosenwald's daughters, and thus an heir to the Sears, Roebuck fortune. In their study of the Northside Center, historians Gerald Markowitz and Mark Rosner show how the Clarks were able to attract the interest and largesse of a small group of mostly Jewish philanthropists and psychiatrists by effectively framing the need for a type of clearinghouse for the most vulnerable of New York's children. Ultimately the Clarks had to struggle against various forms of cultural and professional paternalism in their relations with their board of directors. Even so, the Northside Center was able to operate as a full-time, comprehensive facility in a way that the Lafargue Clinic was never allowed the opportunity to develop.[39] Perhaps the problems of black children were easier for some clinicians, reformers, and philanthropists to face than those of adults suffering from society-induced mental disorders. Perhaps the fact that the Clarks were African American made Northside more legitimate in the eyes of some of its supporters. For some, including Dr. Bernard, the Field Foundation consultant, and even Dr. Brennan of the CMHN, it was of prime importance that black psychiatrists be the advance guard in treating black patients. As there were only a handful of board-certified black psychiatrists in the United States, options for a comprehensive clinic or hospital department of psychiatry headed by blacks were very limited. The fact that Wertham was white remained a problem for some figures and institutions with the power to allocate resources. (Kenneth Clark himself confirmed this point while on a February 1951 conference panel alongside Wertham: "They wouldn't tell *us* that a Mental Hygiene Clinic in Harlem was not needed—they'd tell Dr. Wertham because he is white.") For Bernard and for Brennan, with this opinion went the feeling that white psychiatrists such as themselves were not ideal candidates for directing a mental hygiene clinic within a black community, let alone Harlem, the capital of black America. While a principled and understandable sentiment, it made no room for exceptional figures like Wertham.[40]

The Birth of the Lafargue Clinic

The years of 1945 and 1946 were pivotal to Wertham's frank recognition of who he was and where he stood in relation to the American psychiatric profession. As an outsider, a marginal person—someone who, at his core, identified with the oppressed—Wertham created a space for himself apart from the mainstream of psychiatry, as well as the institutional confines of liberal social reform agencies. Replying to a letter from his erstwhile mentor Dr. Adolf Meyer, shortly after the founding of the Lafargue Clinic, Wertham explained,

> Things stand now in proper proportion. I am now over fifty. Organized American psychiatry, since I left Phipps, has given me nothing and it would be folly to expect any rewards in the future.... Yet I am very satisfied. I have learned what the people of the world are up against, successively organized or re-organized three large mental hygiene clinics in New York [the Court Clinic, at Bellevue and at Queens], [and] recently I started another, for the people of Harlem, in my evening "spare time."... I thank you again for your kind letter expressing an interest in my activities. And I assure you I shall continue the good fight for a decent and scientific psychiatry even though the means of production for it are in other hands.[41]

The time for waiting on the powers that be to endorse Wertham's vision of democratizing psychotherapy was over. In March 1946, without philanthropic or public funding, but with the support and assistance of his friends, colleagues, and students, Wertham found in Harlem a welcoming figure in Rev. Shelton Hale Bishop and a small space to engage in a modestly radical experiment in providing "expert psychotherapy for those who need it and cannot get it."[42] It was simply stated as such in the Lafargue Clinic's brochure—but in back of this plan was a social philosophy and scientific orientation that read black psychological suffering as linked to an oppressive social and economic order and saw therapy as transformative rather than palliative.

In the winter of 1946, Bishop offered Wertham, who continued to serve as director of the Queens General Hospital Mental Hygiene Clinic, the use of two rooms in the basement of the St. Philip's parish house. The Lafargue Mental Hygiene Clinic opened its doors on March 8, 1946, and operated every Tuesday and Friday evening until November 1958. That the Lafargue Clinic was housed in a prominent African American church signaled to Harlem residents that they would be offered legitimate care and treatment with a truly human touch. The Harlem community regarded the church as a safe space where black people would not be toyed with or treated as objects of scientific experiments, to be poked and prodded.[43] Bishop viewed the establishment of the Lafargue Clinic as a Christian service and proclaimed it "the greatest thing to happen to Harlem in many years." In the St. Philip's Church newsletter, published one week after the first night of the clinic's opening, Bishop declared

> there is not one adequate community resource in New York City for the proper psychiatric treatment of colored people. This is well known by all social agencies that serve this community. . . . [The Lafargue Clinic] is for the people in the Harlem community, for both children and adults who have mental or nervous disorders of any kind, and who desire treatment. It is one more attempt on the part of this Parish to meet community needs in a very specific way. . . . We would like to begin especially with the behavior problems of children and with veterans.[44]

It must have been a remarkable experience for residents of Harlem to enter those basement rooms of the parish house. A contemporary report described the scene:

> The little waiting room was crowded. A good looking ex-GI smoked a cigarette nervously. A mother sat holding her 10-year old daughter's hand. Two men sat together quietly.
>
> A young lady in a white smock came in. "Mr. Carson next, please," she announced. He followed her into a large room and they both sat at a small circular table. She poised her pen and asked him numerous questions. When she was through, she led him to one of four cubicles formed by unpainted screens. Here, a psychiatrist was waiting to hear his troubles and start treatment. . . .
>
> From the cubicles came the drone of steady talk as Dr. Wertham's three co-workers consulted with patients. . . . Some patients remain for 15 minutes, others are not through for an hour.

"I got out of the navy three months ago. I can't settle down to my job at the airport. I always worry about my family and about losing my job . . ."

"I don't know how it happened, but when I came to I was lying on the floor. My tongue was bleeding. This is the second time . . ."

"They're out to get me I tell you! I feel sure he put poison in my soup, I'm afraid to eat anything . . ."

"Married? Of course, I want to get married. But if he even shakes hands with me I'm frightened . . ."

"This is Harold, Doctor. He has always been a good boy up until a month ago. Then he started playing hookey . . . Yesterday the man at the newsstand caught him stealing . . ."

And so on, far into the night, thousands of words uttered by hopeful lips in search of peace of mind.[45]

The Will to Survive in a Hostile World

A single page in the collected papers of Fredric Wertham titled "Objectives of Lafargue Clinic" succinctly captured the fundamentally radical, antiracist orientation of the institution:

> Problem of Harlem (racial) is job of Lafargue Clinic
>
> Public should be acquainted with the fact that discrimination exists in psychiatry—example: Psychiatric Institute does not take Negroes as patients.
>
> Individual cases cannot be understood if the above points are not recognized.
>
> Lafargue Clinic to do a higher type of psychiatry besides the ordinary "ABC's of psychiatry"
>
> Political consciousness
>
> Defined by Dr. Wertham as: "knowing what's going on"
>
> Many who have the opportunity to know what's going on do not accept it.
>
> No big theories are needed
>
> No prejudices.[46]

Practicality governed the clinic's method. Each therapy session was only thirty minutes, an hour in special cases. Given the brief amount of time for each patient, the clinic staff had to offer targeted, creative therapy. Thus each member of the staff had to be relatively versatile as counselors and therapists. A September 1952 memo on the clinic's organization read: "The Clinic is entirely oriented to psychotherapy, to all the different forms of psychotherapy. Every staff member with the exception of clerical workers should get instruction in psychotherapy on all levels."[47]

Wertham directed the clinic staff to pay close attention to the broader context of the patient's experiences as sources of discontent, anxiety, delusions, and other mental distress. Upon entering the Lafargue Clinic a patient would answer a series of questions designed to enable an initial impression of a diagnosis, or at least an identifiable category of disorder that was causing a problem for the patient. Each staff member the patient encountered was trained to engender trust and to alleviate the patient's doubts, suspicion, or anxiety about seeking help. Getting patients to feel at ease in telling their story was essential. And the clinic viewed the patient's presentation of his own case history as beginning the therapy process. Dr. Luise Zucker, a psychologist at the clinic, offered these suggestions for first examinations: "Establish a good working relationship with [patient]. This can be achieved by showing him both your sympathy and your respect for him as a human being. Listen carefully to what he says and *how* he says it. Take notes while [patient] is talking, not in retrospect. His own formulations rather than yours can be very enlightening." Zucker further emphasized a focus on the patient's personal information as it related to her attitude to her job and her interactions with friends and other social bonds. Moreover, Zucker warned fellow staff members not to "delude yourself into thinking that you will 'psychoanalyze' your [patient] in seeing him once a week or less often. You may do a good job by using a modified therapeutic approach, based on psychoanalytic principles. Both methods can be helpful, but don't get them mixed up." At the end of each night, Dr. Wertham and Dr. Hilde L. Mosse, the physician-in-charge, would assemble the staff to discuss each case seen that evening, to review the diagnoses, and plan future treatment.[48]

Despite Zucker's admonition, psychoanalysis remained an essential frame and method for the clinic's psychotherapeutic orientation—and Wertham and his staff exceeded the strictures of orthodoxy through a pragmatic polyglot embrace of a variety of methods of treating its patients.[49] Wertham referred to his psychoanalytically based method as analytic psychotherapy and emphasized the necessity of getting to the heart of a patient's story, their life history and current experiences affecting their mental well-being. The clinic's physician-in-charge and Wertham's Queens General Hospital colleague Dr. Mosse explained that "the psychiatrist's skill has to be such as to make the patient feel that the doctor is on *his* side and that he respects the patient as a human being." Together, patient and doctor must become allies in achieving insight into what is ailing the patient, how it occurs, and why. In this therapeutic encounter, Wertham and Mosse emphasized the necessity of offering initial simple reassurance to the patient, as well as giving basic advice guided by a thorough grasp of *who* the patient actually was—hence the importance of the patient's historicizing and ongoing self-narration and self-presentation. "Our analytic insight into the dynamics of the patient," explained Mosse, "makes it possible for us to help him work through his past experiences. It also enables him in the planning of the future."[50]

For the Lafargue Clinic, two psychoanalytic concepts were of great significance to diagnosing and treating its patients. For an oppressed clientele, *gratification* and *sublimation* took on a different cast than they would for the usual white, bourgeois subject of long-term psychoanalysis. Mosse explained that "it is here that Freudian understanding of psychological mechanisms meets the impact of social and economic forces. We have to find a way for the patient to gratify his drives and to sublimate them. To find the right kind of work for the patient, to find a place for him to live, is psychotherapy just as important as the uncovering of the patient's unconscious."[51]

The obstacles to achieving gratification of human drives for sex, for interpersonal and social recognition on one's own terms for a black person in 1940s New York City, were legion. Tools, rituals, practices, and institutions structured to assist the individual's sublimating of his or her drives, of distilling them into a productive and rewarding form, tended either to be denied, or required extraordinary effort to access for African Americans. When confronted with the forms of racial and class subjugation foisted upon African Americans, the Lafargue Clinic was forced to acknowledge the wide impossibility of obtaining "adequate ways of gratification and sublimation for our patient." Taking this as a frank reality of the social world in which its patients lived, the clinic then worked as a group—psychiatrists in collaboration with social workers in collaboration with psychologists and with Reverend Bishop—to "strengthen the patient to such a degree, that he is able to see and face the actual social situation, and to instill in him the will to survive in a hostile world."[52]

A clear example of the clinic's approach to its patients can be seen in the case of a twenty-three-year-old woman who came to the clinic in early 1947 with the chief complaint of "nervousness" and repeatedly waking with a severe pain in her breasts after a night full of sexual dreams. She met with a Dr. Husserl (a relative of the founder of phenomenology Edmund Husserl), who soon diagnosed her with mild hysteria, psychoneurosis with conversion. This meant that she was converting her nervousness into physical symptoms. This young black woman was a domestic worker, who lived on her own in Harlem. Both her parents had died when she was four years old. Her grandmother raised her until she was eleven, at which point she was sent to a boarding school. She returned to New York and lived briefly with her grandmother. The patient expressed the feeling of being unwanted both as a child and later as an adult. She stated that from a young age she had been made to feel ugly, which in turn made her feel as though the whole world was hostile to her. She felt this even in romantic relationships with men. On her second visit, Dr. Husserl noted that this young woman's physical symptoms were spreading to headaches and to arm and back pain. The sexual dreams persisted, almost every night. The doctor reported "encouraging" her that she was not unattractive and urging her to "integrate her life [with] a social group." A week later this patient returned for another visit, after having a full physical with X-rays as well. There were no apparent organic causes for her pains, and the patient reported that all her symptoms, except for pains in her breasts, had disappeared. She then said that the intense sexual dreams had disappeared as well. The patient also reported feeling better because she was pursuing other work, beginning with taking a "vocational aptitude test." The doctor's diagnosis was kept as mild hysteria, but he noted a significant improvement. Based upon what was in the report, Dr. Mosse noted in a 1949 review: "Neurosis Recovered."

This patient's case is rather unremarkable, to be sure. But it demonstrates the straightforward, practical work done by the clinic. She had, in psychiatric terms, a "complaint" and told the doctor what she thought of the reasons for it; Dr. Husserl countered her negative feelings about herself by persuading her to see the reality that she was not ugly. She had obviously held on to negative feelings about herself from childhood, and Husserl knew that she needed to make the adult decision to place herself in a fruitful social situation where she would be involved in productive activities with other adults.[53]

Culture and Society in Postwar Psychiatry

By the time the Lafargue Clinic had opened in the late winter of 1946, a number of schools of "environmental," "interpersonal," and "cultural" psychiatric thought had come to fruition. One important group coalesced around the work of the psychiatrist Harry Stack Sullivan, cultural anthropologist Louis Sapir, and Harold Lasswell at the William Alanson White Foundation.[54] Another was the "culture and personality" group whose primary home was Yale University and was best represented in the work of Dr. Karen Horney and the group of psychoanalysts who came to be known as "neo-Freudians" or "post-Freudians."[55] Throughout the life of the Lafargue Clinic, though, Wertham remained critical of the major trends in psychoanalytic psychiatry that explicitly incorporated what he termed "supra-personal" factors into the total picture of human personality and mental health. He resisted the two predominating paradigms that contributed most to the environmental turn in psychiatry, namely "culture and personality" and (ironically) "social psychiatry."[56]

It would appear that Horney's brand of psychoanalytic environmentalism would have considerable insight to offer Wertham in his work. Horney and the so-called neo-Freudians challenged the *biologism* of both traditional somatic psychiatry and the orthodox Freudians insistent on the primacy of the sex and death drives in man's personality. And more fundamentally, Horney challenged scientists and the public to confront the cultural forces that make people think and act the way they do, apart from their supposed instinctual drives fixed in their bodies and minds. But Wertham argued that the neo-Freudians did not offer a substantive advance in psychotherapy, because they still failed "to take into full account the dynamic interaction between personal and impersonal [social] factors." In Wertham's view it was not good science to equate cultural factors with social factors, namely because the former remained in the arena of the subjective. This meant that psychiatry, cultural or otherwise, would still treat the individual in terms of how he negotiated psychologically the culture of which he was a member. Wertham argued that a focus on culture elided the relationship of individuals and classes of people to the means of production and their place in the larger social structure, particularly how race and class intersect to structure individual and group experience.

Other contemporary scientists and doctors were using the term social psychiatry, as well, to describe a desired rapprochement between psychodynamic psychiatry and the social sciences of psychology, anthropology, and most especially sociology. Historian Gerald Grob situates social psychiatry in the larger trend of post–World War II psychiatry's deinstitutionalization.[57] After the war a new generation of psychiatrists made the whole of American society the home of psychodynamic research, treatment, and prevention. The psychodynamic paradigm of psychiatry had its roots in psychoanalysis and the mental hygiene movement but was very much the child of World War II. Many psychiatrists took notice not only of the individual patient's relationship to his or her mother and father but began focusing on the place of that individual in the social order and how the sociocultural environment might play a role in the development of a mental disorder. One prominent exponent of social psychiatry expressed the main thrust of the new framework, "If psychiatry is truly to move into a vigorous period of real preventive work, it must begin to look beyond the individual to the forces within the social environment which contribute to the personal dilemma." The psychodynamic framework's focus on a variety of causes—somatic, constitutional, and environmental—of personality problems and mental disorders and its use of psychoanalytic clinical methods provided the theoretical and methodological compass directing the development of social psychiatry in the early postwar era.[58]

By the mid-1950s an interdisciplinary consortium of psychiatrists and sociologists in the United States and Britain were making a coherent attempt to define the meaning of social psychiatry.[59] In the wake of the war, the concern over mental illness had grown, and the experience of some psychiatrists working in the military and then in outpatient clinics had bolstered their confidence in preventive measures. Moreover, these doctors and scientists wanted to make it possible for all psychiatrists and affiliated professionals to develop and apply new scientific knowledge about the sources and nature of mental illnesses in individuals and in particular communities. In the editorial of the first issue of the *International*

Journal of Social Psychiatry, Dr. Joshua Bierer of London explained: "The causes of most mental and social illnesses and maladjustments have not yet been fully explored. If we are to find these causes, we must change our attitude and our approach. Our attitude so far has been either *particularistic*—concentrating on one part of the body or of the mind, or *total*—concentrating on the person as a whole, or on the 'total personality.' Our future attitude should be a 'universal' one; we must concentrate on the '*whole situation*'—i.e. the total personality plus environment and relationships."[60] But what would this concentration on the "whole situation" mean in terms of a new discipline or specialty within psychiatry? And how might broadening the purview of psychiatry through the sociological study of mental illness affect actual psychiatrists and social workers who cared for and treated the mentally ill (or those simply suffering from everyday mental stresses)?

Some historians have argued that social psychiatry was never a coherent field or specialty with which psychiatrists could apply specific clinical methods to real mental illnesses. Social psychiatry, some argued, could indeed be viewed as part of a larger revolution in understanding personality and behavior taking place since the early 1940s, a paradigm shift stressing the interrelatedness of physical, biological, cultural, social, and psychological factors in human behavior. But social psychiatry supposedly had little to offer in the way of specific tools or methods for actual practice. One team of authors wrote in 1966 that

> apart from its usefulness as a label for a certain type of crossdisciplinary research training and research procedure, the term, "social psychiatry," would appear to have no logical meaning. There is little merit in applying it to the many and heterogeneous methods of practice and prevention in the area of community mental health now being elaborated in an experimental fashion.

Writing a generation later, historian Gerald Grob concluded that "at best social psychiatry was a label for cross-disciplinary research training and research procedure; it lacked many of the attributes of clinical practice."[61]

None of these historical accounts of social psychiatry mention the ideas or work of Fredric Wertham. None of the surveys of the field written during the years of the Lafargue Clinic's operation mention him or consider the clinic's efforts to implement the social psychiatric paradigm.[62] Perhaps this was because Wertham was not a part of the Group for the Advancement of Psychiatry (GAP), a psychodynamic-oriented association within the American Psychiatric Association (APA) committed both to environmental explanations of etiology and to social activism informed by psychiatry. Its most prominent members were Karl and William Menninger, Thomas Rennie, Robert Felix, Daniel Blain, and Marion Kenworthy.[63] None of Wertham's articles, clinical or otherwise, appeared in the *American Journal of Psychiatry* (*AJP*) during the 1940s or 1950s.[64] He chose instead to submit his scientific studies to the *American Journal of Psychotherapy*, published by the Association for the Advancement of Psychotherapy, of which he was president for the years 1943 to 1948. We can only wonder whether initial retrospective assessments of the "coherence" of social psychiatry might look different had they considered the work of Wertham and his colleagues at the Lafargue Clinic.

Wertham's brand of social psychiatry gave answers to the basic question of the origins and manifestations of mental disorders that addressed the concrete, reality-based nature of human personality and psychological problems people confronted. In order to treat anxieties, for example, a doctor had to grasp the origin and character of those anxieties. In New York City both before and after World War II he saw racial discrimination and class exploitation and made the step that his putative colleagues had not, could not, or would not: he opened a clinic "in and for" the community of Harlem for the practical treatment of socially induced anxieties and mental maladies. Wertham's problem with the putative social psychiatrists the culture and personality psychoanalysts was, therefore, never theoretical or methodological alone. His main criticism was quite basic. All the progressive theories and treatments in the world would mean little if the majority of people never had access to psychotherapy.

Wertham's contempt for various brands of psychiatry and some of the leading figures in the field may have blinded him, though, to the changes going on within the American Psychiatric Association. By the late 1940s more and more members of the Group for the Advancement of Psychiatry assumed positions of leadership and implemented psychodynamic approaches within the association, within the pages of the first *Diagnostic and Statistical Manual of Mental Disorders* (DSM-I), and at medical schools. Wertham may have simply chosen to be marginal, to be an antagonist, where he could remain a critic and not a more conventional participant in the changes taking place within psychiatry at mid-century. Or maybe Wertham just thought he was right and that others, even putative allies in social psychiatry, were wrong both conceptually and clinically—that they were blind to the *social* in social psychiatry. Nevertheless, Wertham, despite his pedigree, his scholarship, and the positions he held, was not a member of the circle of social scientists and psychiatrists most prominent in defining and implementing a form of social psychiatry held in common and based upon the work of men like William Menninger and Thomas Rennie, professor of psychiatry at Cornell University. Wertham's problem with his colleagues in the social and mental sciences led him to be marginal to the very field in which he sought to make his greatest contribution. And his marginality led to a great silence on Wertham and the Lafargue Clinic in the relevant scientific literature of the day.[65]

Diagnosis and Treatment at Lafargue

The establishment and operation of the Lafargue Clinic also coincided with the years in which the first *Diagnostic and Statistical Manual of Mental Disorders* was drafted and ratified by the American Psychiatric Association. Commonly known as DSM-I, this manual appeared in 1952 and presented board-certified psychiatrists with a systematized definition and classification of mental disorders and identified which symptoms of speech and behavior when taken together composed a diagnosable syndrome or "reaction-type," in language still beholden to Wertham's erstwhile Phipps Clinic mentor, Dr. Adolf Meyer. Psychiatrist and historian Jonathan Metzl explains that though the DSM-I "retained a good amount of diagnostic language from earlier classification systems," it also reflected the psychodynamic turn in psychiatry in the wake of World War II—so that "the [psycho-]analytic presence helped shape the first postwar classification of psychopathology" and had the result of codifying "the belief that mental disease resulted, not only from biological lesions, but from early life conflicts."[66]

While an advance from the exclusive somatic paradigm as the basis for diagnosing mental disorders, the DSM-I failed, in Wertham's eyes, to account for the social context and basis for the emergence of mental disorders among the American populace, especially among the oppressed. There was at this time in postwar America, according to Wertham, "a great contradiction between the tendency to apply psychiatric and psycho-analytic ideas to the social sciences and the failure of psychiatry so far to study adequately even those social problems which are most closely related to the care and treatment of mental patients."[67] Wertham's fundamental critique of psychiatry and psychoanalysis was that its practitioners focused too much on either the individual or the biological aspects of human thought and behavior to the exclusion of their social basis. He wanted his fellow psychiatrists to understand that a patient must be understood first and foremost as belonging to a class, each patient positioned with a distinct social relation to the means of production, with specific concerns and problems based on this relation. The psychiatrist must be concerned with whether one was a boss, worker, or part of that group of have-nots that some have called the underclass, which Marx called the *Lumpenproletariat.* By paying close, clinical attention to the social basis of mental life, psychiatry would advance itself as a science. Wertham argued that "there is no contradiction between scientific and social psychiatry. Psychiatry cannot be social if it is not truly scientific, and it is certainly not scientific if it is not social. The road to progress is the integration of Kraepelin, Freud, and Marx—which means to do justice to the dynamic dialectic interaction of conscious, unconscious, and social factors."[68]

While this Kraepelinian-Freudian-Marxian integration served as the framing point-of-view for encountering the patients who came to Lafargue, Wertham repeatedly stressed to his staff the importance of proper individualized diagnosis of discrete mental disorders: "Diagnosis is the cornerstone on which all scientific medical therapy and psychotherapy rests. Diagnosis should not consist of a single label but be a formulation of the structure of the interplay of personality, illness and situation."[69] The clinic encountered among its patients the full gamut of mental disorders extant in American society in the early postwar era. Exactly ten years after the clinic first opened its doors, three staff members drafted a statistical report on the clinic's patients. It is the only comprehensive report in the clinic's archival records. From a total of 1,489 files, the report's authors examined and categorized 250 patient charts. There is no explanation in the report of how the authors chose this sample of 250 charts; 185 were adults (69.4% of patients), 65 children under the age of sixteen (30.6%).

The report also included 31 court cases (12.3%), of which 16 were adults, 15 children. The clinic diagnosed 113 adults (62.5%) and 8 children (14%) with neurosis; 38 adults (21%) and 1 child (1.8%) with psychosis; 2 adults (1.1%) and 4 children (7%) with organic conditions; 6 adults (3.3%) and 2 children (3.5%) with physical problems; 22 adults (12.1%) with "social and family problems"; and 42 children (73.7%) with "behaviour problems." The results of treatment were then divided as follows: 34 adults (25%) and 6 children (14.3%) unimproved; 64 adults (47.1%) and 17 children (40.5%) improved; 22 adults (16.2%) and 16 children (38.1%) recovered; and 16 adults (11.7%) and 3 children (7.1%) hospitalized.[70]

The Lafargue Clinic often questioned and challenged the diagnoses and treatment plans of other agencies in New York. In a 1956 statistical report on the clinic's diagnoses over the years, there was a note reading: "*Re: Psychoses*: When we diagnose psychosis we mean it. We do not mean what all the other clinics and papers talk about, namely what they call 'latent' schizophrenia. We diagnose unquestionable psychoses . . . usually not recognized before they came to the Lafargue Clinic. . . . It is still amazing how many patients with major mental diseases are undiagnosed and untreated in spite of the increase in mental hygiene facilities in the past 10 years."[71]

There were a number of cases in which other New York public and private agencies had diagnosed both children and adults as being a "problem personality" or as being a "malingerer." In one notable case, a twenty-six-year-old man, originally from Norfolk, Virginia, came to the Lafargue Clinic in January 1951 with a pain in his head and hips. He also complained of nervousness and "bad thoughts, [wishing] I was dead, thinking about killing myself." This man told a staff doctor that he had been referred to Lafargue from a fellow patient at the Bellevue Hospital Psychiatric Division, where the twenty-six-year-old had been hospitalized during March and April 1949. He stated that his current symptoms had been present for at least three years. He had previously sought help at Bellevue Mental Hygiene Clinic, Montefiore Hospital, and Metropolitan Out-Patient Department (better known as Welfare Island). The diagnoses of each agency were, respectively: schizophrenia, neurosis, and "too lazy to work." The report from Welfare Island declared "this is a 26 year old man who does not like to work; there is nothing in the history or findings to justify his visits here; Discharge: Rx heavy work"![72]

Wertham discussed this case at one of the staff meetings held at the end of each evening's work. Based upon the evidence of neurological, psychological, and clinical examinations, Wertham concluded that this young man's problems were most likely the result of an organic disorder, although schizophrenia could not be ruled out. The clinic gave a provisional diagnosis of Picks Disease, a form of premature dementia caused by atrophy of the frontal and temporal lobes of the brain, which resembles the organic aspects of Alzheimer's disease, and the symptoms of some forms of schizophrenia.

In another case, a young woman came to the clinic first in 1952 and was seen a number of times over the next two years. She discussed her anxiety over what the staff termed "problems of everyday living." She hated her job as a domestic and was having difficulty as a single mother with three young boys. The clinic staff never diagnosed her as neurotic or having any other type of mental disorder; nevertheless, she continued to come to the clinic because the staff was helping her in ways that other social service agencies had failed to do. This young, single mother was behind three months' rent on her Harlem tenement apartment. So one of the clinic's social workers helped her apply for public housing and other aid. Her son was diagnosed by the clinic staff as having a severe behavior disorder, so the staff worked to place the boy in Rockland State Hospital, just north of New York City, where he could receive intensive treatment.

The outcome of this woman's case is not in the Lafargue Clinic records, nor is that of her son. But we can see that the clinic addressed this woman's anxiety in practical terms by assisting her in attaining her basic needs. And by intervening to help place her son in a hospital, the clinic enabled this young woman to attend to the needs of her two other, younger sons, who according to one staff member were being neglected as a result of the mother having to deal with the elder son's behavior problems. We may wonder exactly how this family's experience of the clinic compared to its encounters with the other institutions in New York City designed to aid those in similar circumstances. It *is* clear though that the variegated service that the clinic provided is evident in this case, as is its comprehensive aim of taking social circumstances seriously in treating each patient.[73]

In November 1950, Wertham referred a young black boy to the Lafargue Clinic. Wertham had seen the six-year-old at the Queens General Hospital Outpatient Clinic because the boy was acting out at school and resisting his mother and father at home. He had been aggressive several times with his baby sister as well. A year prior, the family had moved from Harlem to Jamaica, Queens, into a predominantly white neighborhood. In September of that year (1949), the boy began attending public school in the new area, and soon after had an acute asthma attack. He had never had asthma before, but soon had daily minor attacks. The clinic staff spoke at length with the boy's mother and soon recommended putting the boy in playgroups, as a form of examination and therapy. The child's mother told the staff that her son had shown an early preference for light skin and having white playmates. The mother suggested that part of the reason for the child's resistance to her and her husband was that the boy resented their dark color, and possibly even his own. Dr. Florence Brand-Grossman, one of the clinic's psychologists, wrote that on one occasion the boy remarked to his mother "that some of his white playmates expressed a fear that if they touched him they would turn colored. [Patient] very much disturbed by this." Dr. Mosse, the physician-in-charge, noted in the child's file that the asthma likely had a psychological basis, and she prescribed attending the clinic's child playgroup.

Over the next five months, the young boy attended the playgroup once a week. By January 1951, the child's mother told Dr. Grossman that the boy was doing much better since coming to the playgroup, that he no longer sucked his thumb, and that he hadn't had any asthma attacks since the fall. The sociogenic nature of this boy's problems is clear from the reports in his patient file. The hostile social world in which the boy was thrust engendered "pathological" physical and emotional responses. This child lived the paradox of attraction to and repulsion from whiteness. The clinic's playgroup offered this boy a space and a form of interaction with an interracial group of children that countered the experience of displacement and alienation in his new whiter environment. The clinic did not *adjust* the child to antiblack racism. Rather the clinic presented another mode of play and interaction for the boy, one that countered the hostility of his school and neighborhood environments.[74]

"Freud Turned Upside Down"

Contemporary newspaper and magazine articles about the Lafargue Clinic focused on its novelty and hardscrabble operating conditions. Journalists portrayed the work of the clinic in terms that would appeal to a broad

American audience in the early postwar years. One report exemplifies this approach:

> [More] than half a year was devoted by staff workers to starting an entire family on the road to mental rehabilitation. A 16-year-old who had served a reformatory term for truancy and shoplifting was referred to the Clinic. Social workers found that her mother was psychotic, and vented her delusions on the long-suffering daughter and husband. Step by step, the Clinic arranged for the mother's hospitalization, helped the husband adjust himself to the situation, and not only persuaded the girl to return to school but also found her a part-time job. Her self-respect restored, and with the prospect of a normal home environment, the girl is now a model student and daughter. When the mother completes her recovery, the Clinic will have saved a family.[75]

Such articles offered narratives of redemption aimed at making their audience sympathetic both to the travails of individuals and families struggling with mental disorders and to the work of the clinic. Reporters often referenced the conditions of discrimination against Negroes that precipitated its founding. But they avoided discussion of the clinic's radical orientation linking racism and class subjugation to the increased anxiety and full-blown mental disorders among black New Yorkers.[76]

Richard Wright, however, presented the Lafargue Clinic as an underground anomaly, radically subverting the foundations of psychiatry. In his essay "Psychiatry Comes to Harlem," published in 1946, Wright used various literary tropes alongside "the underground" to describe the Lafargue Clinic. He explained that "though the Lafargue Clinic does exist, there is a widely prevalent feeling among many of the people that it does *not* exist." Wright and Ralph Ellison both would use the trope of absence or nonexistence in their essays on Lafargue and its place in the world of 1940s Harlem. As a form of framing the reality of the clinic's existence, both "absence" and "the underground" could easily be counterposed to the truth of the historical presence of the Negro in American society and the need for psychiatrists and the rest of white America to recognize the reality of black Americans' need for mental health services. In his essay, Wright likened the establishment of Lafargue to the appearance of that which has been psychologically repressed in the individual. "Social needs," he wrote, "go underground when they have been emotionally or morally rejected, only to reappear later in strange channels." Like individually repressed needs, socially repressed needs such as basic medical care—in this case psychiatry—are realized often through methods that subvert the sanctioned order of things. People form institutions that begin on an underground level when they do not have their basic needs met in those institutions already established within society. It is the underground, the absent from daylight, that is the subsoil for radical social upsurges.

In his essay on Lafargue and the Harlem community, Ralph Ellison noted that when asked how they are doing, many Harlemites very often replied, "Oh, man, I'm *nowhere*." Ellison argued that this phrase expressed "the feeling borne in upon many black people that they have no stable, recognized place in society. One's identity drifts in a capricious reality in which even the most commonly held assumptions are questionable. One

photo by GORDON PARKS

A patient waiting in one of the cubicles of the LAFARGUE CLINIC.
The Lafargue Clinic aims to transform despair, not into hope
but into determination.

Figure 6. Lafargue Clinic patient waiting for treatment; caption written by Ralph Ellison. Photo by Gordon Parks, 1948. Courtesy of the Gordon Parks Foundation.

'is' literally, but one is nowhere; one wanders dazed in a ghetto maze, a 'displaced person' of American democracy."

Ellison and Wright devoted themselves to exploring the black American experience of migration, urbanization, and, ultimately, modernization. They joined many other fiction writers and social scientists at midcentury in their concern over the effects of modernity on the personality of African Americans.[77] Ellison was concerned that in leaving behind the folklife of the rural South, African Americans had jettisoned modes of being and thinking that equipped them for keeping their personality intact in a hostile world. Ellison expressed in "Harlem Is Nowhere" a profound worry that in surrendering those cultural practices and institutions that gave them meaning and sustenance, black people were left untethered and unmoored from their roots and simultaneously segregated from the institutional life of the rest of society. Ellison explained that *"they lose one of the bulwarks which men place between themselves and the constant threat of chaos.* For whatever the assigned function of social institutions, their psychological function is to protect the citizen against the irrational, incalculable forces that hover about the edges of human life like cosmic destruction lurking within an atomic stockpile. And it is precisely the denial of this support through segregation and discrimination that leaves the most balanced Negro open to anxiety."[78]

Fredric Wertham's efforts at addressing how black Americans at midcentury reacted to the degradations of antiblack racism derived both from his conversations with Wright and Ellison as well as a combination of life experience and social psychiatric theorizing. Wertham's entry point into the conversation had been through his work as a clinical psychiatrist in Baltimore, where blacks and whites were legally segregated, and in New York City with its peculiar type of de facto Jim Crow. Public spaces and facilities were not legally segregated in New York, but through code and custom, whites made it quite clear to blacks where they were allowed to live, work, shop, and seek services, including medical care.[79]

Wertham's clinical experience treating black people was only part of a broad-ranging process of gauging the social problem of "race relations" and class exploitation. He encountered black patients in prominent mental hygiene institutions, and this firsthand knowledge of the manifestations of mental disorder among African Americans coalesced with his habits of mind oriented toward comprehending and challenging both oppressive and repressive forces in modern society.

At the very moment the Lafargue Clinic hit its stride, Richard Wright chose exile in France. In a letter to Gertrude Stein just after the war ended, he informed her that he would like to see France and maybe stay for a good while. With his wife Ellen and daughter Julia, Wright visited Paris from May through December 1946 as a guest of the French government. As the clinic gained notoriety and prominence through the publicity of several articles, including his own, Wright was not only in the process of reconsidering his relationship with his native land; he was beginning to think of himself less and less an American, more and more a citizen of the world. He had seen in the clinic an opportunity to address in practical terms the psychological impact of being black in a hostile society. With Wertham he had created a new type of institution in the most prominent black community in America, but he was exhausted by the daily trials of trying to live an ordinary life without the basic freedoms taken for granted by his fellow white citizens, not to mention his fellow men of letters.

When Wright returned from Paris at the end of 1946, he gave no indication that he considered moving permanently to France. One reporter asked why he had even come back to the United States, given his newfound love for Paris. "I live *here*," he replied. "My work is here." But in New York, he soon encountered one racist humiliation after another: salt placed in his coffee at a New York diner, a sign to all Negroes letting them know they were not welcome; menacing looks and threatening words from his Italian neighbors in Greenwich Village; a thwarted attempt to purchase a summer home in rural Connecticut, a house he afterward saw advertised for sale in a New York newspaper. These reminders of American racism hurt him personally and deeply. But the defining issue for Wright revolved around his imagination of what racism would do to his five-year-old daughter, Julia.

In the end he could not stomach the idea of Julia developing the same circuit of fear and hatred Wright knew in his core was endemic to black children in racist America. So on July 30, 1947, Richard, Ellen, and Julia Wright boarded the aptly named SS *America*; they brought along the necessary items they knew would be difficult to acquire in a France rebuilding itself after the war, and they brought their cat Knobby. The Wrights had quit America. Wertham's wife, Hesketh, wrote later to the Wrights, apologizing for her husband and herself for not being able to see them off. In her long letter she asked Wright if he would seek out Dr. Edgar Longuet, the nephew of the clinic's namesake Paul Lafargue, to get some of his uncle's writings not available in the United States. Wright wrote back, agreeing to do so. Soon after arriving in Paris, the Wrights received a follow-up telegram from the Werthams: "MANY THANKS WONDERFUL CABLE LAFARGUE CLINIC FLOURISHING."[80]

THE CLINIC hours are from six to eight P. M. on Tuesdays and Fridays. Appointments can be made by telephone or in person during these hours. The LAFARGUE CLINIC is designed to provide expert psychotherapy for those who need it and cannot get it. Its services are available to any child or adult with or without referral from any public or private agency. A nominal fee of 25 cents (50 cents for court testimony) is charged for those who can afford it.

LAFARGUE CLINIC BOARD

Earl Brown   Rev. Shelton Hale Bishop
Richard Wright   Marion Pettiford Hernandez
Frederic Wertham, M. D.

THE LAFARGUE CLINIC

A Mental Hygiene Clinic
in and for the
Community of Harlem

PAUL LAFARGUE [1842-1911]

215 West 133rd Street • New York 30, N. Y.
Telephone: EDgecombe 4-7950

THE LAFARGUE CLINIC takes its name and inspiration from Paul Lafargue, physician, philosopher and social reformer. Born in Cuba, of Negro parentage on his father's side, Lafargue devoted his whole life to the fight against oppression, prejudice, bigotry and false science. He was a member of the Paris City Council and of the Chamber of Deputies. More than any other scientific writer on social subjects, he gave social progress meaning in terms of human happiness.

THE LAFARGUE CLINIC is a clinic for the treatment of all kinds of nervous and mental disorders and behavior difficulties of adults and children. Its emphasis is not on testing and retesting, but on practical, intensive and if necessary prolonged psychotherapy. The diagnostic and psychotherapeutic methods employed are in accordance with the highest modern scientific standards.

Figures 7 and 8. Lafargue Mental Hygiene Clinic brochure. Courtesy of Dr. Elizabeth Bishop Davis Trussell.

CHILDREN AND THE VIOLENCE OF RACISM

The Lafargue Clinic, Comic Books, and the Case against School Segregation

In the spring of 1946 the *New York Amsterdam News* ran a series of articles examining the nature of mental health services for African Americans in New York City. Its findings were damning. The articles highlighted discrimination against blacks at the hospital and outpatient clinic of the state-funded Psychiatric Institute, at the Mental Hygiene Clinic at Belle-vue Hospital, and in the treatment of chronic alcoholics at city facilities. The final article in the series lambasted the disproportionate placement of black children in "retarded classes" by the Bureau of Children of Retarded Mental Development.[1] The April 27 lead editorial announced the impor-tance of the newspaper's exposé: "The whole sordid story of the harsh race bars which doom Negro children to creeping insanity, until they are 'crazy enough' to be institutionalized, is being told in the news columns of the AMSTERDAM NEWS for the first time."[2] Three weeks later, Constance Curtis, the author of the other articles in the series, got a scoop: a mental hygiene clinic would soon open at Harlem Hospital, "making it the first such service offered by the City to citizens of the community of this area." Curtis wrote,

The new clinic, when it is opened, will be the direct outgrowth of the Lafargue Clinic, which began to function just two months ago in the basement of St. Philip's Parish House. Vacillating city officials have been forced to recognize the existence of the successfully operating mental hygiene clinic, which was the first of its kind to open in the congested Harlem area. Since its beginning, the Lafargue Clinic has given aid to countless patients who have come to the clinic to seek the services of the highly trained psychiatrists and social workers who are giving their time without pay so that the clinic may be successful.[3]

In the year following the Lafargue Clinic's opening in 1946, a small yet significant group of psychiatrists, psychologists, and social workers coalesced in Harlem to address the problems detailed in the *Amsterdam News*. On May 6, 1947, the Lafargue Clinic hosted a symposium to inaugurate the Joint Committee on Mental Hygiene Services in Harlem. Appointing himself chairman of the committee, Fredric Wertham hoped to establish a dialogue among representatives from the Harlem Hospital clinic and the Northside Center for Child Development. One important participant was Dr. Kenneth B. Clark, cofounder of the Northside Center (also founded in March 1946), who would later become the most prominent race relations expert of the civil rights era.[4] What seemed to be the founding moment of an important collaboration between Clark, the leading African American social psychologist in New York, and Wertham, arguably the most vocal advocate for democratizing the practice and provision of psychiatry in America, turned out to be the first and last formal meeting of the Joint Committee for Mental Hygiene Services in Harlem. Though the two men shared a concern over the mental health needs of black Americans, their commonality ended there. What precisely transpired at the symposium is unfortunately lost to history. But the meeting may have sown the seeds of discord that would have a lasting impact on Wertham's status in the postwar social scientific movement to combat racism and its effects. While both men participated in the historic school desegregation movement culminating in the *Brown v. Board of Education* case in 1954, Clark would become the public face of American social science on matters of race, while Wertham receded into relative obscurity. And with him went the fortunes of the Lafargue Clinic.[5]

For a time, though, in the 1950s, the antiracist social psychiatry inaugurated in the Lafargue Clinic did play a pivotal role in two of the most important social debates of the day: juvenile delinquency and public school segregation. In both cases, Wertham's initially most effective tool, clinically derived testimony from young people most affected by the problem, became his greatest liability in the hands of skeptics and critics. At issue was the basic question of scientific truth. Wertham's central argument in both his testimony against segregation and his attack upon comic books was that both contributed to a hostile climate that interfered with the emotional and mental health of young people. Moreover, the argument was founded on evidence derived from the clinical methods of social psychiatry practiced at Lafargue.[6]

"I Don't Like the Jungle"

During its entire existence, much of the Lafargue Clinic's work was dedicated to identifying and countering sources of violence directed toward Harlem's youth. In the hands of children and adolescents at Lafargue, Wertham discovered a recurring source of antiblack images and messages: crime comic books. Images of black men being bound and whipped, of white men and women "taming" African "natives," and of black children being ridiculed and abused pervaded the little magazines that circulated so widely among the youth Wertham and his colleagues saw at the clinic. He wondered not only how these comic books were affecting the black children of Harlem, but also how they shaped white children's perceptions of the legitimate treatment of the black people in their midst.

Soon Wertham was suggesting that crime comic books were manuals for the promotion of stereotypes that engendered low self-esteem among black children, as well as antiblack sentiment and action among whites. At the core of his concern was the conviction that crime comic books contributed to the already existing hostile atmosphere in American society for black people. It would take a Herculean effort not only to demonstrate their harm, but also to convince policy makers and the public that comic books contravened the healthy development of young people.

As early as 1948, Wertham had become engrossed in studying the effects of comic books on the minds and behavior of young people. In an article first published in the *Saturday Review of Literature* and later condensed and republished in *Reader's Digest*, America's widest circulating periodical at the time, Wertham recounted several cases of boys and girls brought to the Lafargue Clinic who had committed delinquent acts ranging from stealing and sexual assault to murder. Were these acts the result of the "natural aggression" in the human organism? Were they manifestations of the sex instinct? Were they the "release of natural tendencies?" In posing these questions, Wertham gestured toward the commonly stated explanations for juvenile delinquency by both expert and lay commentators under the sway of a bowdlerized psychoanalysis, one that naturalized childhood aggression as an instinctual fact. Wertham rejected the notion that aggression was intrinsic to human nature and offered instead a social answer to the questions he posed.

In each case he recounted, the common denominator was comic books. He observed a direct correlation between the specific antisocial activity of young people—including a group of boys ages three to nine who handcuffed a four-year-old neighbor and used her for bow-and-arrow target practice—and the glorification of such cruelty and violence in the pages of horror and crime comic books. Comic books did not have the power to induce delinquency in all children, he noted. But because their depiction of violence and depravity threatened the ethical development of young people, according to Wertham, they constituted a threat to the mental and emotional health of all children.[7]

Some six years later, Wertham published *Seduction of the Innocent*, a study of the effects of crime comic books that would come to define his public persona and for many his historical legacy, for better or worse. *Seduction* was written for a popular audience, using primarily nontechnical language and a lively, acerbic tone. Yet the book offered a coherent set of clinically based arguments about the perils of crime comics based on evidence drawn from the Lafargue Clinic and Queens General Hospital's Mental Hygiene Clinic.

Wertham's anti-comic book campaign required a good deal of persuasion, and he sometimes seemed to relish indulging in hyperbole to push his case. His first task was to counter the widely held belief of child psychology experts and many parents that comic book reading had no effects at all on the minds and behavior of children and adolescents. Next he had to demonstrate that the delinquency resulting from youngsters' contacts with comics was symptomatic of a broad social problem rather than an indication of pathology endemic to the individual child. And his final task was to argue for a remedy for the pathogenic effects of comics. It was this last dimension of the project that made Wertham so controversial, as he wanted the state to enact laws to restrict the sale of crime comics to children under the age of sixteen.[8]

Seduction of the Innocent became the bible of the anti-comic crusade of the 1950s and had the effect of transforming the entire comic book industry.[9] The book remains the subject of study and criticism by scholars and champions of popular culture. Most critics of *Seduction of the Innocent* have tended to characterize the book as a moralistic, polemical screed masquerading under the guise of science. Published material on *Seduction* tends to frame the interpretive issues involved in terms of the validity of Wertham's argument and the vehemence of his attack on comic books. *Seduction of the Innocent* is best understood, though, within the broader context of Wertham's social psychiatry in the late 1940s and throughout the 1950s, and most specifically in light of the psychiatric practice of the Lafargue Clinic.[10]

Wertham and his Lafargue colleagues recognized racism, however it was experienced, as traumatic for black children. Wertham's arguments about the effects of racial stereotypes and racial violence in comic books were representative of his ethical concerns, as well as indicative of his clinical approach. The general effect of racist depictions in comics, he claimed, was that children came to accept a division between two groups: "regular men who have a right to live, and submen who deserve to be killed." But the problem reached even further, into the depths of young people's psyches. Racist images insinuated themselves into the dream and fantasy life of children: "A large part of the violence and sadism in comic books is practiced by individuals or on individuals who are depicted as inferior, subhuman beings. In this way children can indulge in fantasies of violence as something permissible." While many young whites unconsciously assimilated degrading images of dark-skinned peoples in comics, "for others they constitute a serious traumatic experience," explained Wertham.[11]

The core of Wertham's arguments reflected a concern for the positive mental health of all children. Wertham suggested that few child psychologists and psychiatrists paid attention to the health effects of comic books promoting "race hatred." He told of a twelve-year-old black girl with whom he had discussed comic books at the Lafargue Clinic. "I don't like the jungle," she informed him. "I don't think they make the colored people right [in those comics]. The way they make them I never seen before—their hair and big nose and the English they use. They never have an English like we have. They put them so dark—for real I have never seen anybody before like that. White kids would think all colored people look like that, and really they aren't." In the very next sentence she alluded to fights that broke out at her school sparked by racial animosity. He concluded: "This influence, subtle and pervasive but easily demonstrable by clinical psychological methods, has not only directly affected the individual child, but also constitutes an important factor for the whole nation."[12] Wertham's emphasis on the importance of the individual child's case as illustrative of what clinical psychiatry could discern about the deep experience of racism—in ways that other methods such as lab-like experiments and surveys could not—put him at odds with the emergent quantitative paradigm in psychological science.[13]

Wertham never argued, though, that crime comics alone were the cause of juvenile delinquency. He contended instead that "crime comics are certainly not the only factor, nor in many cases are they even the most important one, but there can be no doubt that they are the most unnecessary and least excusable one. In many cases, in conjunction with other factors, they are the chief one."[14] His main point was that children and adolescents were vulnerable and consistently left unprotected, most especially in their leisure time. Wertham argued that parents and other adults failed to understand this vulnerability and the variety of forces and sources that preyed upon what he called "unprotectedness."

Wertham's broader argument in *Seduction of the Innocent* (and in his later works he would return to this point) was that the social and behavioral sciences, and thus the broader public, had grossly misunderstood the nature of juvenile delinquency. The paradox of this misunderstanding was that scientists emphasized the individual even in the midst of a social panic over a widespread phenomenon. While clearly a social phenomenon, with socially frightening effects, juvenile delinquency elicited a heightened attention to the individual nature of the phenomenon and the perpetrator. Wertham wrote that "juvenile delinquency is not a thing in itself. It can be studied only in relation to all kinds of other child behavior. And it is a mass phenomenon which cannot be fully comprehended with methods of individual psychology alone. Children do not become delinquents; they commit delinquencies. The delinquency of a child is not a disease; it is a symptom, individually and socially. You cannot understand or remedy a social phenomenon like delinquency by redefining it simply as an individual emotional disorder."[15] Wertham's argument and the manner of presentation, and the venues in which he made his case, thrust him into the roles of social critic and public intellectual. Yet Wertham was a psychiatrist and in his own view a scientist, who had come to his conclusions about comic books and juvenile delinquency through the clinical method of psychiatric observation. Wertham's social psychiatry mandated that the clinician and social worker take into account the total environment when explaining and treating behavior problems in children. Crime comic books were an identifiable, tangible part of the everyday lives of children, components of the environment that shaped how they viewed themselves and others, and guided their thoughts and actions.[16]

Seduction of the Innocent, along with Wertham's appearances on radio and television programs lambasting comic books, forced the comics industry in late 1954 to adopt an editorial code "to rule out offensive material." To avoid complete censorship, the Comic Magazine Association appointed a "czar" who would mark all "acceptable" comics with a seal of approval. Many comic book publishers believed that the resulting editorial code would appease critics such as Wertham and the politicians and parents who joined him in the anti-comics crusade. The comic book industry had been devastated, however, by Wertham's blows against it. Only the biggest companies able to diversify their publications survived the torrent of anti-comics activism in the 1950s. Within "a few years of the publication of *Seduction of the Innocent*, twenty-four of twenty-nine crime comic publishers went out of business."[17]

Wertham had argued in the mid-1940s that mental disorders among black Americans and other oppressed people required a social psychiatry. The social psychiatry that Wertham developed at the Lafargue Clinic regarded the individual patient as possessing a social identity with real-world experiences that had to be incorporated into the total picture of his or her mental health. Just as he had with racism, Wertham argued that violent forms of juvenile delinquency, especially those precipitated by the influence of comic books, could not be understood individually but instead needed to be approached in social terms. The importance of *Seduction of the Innocent* and Wertham's broader campaign against mass-media violence thus emerged from the same combination of politically inflected moral outrage and medical concern that undergirded the establishment of the Lafargue Clinic.

The Lafargue Clinic and the Effects of School Segregation

The period in which Wertham mounted his campaign against crime comic books coincided with the Lafargue Clinic's integral involvement in one of the most important phases of the struggle for racial equality in American history. Wertham and his colleagues would come to play a pivotal, though unheralded, role in the campaign to end public school segregation in America. In the fall of 1951, the Lafargue Clinic came to the attention of the Legal Defense and Education Fund (LDEF) of the National Association for the Advancement of Colored People. At this time the NAACP-LDEF was immersed in a decades-long campaign to dismantle public school segregation. By the early 1950s, the LDEF had begun to look to social science, seeking scientific evidence of the effects of Jim Crow education on black children.

In the mid-1940s, the NAACP-LDEF launched a direct attack on segregation per se. One of the NAACP-LDEF's central strategies was to demonstrate that segregation was inherently unequal, because no matter how much parity existed between a white school and a black school, the underlying principle of segregation imposed a stigma of inferiority on black students. As the NAACP-LDEF mounted its legal campaign, members of the staff began to look for experts who could provide evidence that black students in segregated schools not only experienced marked educational inequality, but that they had been psychologically harmed because of state-sanctioned Jim Crow schools.[18]

The NAACP-LDEF's incorporation of social science evidence reflected the antiracist turn in the human sciences since the 1930s, as well as the rising popular stature of social and behavioral science. By the start of World War II, the sciences of psychology, sociology, and anthropology became prominent domains of research into the reasons why people held prejudices against minority groups such as African Americans and Jews. There was no more influential World War II–era social scientific work on prejudice and discrimination than Swedish economist Gunnar Myrdal's *An American Dilemma*. Its publication in 1944 ushered in a period of unprecedented alliance between social scientific research and practical efforts to ameliorate the race problem in American society. A massive text consisting of nearly fifty chapters pertaining to the economic, social, political, cultural, and mental life of the black Americans, *An American Dilemma* consolidated a vast swathe of facts about the origins, development, and current state of relations between blacks and whites. Myrdal and his team of researchers sought to provide both policymakers and ordinary citizens with a foundation for re-engineering American society.

An American Dilemma was the culmination of efforts by countless social scientists in the previous decades to demonstrate that racial hierarchy and race conflict derived from historical rather than natural, or so-called organic, sources. Social scientists had identified economic, social, and psychological factors in race relations that produced and maintained racial enmity irrespective of any supposed natural or biological basis. Myrdal fused the findings of social science with a moral argument. In effect he declared: *Here, America, are the facts of the problem and it is now up to you as individuals and as members of government and civil society to align your social order with the fundamentally liberal American creed of equality for all.* It would be difficult to overstate the influence *An American Dilemma* had on postwar American race relations policy, as well as social scientific research related to race.[19]

As the psychological roots of prejudice and discrimination became a legitimate topic of research, and a subject of widespread popular concern, a number of social scientists also turned their attention specifically to the effects of racial discrimination and segregation on American minority groups—and prominent among these scholars were members of those minority groups.[20] By the late 1940s, Drs. Kenneth and Mamie Clark, the young psychologists who had founded the Northside Center for Child Development in Harlem, emerged as two of the most important contributors to the growing scientific literature on racism's impact on the minds of African Americans. Beginning just before the outbreak of World War II, the Clarks published a series of articles demonstrating black children's emotional and psychic responses to living in an antiblack world. As social psychologists, the Clarks were concerned with the question of how children viewed themselves in relation to the wider society: What was their self-image, and how was it shaped by the social environment?[21]

The Clarks' primary method of studying children's psyches involved the use of projective tests, presenting subjects with images or objects to elicit their unconscious and conscious associations. Though best known for their use of toy dolls in their studies of black children, the Clarks' first projective tests involved a coloring test, administered to some 160 children, ages five to seven. The tests were designed to reveal how black children identified themselves and what they had learned of racial categorization and the relative values of whiteness and blackness. The Clarks observed the children's use of colored pencils to depict everyday objects such as leaves and oranges, then asked them to depict themselves, using such prompts as, "Color this little boy (or girl) the color that you are." As one historian notes, "What the Clarks found was that the children consistently portrayed themselves as distinctly lighter than the actual color of their own skin. Further, the gap between realistic and unrealistic coloring was largest among children whose skin was darkest." "It is clear that the Negro child, by the age of five is aware of the fact that to be colored in contemporary American society is a mark of inferior status," the Clarks concluded. This awareness, they added, "introduces a fundamental conflict at the very foundations of the ego structure."[22] Although the Clarks had not conducted their research expressly for the purpose of providing evidence for social and legal policy, their findings would lend support to the claim of NAACP lawyers that segregation not only marked "the Negro child" as inferior but that it also infiltrated children's own self-concept.

Robert L. Carter, a Columbia University–trained black lawyer for the NAACP-LDEF, was the chief proponent of incorporating social scientific findings such as the Clarks' into the legal campaign to challenge segregated schools in the United States. As early as 1945, Carter made use of *An American Dilemma* in desegregation briefs filed on behalf of Mexican American and African American litigants in California and throughout the South. Carter presented general social scientific evidence of the effect of segregation, irrespective of the particular conditions of a putatively "separate but equal" institutional setting. As one NAACP-LDEF lawyer noted, other "lawyers had already been calling on social scientists for aid in public-law cases," with earlier cases involving "problems affecting great portions of our populations."[23] But Carter's application of social science was specifically tailored to the effects of segregation on personal achievement and professional advancement.[24] In his brief for *Westminster v. Menendez* (1945), for example, Carter used sociological evidence to show that "a consequence of the policy of segregation has been to deprive the individual Negro citizen of the skills necessary to a civilized existence, the

Negro community of the leadership and professional services it so urgently needs, and the nation as a whole of the full potential embodied in the intellectual and physical resources of its citizens." The appeals court that heard the *Westminster* case ruled that segregation of Mexican American children violated the Fourteenth Amendment on narrow legal grounds, making no reference to Carter's social science–laden brief. But in the coming years, Carter would build on his first foray into social scientific jurisprudence to marshal a phalanx of experts to underscore the damaging effects of segregation on African American children.

The central problem that social science could address was whether segregated schools harmed "the Negro student's" educational achievement, stunted his aspirations, and generally blocked his emotional, educational, mental development—thus *damaging* the individual student.[25] By September 1951, when Jack Greenberg, a twenty-six-year-old Jewish Columbia Law School graduate who had joined the LDEF in 1949, contacted Fredric Wertham, Carter had convinced several of his fellow lawyers at the LDEF, most importantly its director Thurgood Marshall, that testimony from social scientists like the Clarks might play a pivotal role in a set of cases challenging segregated schools.

After successful challenges to segregation in professional and graduate education in *Sweatt v. Painter* and *McLaurin v. Oklahoma Board of Regents* (1950), the LDEF set its sights on confronting "separate but equal" as established in the landmark 1896 ruling, *Plessy v. Ferguson*, with the aim of forcing the U.S. Supreme Court to rule on segregation in American public schools. Between 1949 and 1951, five cases emerged that brought the question of "separate but equal" to the fore and became the staging ground for the incorporation of social scientific testimony that would eventually be heard in arguments before the Supreme Court in *Brown v. Board of Education*. In addition to *Brown*, the cases were *Briggs v. Elliot* (South Carolina), *Davis v. County School Board of Prince Edward County* (Virginia), *Bolling v. Sharpe* (District of Columbia), and *Belton/Bulah v. Gebhart* (Delaware). *Bolling* was the only one of the cases in which social science experts did not testify.[26]

Assigned the task of finding social scientists who would participate in the cases before state courts, Carter sought advice from one of the indisputable experts in the study of race. Since his time as a Columbia Law School student, Carter had been aware of social psychologist Otto Klineberg's important studies published in the 1930s that demonstrated that differences among races were not genetically inherited. Klineberg also served as a major adviser to Gunnar Myrdal as he prepared *An American Dilemma*, drafting a long memorandum titled *Characteristics of the American Negro*, which consisted of a survey of psychological research on African Americans and was later published independently. Carter and Thurgood Marshall hoped that Klineberg would not only be their star witness, but that he would also organize his colleagues for the cases. Klineberg declined the invitation to lead the consolidation of social scientific evidence and experts but directed Carter to his former student at Columbia, Dr. Kenneth B. Clark.[27]

Carter found in Clark someone who was both scientifically prepared and temperamentally suited for the task. And the timing was perfect. At their first meeting in his office at the Northside Center in Harlem, in February 1951, Clark handed Carter a copy of a manuscript titled "The Effect of Prejudice and Discrimination on Personality Development," which he had written the previous year as a report for the White House Midcentury Conference on Youth. In his report, Clark synthesized the current scientific views on how prejudice and discrimination gave rise to pathological personalities in both victims and perpetrators. The section that struck Carter as most useful was a summary of "the effects of prejudice, discrimination, and segregation on the personality of Negro children in the United States."[28] A few days after reading the White House Conference report, Carter returned to Clark's office. "He was enormously enthusiastic," recalled Clark. " 'It's just what we're looking for. It's almost as if it were written for us,' " he remembered Carter saying. Carter asked Clark to testify in South Carolina's *Briggs* case and to call upon his most prestigious colleagues to join him.

Clark was calm in the midst of Carter's excitement, immediately grasping the difficulties of conveying the meaning of scientific material in a court of law. Nevertheless, Clark agreed to participate; he had always envisioned his science as part of a broad contribution to understanding and addressing social problems, particularly those centering on race. And as an active member of the growing community of liberal-minded social psychologists, particularly the Society for the Psychological Study of Social

Issues (SPSSI), Clark was well positioned to enlist other social scientists to testify in the upcoming cases.[29] Not all the lawyers at the Legal Defense Fund were as enthusiastic as Carter about putting social scientists on the witness stand, but Thurgood Marshall supported Carter's efforts and gave Clark his seal of approval to begin his recruitment of experts.

Fredric Wertham was not on the list of scientists Clark identified as "real top-notchers" who should be asked to testify—despite his being a professional neighbor in the Harlem community and having shared a podium with Clark at the first and only meeting of the Joint Committee on Mental Hygiene Services in Harlem. Instead, Clark supplied the NAACP-LDEF with a list of men and women who had conducted experimental psychology and sociological analysis within the framework of the emerging field of intergroup relations. Intergroup relations was not simply a new name for race relations. An interdisciplinary field, it conjoined the new psychodynamic orientation in the behavioral sciences to experimental and proto-ethnographic research aimed at reducing or eliminating prejudice and discrimination.[30] Clark invited figures such as Klineberg, Robert Redfield, Jerome Bruner, Alfred McClung Lee, Isidor Chein, M. Brewster Smith, Theodore Newcomb, and his own wife, Mamie Phipps Clark.[31]

The selection of experts tilted toward experimental social psychologists whose research employed quantitative methods found in the so-called hard sciences. While critics from within and without the social sciences would later famously challenge the research performed by the Clarks and their colleagues on the effects of segregation, their core methods and evidence reflected the quantitative paradigm that undergirded postwar social psychology's claims to legitimacy.[32]

Delaware

The school cases in Delaware captured the quotidian hindrances of Jim Crow, as well as the profundity of black children's early, yet lasting, encounters with antiblack racism. Sarah Bulah of Hockessin, just outside Wilmington, petitioned the state to have the school bus that passed by her house bringing white children to school also transport her six-year-old daughter Shirley to an all-Negro schoolhouse two miles away. Mrs. Bulah's aim was not to challenge school segregation; rather, she simply wanted a bus to take her daughter to school. After many unanswered letters, the state superintendent finally wrote back to Mrs. Bulah, declining her request, "since the State Constitution requires separate educational facilities for colored and white children, your children may not ride a bus serving a white school." Initially hoping to force the state to provide any form of transport, even if it were segregated, Sarah Bulah soon agreed to have her case become a direct challenge to school segregation.

Belton v. Gebhart from its inception explicitly attacked the issue of school segregation. Ethel Belton of Claymont resented the fact that her daughter Ethel Louise had to travel at least two hours per day to attend the only Negro high school in all of Delaware, located in downtown Wilmington, when all-white Claymont High School sat only a mile away from the Belton home. Ethel Belton and seven other black Claymont parents petitioned the State Board of Education to allow their children to attend Claymont High School. The entreaty was of course denied.[33]

In early 1951, the NAACP-LDEF filed the two conjoined cases, *Bulah v. Gebhart* and *Belton v. Gebhart*, in the U.S. District Court in Wilmington. In response to a request from Delaware's attorney general, the cases were transferred to the State Chancery Court. Louis Redding, Delaware's sole black lawyer in 1951, would be the lead counsel representing the plaintiffs in the cases. Jack Greenberg was to aid him, especially with the social science experts. Redding was surprised and delighted that the cases would be heard by the same judge who had ruled in *Parker v. University of Delaware* in favor of desegregating the University of Delaware the year before, Judge Collins J. Seitz. The fact that these cases were tried in a state court, rather than a federal court as the other desegregation cases had been, represented the first aspect of the trial that made it unique—but its outcome was what truly distinguished the Delaware cases within the campaign to overturn separate but equal.[34]

With the trial date set in Wilmington for the week of October 22, 1951, Greenberg worked with Clark over the summer and fall to organize and prepare the social scientists who would testify. They were particularly concerned that in the first of the school segregation trials soon consolidated into *Brown*, social scientific testimony had had little effect on the outcome of the trial. In South Carolina's *Briggs v. Elliott* (May 1951), Kenneth Clark presented evidence from a projective test he conducted with black children in Clarendon County, in which he used two plastic dolls "equal in every respect," except one represented a white child and the other a "Negro child." The test consisted of asking sixteen black children individually a set of questions to determine their "sensitivity to racial discrimination and its effect on [their] personality and development." The most telling finding of the doll tests was that eleven of sixteen children chose the brown doll when asked to select the doll that "is likely to act bad." "The conclusion which I was forced to reach," Clark informed the court in Charleston, "was that these children in Clarendon County have been definitely harmed in the development of their personalities; that the signs of instability in their personalities are clear, and I think that every psychologist would accept and interpret these as such." Clark would go on to conduct the same now-famous doll test with forty-one black Delaware children, producing similar results.[35]

In both cases, the states' attorneys sought to trivialize and render suspect Clark's doll test, questioning its representativeness and overall scientific validity. "I was concerned about findings of fact," South Carolina's state's attorney Robert Figg recalled, "and once we determined that his testimony was based on very few children, that there were no witnesses to the tests, and that this was his own test method and not a well-established one, I didn't press the matter. . . . Nobody took it seriously." But Clark's testimony had now entered the court record, and Figg could not have known that once *Briggs* and the rest of the *Brown* companion cases reached the Supreme Court the social scientific "finding of fact" would play a prominent role in justifying the Court's ruling.[36]

Even so, in the summer of 1951, the NAACP-LDEF was hardly assured that the testimony of social and behavioral science experts like Clark would prove effective at establishing segregation as inherently a violation of the Fourteenth Amendment. Attorney Greenberg believed something substantive was missing from the scientific evidence used previously by the NAACP-LDEF. He wanted to present to the court a qualitative assessment of the harm done to children by official segregation. Aware of the Lafargue Clinic's psychiatric work in the Harlem community, Greenberg sought Wertham's help. "We would like you to testify for us," Greenberg told Wertham, "both on the basis of your broad general experience, and on the basis of investigation of the particular plaintiffs, some of whom we will make available to you." With just over a month before the trial date, Wertham agreed, though he insisted that he examine both black *and* white students to determine whether school segregation was "injurious to the mental health of children" of both races.

Unlike Clark, Wertham did not travel to the plaintiffs' community; instead a member of the Wilmington NAACP arranged to bring thirteen randomly selected boys and girls to the Lafargue Clinic. Eight of the students were black and five were white, and they ranged in age from nine to sixteen years old. "They obtained the white children," notes one historian, "by explaining to their parents that the clinic was conducting experimental research in race relations. Segregation was not mentioned." And so, on five occasions, beginning on October 4, all thirteen children boarded a train in Wilmington together and made the two-hour trip to New York's Penn Station, where Greenberg met them and brought them by subway to Harlem. The clinic at this time was open only on Tuesdays and Fridays, and much of its October operating schedule had to be dedicated to examinations of the Delaware children.[37]

The Problem with Clinical Evidence

Wertham's frame for the study of social and psychological problems differed from that of the scientists enlisted by the NAACP-LDEF. While he acknowledged the utility of experimental social psychological methods, he regarded them as supplementary to a broader examination of the individual's psychic life. As a clinical psychiatrist, Wertham certainly employed nominally objective measures of psychological evaluation in his examinations, such as intelligence and projective tests that might be uniformly applied to any patient. But most importantly, his clinical psychiatry involved ascertaining the facts of an individual's experience that had a determining influence on his or her basic psychic functioning. And within Wertham's social psychiatric paradigm, awareness of objective, ascriptive factors such as race, class, and gender fused with subjective, interior forces to provide a picture of the whole individual.

Clinical evidence posed a problem, though, at the basic level of fact. Because the psychiatrist was a subjective observer and interpreter of an individual's inner mental life, the clinical method's claim to truth depended upon *trust*—trust between psychiatrist and patient, and trust between the psychiatrist and whomever he was trying to convince of the mechanisms at work in the patient's emotional and mental life. A significant test for clinical evidence arrived when Jack Greenberg called upon Wertham to discern what effect state-sanctioned school segregation had on the mental health of both black and white youth in Delaware and to argue generalizable claims regarding those effects. The crucial question was whether Wertham's findings could be said to apply beyond the small cohort of students he and his Lafargue colleagues observed.[38]

By the fall of 1951, the Lafargue Clinic had established a solid base in the Harlem community, but its status in the field of mental health care in New York City was more ambiguous. While the clinic attained a considerable degree of prominence through being featured in the local and national media, it had yet to obtain significant government or philanthropic support. And though the clinic provided a model of offering inexpensive psychotherapy among an oppressed population, the wider community of psychiatric and social welfare professionals expressed little interest in adopting Wertham's techniques. Administrators of mental health programs and institutions rarely said so explicitly, but they were clearly skeptical of the linkage Wertham posited between the social conditions of oppression and the manifestation of psychic strain among African Americans, and skeptical as well as of the socially based psychotherapeutic techniques he championed.[39]

Yet the community of Harlem had embraced the clinic, and many sought out its services. And the clinic attracted a new generation of psychiatrists, psychologists, and social workers committed to the anti-oppression social psychiatry of Dr. Wertham. Some of these young mental health care workers would later go on to play prominent roles in the expansion of public mental health services in New York City's black and poor communities.[40] And so, by the time Greenberg and the group of Delaware students arrived at the 135th Street IRT stop, the Lafargue Clinic had wide renown, a full staff of thirty professionals, and a full appointment book, but it still remained on the margins of mainstream psychiatric practice in New York City.[41]

Wertham incorporated the Delaware students' examination into the routine clinical procedures already in place at Lafargue. Rather than creating a laboratory-like setup for experimentation, he employed the clinic's regular intake and examination methods, which he believed lent themselves to patients' spontaneous expression. "The methods employed consisted of the taking of individual case histories, individual interviews, group observation and group discussion, and standard tests such as drawing tests, mosaic tests and Rorschach tests," Wertham later explained. The team that examined the children represented the fully developed Lafargue Clinic staff, including psychiatrists, psychologists, social workers, teachers, probation officers, and guidance counselors.[42]

The clinic staff's approach to these specific students and the students' response to the open atmosphere of the clinic's therapeutic context were symbolic of the wider significance of Lafargue's practice in the Harlem community. Over the course of the five visits, the clinic staff aimed to build "a relationship of complete trust" on the part of the students. According to one historian, "the black youngsters in particular were responsive to

Figure 9. Play therapy at the Lafargue Clinic, February 1948. Photo by Lisa Larsen. Courtesy of the Library of Congress.

the Lafargue clinicians, in part because they had so long bottled up feelings that they had not been able to discuss comfortably with their parents, whose own sense of insecurity, the children guessed or sensed, would have left them embarrassed by the subject of segregation." As with the Delaware students, the clinic offered a space in which African Americans and any others who sought treatment could express themselves freely, trusting that their feelings would be taken seriously and that they would receive professional care. No other contemporary psychiatric clinic in the country could make the same claim.[43]

Positive Mental Health and the Public Health Problem of Racism

Wertham claimed that the Lafargue Clinic examined the issue of segregation from an entirely new point of view: racism was not exclusively a social and political problem but represented a community health problem as well. Irrespective of individual attitudes or behavior, segregation, both in the South and the North, was embedded in the American societal structure. And segregation engendered obstacles to the development of the American public's mental health. The questions he aimed to address with the help of his staff in the Delaware cases were, "Is school segregation injurious to children's mental health, and for that reason is it a public health problem?" It was somewhat disingenuous for him to suggest his own originality in considering the problem of segregation in terms of injury to the child's mental health, since the bulk of Kenneth and Mamie Clark's testimony famously sought to address just that question. But his framing of discrimination and segregation as a public health problem was indeed original.[44]

Wertham employed the concept of "positive mental health" as the basis for his entire approach to clinical psychiatry. Most psychiatrists at midcentury "operated on the assumption that the absence of illness denoted health."[45] Though many psychiatrists were increasingly revising their conceptualization of mental health and illness in order to place the individual patient along a continuum of normality and pathology, psychiatry on the whole concerned itself with the prevention, diagnosis, and treatment of *mental disease*. Wertham's focus on positive mental health aimed to reorient the primary focus of psychiatry from illness and disease, with a circumscribed emphasis on the individual, to the factors and conditions constituting the total environment in which a person developed. "It wasn't enough to look at the child and say, "This little girl doesn't have nightmares, she gets by in school, she doesn't annoy anyone at home, she isn't a juvenile delinquent," Wertham argued. "That is not enough. I hold the scientific opinion that if a rosebush should produce twelve roses and if only one rose grows, it is not a healthy rosebush. It is up to us to find out what is interfering with its growth and with its health."[46]

For Wertham, the positive mental health framework could be enacted best through aggressive public health measures that confronted the root causes of psychological disturbances. His favorite analogy for promoting public mental health came from tuberculosis prevention: "Thousands of people in large cities inhale tubercle bacilli into their lungs. And yet only a relatively small number of these infected multitudes come down with the disease tuberculosis. We do not say that we do not have to pay any attention to the tubercle bacillus because enormous numbers of people do not become overtly ill from it." Wertham's blending of positive mental health and public health was confusing at times, given his divergence from the disease model of mental health and illness—especially since he made clear that the problem of racism, like the tubercle bacillus, constituted a pathogenic source of disease. Despite the possible terminological slippage in his conceptualization, Wertham's framework for assessing the effect of segregation on both black and white children would soon offer the Delaware court a novel scientific basis for deciding the fate of segregated public schools.[47]

"Very Subtle Things, Very Subtle Testimony"

Wertham had testified in court many times before, but in those instances his focus was the psychological makeup of one individual. Now he was called upon to present a set of general findings on the effects of school segregation on the basis of the Lafargue Clinic's evaluation of the group of Delaware students. And this time, there was no individual on trial for a crime, no person to be judged either sane or insane. In Delaware it was the state that was on trial, and Wertham believed he held the evidence to prove that state-sanctioned school segregation was guilty of "interfering with the healthy development of children."[48]

Unwilling to be responsible for defending statements made by other social scientists, Wertham insisted on being the first expert to testify at the trial in Wilmington. Jack Greenberg recalled that throughout their collaboration Wertham had been temperamental and imperious, and "everything had to be precisely as he wanted it." It was true that Wertham had developed the standpoint that *his* was always the correct way of doing things. After so many years of being marginalized by the mainstream of psychiatry and failing to convince those who wielded power in institutions that could aid the Lafargue Clinic, he had concluded that the only way to advance his vision for social psychiatry was to take an uncompromising approach to conducting and presenting his work.

Wertham treated his appearance in the Wilmington courtroom on October 22, 1951, as though he were offering a seminar on the psychological development of children. As he began to present this material, Wertham captivated the courtroom with the clarity, depth, and tone of his testimony.[49] His testimony that day encapsulated the entire social psychiatric orientation instituted in the Lafargue Clinic since its opening in 1946. In order to prove his thesis that state-imposed school segregation constituted a threat to the mental health of Delaware children, he sought first to establish for the court a general scheme of potential obstacles to the child's healthy development. He identified three categories of injurious factors: *personal, infra-personal,* and *supra-personal*. Personal factors were those emotional experiences derived from contact with one's family members from the earliest moments of one's conscious and unconscious life. Infra-personal factors referred to physical facts—matters of constitutional inheritance, organic defects, or physical handicap. Supra-personal factors, Wertham explained, "are identical with what we speak of as social factors. They have little to do with the personality of the individual child . . . and one can make a statement about a whole group of children" by studying supra-personal factors. While these factors taken together formed the nexus in which a child developed, it was possible to identify, isolate, and possibly eradicate specific sources of injury to the child. Segregation represented a salient example of a supra-personal, thus

Figure 10. Fredric Wertham in his home at 44 Gramercy Park in New York City, 1954.
Photo by Gordon Parks. Courtesy of the Gordon Parks Foundation.

social, factor causing a disturbance in the child's progression to healthy development.[50]

Wertham found that segregation produced an "unsolvable emotional conflict" in the black Delaware children he had examined. The central component of this conflict was children's inability to obtain a coherent explanation of segregation from either their parents or other authority figures. Comparing the topic of segregation to sex, Wertham noted that although sex was difficult for parents to discuss with children, there were many adults able to do so. "But this race problem is so difficult and creates such an insecurity even in mature people that either their children don't care to ask their parents, or don't want to ask, or if they ask would get the same evasive answers they would get to an inquiry of 'where do babies come from?' because their parents have to tell them fairy tales." The child then failed to resolve the conflict through a "realistic rationalization"—a clear and reasonable explanation of segregation—provided by a parent or alternate authority figure.[51]

Having failed to obtain a realistic rationalization for segregation, the child attempted to overcome the "unsolvable" conflict by repression or overcompensation. But repression did not work as it might in other responses to rebuffs in one's life, because the issue of segregation continued to reappear everyday as part of school life—in the distance the child had to travel to reach school, in the unequal facilities, in the different subjects taught and the materials used by the teacher. The child was not allowed to forget or evade the fact of segregation for very long. At times, black children might hope to overcome the stigma of segregation by "excelling in one field or another," or by forging "a complete identification with the non-Negro group." But sooner or later, the child who strove to overcome the condition of conflict bumped up against reality—at some point the fantasy that one could outrun racism dissolved.[52] The child was thus thrown back upon himself, forced to struggle for a healthy sense of himself and his world without recourse to common psychological mechanisms used to fend off the threats of anxiety and disorientation.

It was at this point in his testimony that Wertham introduced the state, that fundamental repository of official power and authority. He argued that the state "interferes with the way in which children can use any defenses they have, because the State itself is doing something wrong." He then read to the court a dialogue between himself and one of the Delaware students:

"Who forbids you to go to the schools?"
—And I quote—the child says "the State."
And I said, "Who is the State?"
And the boy said, "The State is the government."
And I said, "Why does the government forbid it?"
And he said, "That I don't know."

This exchange, Wertham testified, exemplified the fundamental conflict in the black child's mind, because of the special role that authority played in the development of young people's mental health. The emotional conflict engendered by segregation was especially acute because the state stood at the apex of authority. "If you have an emotional conflict about the very source of authority, namely the State, then this particular mental growth is endangered, interfered with, or even jeopardized," Wertham declared. In one of the most evocative moments in his testimony, he explained that the children he examined interpreted segregation as punishment. These children believed they were being punished for something not explained to them, for something they had not done.[53]

The central problem for the NAACP-LDEF was to distinguish the singularity of state-sanctioned school segregation. What made it a unique cause of emotional damage to black children within the wider context of racism and stigma in American society? In other words, the burden of the case was to prove why segregated schools in particular impaired the healthy development of Delaware's children, thus violating the equal protection clause of the Fourteenth Amendment. Wertham acknowledged that school segregation was not the only threat to "the Negro child's emotional health." In fact he admitted that it was just one part of a broader complex of a society that stigmatized black people. He insisted, however, that within the context of discrimination that a black child encountered in a segregated society—for instance in places of commerce such as restaurants, movie theaters, and drug stores—the public school superseded all other institutions in its importance as a contributing source of emotional conflict in the child.

Wertham listed the reasons why school segregation was of paramount importance: (1) it was absolutely clear-cut—you either go to one school or the other; (2) the state does it and does it by law (here he contrasted this circumstance with the fact that if one store owner denied a Negro service, another proprietor might let him in); (3) it is discrimination of long duration—"it is not just Monday or Tuesday, or once when you want to go to the store, but . . . always so, a part of your absolute daily life"; (4) "it is bound up with the whole educational process, which I consider part of the mental life of the child. It hits the child at two very important moments in his life . . . where a child steps forward from the . . . more or less sheltered family [and in adolescence where for] the first time the person must find a social group for himself."[54]

Having established that school segregation injured the mental health of children, Wertham trained his sights on segregation as a problem of public health. He conceded a point that many contemporary and latter-day

critics of the psychological-damage argument tended to overlook or deliberately disregard: the psychological harm of segregation was potential, and
it was "wrong to ascribe an emotional disorder or the presence of 'hostility'
to every child so affected."[55] Rather than affecting all children uniformly,
segregation, like other supra-personal pathogenic factors, acted as a "foreign body" in the children's psyches, as an interfering element in healthy
growth. Each child might not succumb to the emotional disturbance that
segregation might produce, but the potential harm to the child's mental
health remained constant.

Wertham found that white children were not immune to the potential
harm of segregation. White children tended either to identify themselves
with the plight of black children or to assume "the illusion of superiority"
over "the Negro." He illustrated this potential by referring to the words
of the Delaware children themselves. One nine-year-old white girl had
remained quiet during the group sessions held at Lafargue. Wertham
asked her why she had not participated in the discussion. Far from being
uninterested in school segregation, she declared that, no, "I care a lot about
it myself." When matters of racial discrimination came up, she could not
help thinking of her black playmate, "the daughter of a woman employed
in her family." The girl told the Lafargue Clinic staff about how the boys
in her class at school suggested that "colored children should be tied up."
"They shouldn't be tied up always," the boys would say, "but they should
work . . . while we are playing." With remarkable gravity, this young girl
declared, "People don't care. They don't think about others, they just think
about themselves, so they think they are better than the Negro." Wertham's recounting of the girl's comments provided texture to the overarching argument that segregation constituted a "potential health hazard for
all children."[56]

Delaware Chancery Court judge Collins J. Seitz had allowed Wertham considerable time and latitude during the direct examination phase
of his testimony; in the comparatively brief cross-examination Delaware
attorney general Albert Young restricted his questioning to three primary areas. First he asked Wertham whether all that he had testified to
was a matter of opinion, not an exact science; second, he returned to the
question of what made de jure segregation any different from de facto;
and third, he wanted to know whether ending segregation in Delaware

would "cause or eliminate the effect of this emotional disturbance and this frustration that you say exists in Negro children." To the first question Wertham was adamant that his opinion on the matter of segregation was "as exact as a doctor's science when he says someone has measles." Moreover, he asserted that it mattered little that he had examined only thirteen children of varying ages, because these children's responses represented confirmation of general scientific conclusions he had reached through long years of clinical contact with a wide variety of children experiencing emotional disturbances—including those who attended schools segregated by law as in Baltimore and those segregated by custom as in New York. It was actually this response that prompted Attorney General Young to inquire about the distinction between de jure and de facto school segregation. Wertham's response encapsulated the primary message of his entire testimony that day:

> I would say that segregation as it exists in New York, especially in the district where [the Lafargue Clinic] is located ... I think the effects are bad too, and the only difference is that if the state directs the segregation it intensifies this conflict on the one hand, and on the other it deprives the child ... of any rationalization about it, because they could say where it is not decreed by law, "Well, there is a bad official here, or a bad feeling," and they could blame someone, and legitimately, if they wanted to. But if it is decreed by law we deprive the child of his ethical hold because the state does it, and we want by education to inculcate in the child that the state, the whole group as whole [*sic*], is the symbol of ethics.[57]

Wertham later suggested to one historian that his frank acknowledgment of school segregation in New York along with his rationale for distinguishing that type of segregation from Delaware's disarmed Young, "melted the judge's disbelief," and "contributed to the exceedingly loose tether Seitz kept on his testimony."[58]

Wertham deftly handled the attorney general's final line of questioning. The basis of the state's case was the argument declared by Young at the outset of the trial: "We cannot by judicial fiat impose upon a people against their will what they have accepted by heritage, tradition, and governmental sanctions ... for so many years." Young's questions about the possible impact of desegregation derived from this argument, and they ended up eliciting from Wertham two significant interrelated ideas regarding the likely impact of desegregation on both black and white children. Wertham called upon the court to take the perspective of the children on the question of whether the duration of segregation as a fact of custom and community life mattered in his analysis: "We are dealing with the mind of a child and the emotions of a child of nine, who is late for a bus going to a segregated school, and the state decrees it, and the bus for white children passes and children stick out their tongues and say, 'You nigger.' What difference does it make if it is one year or one hundred years?" The second point Wertham made in reply to Young emphasized his faith in the law as an educational force in society. "I think laws are one of the best educational measures we have," declared Wertham. At present the law of segregation ratified the beliefs of Delaware society's "most bigoted citizens," and the damaging educational effect was clear. He suggested that both adults and children learn from the law and that change in the law would at the very least eradicate the primary source of injury to the emotional health of Delaware children. With this Young concluded his cross-examination. The central point of Wertham's testimony was a persuasive explanation of the power of the state and its singular importance as a determining force in the lives of Delaware children. Ultimately, the state's laws could be a force harming or ensuring its citizens' health.[59]

On April 1, 1952, Chancellor Seitz ruled that school segregation as practiced in Delaware violated the doctrine of "separate but equal." Of the five companion cases argued collectively as *Brown v. Board of Education*, the Delaware cases were the only ones in which the state ruled in favor of the black plaintiffs. Seitz ruled that "State-imposed segregation in education itself results in Negro children, as a class, receiving educational opportunities which are substantially inferior to those available to white children similarly situated." He stopped short of "dismissing the *Plessy* decision as precedent," noting that he believed "the 'separate but equal' doctrine in education should be rejected, but its rejection should come from [the Supreme Court]." Finding the Delaware schools unequal, Seitz ordered the immediate admission of Shirley Bulah, Ethel Louise Belton, and the other plaintiffs in Claymont to the currently all-white schools in their communities.[60]

Wertham's testimony proved crucial in shaping the opinion of Chancellor Seitz. Despite having his legal opinion constrained by *Plessy*, Seitz recognized as a finding of fact Wertham's argument that segregated schools hindered the educational opportunities and posed a public mental health threat to Delaware's black children. Referring to Wertham in his opinion, he wrote, "One of America's foremost psychiatrists testified that state-imposed school segregation produces in Negro children an unsolvable conflict which seriously interferes with the mental health of such children." Thurgood Marshall glowingly reported to Wertham that "the Chancellor in Delaware came to his conclusions concerning the effects of segregation largely upon the basis of your testimony and the work done in your clinic." Wertham would later claim that his testimony in Delaware laid the scientific foundation for the Supreme Court decision overturning "separate but equal." Wertham's boast was to a significant degree quite accurate, as Chief Justice Earl Warren later cited Seitz's finding of fact in his opinion for the *Brown v. Board of Education* ruling.[61]

Fredric Wertham and the Social Science Statement

Despite having delivered arguably the most potent scientific ammunition to the desegregation fight, Wertham failed to secure a place for himself among the circle of social scientists most closely associated with the NAACP-LDEF's campaign. As the hearings in Wilmington concluded in October 1951, Robert Carter asked Kenneth Clark to begin work on a brief consolidating social scientific evidence on the effects of segregation and the projected ramifications of desegregation—a brief to be included in materials submitted to the U.S. Supreme Court, should it agree to hear the cases. Clark did not ask Wertham to participate in preparing the brief. The committee that produced the brief consisted entirely of members of the Committee on Intergroup Relations of the Society for the Psychological Study of Social Issues, an association of progressive psychologists established in the 1930s. In addition to Clark the brief committee consisted of a number of social psychologists and psychiatrists who had been or were slated to be NAACP-LDEF witnesses in the South Carolina, Kansas, Virginia, and Delaware cases. One of the committee members was Dr. Viola W. Bernard, the Columbia University psychiatrist who had advised the Field Foundation against funding the Lafargue Clinic in 1945, suggesting that the time was not right for the clinic and that Wertham, a white psychiatrist, was certainly not the appropriate person to run a Harlem-based clinic.

Perhaps the committee failed to include Wertham because he was not a member of Society for the Psychological Study of Social Issues. Perhaps one New York psychiatrist, Dr. Bernard, was sufficient. Or more likely, Clark and Bernard were wary of Wertham. They probably recognized that Wertham's "imperious nature," as Jack Greenberg had characterized it, would prove an obstacle in preparing a statement reflecting the current state of psychological knowledge on segregation and desegregation.

The social science brief thus took shape without Wertham's input. And it reflected the aim of providing the court with a dispassionate digest of the current state of scientific knowledge on the effects of segregation and prospective consequences of desegregation. Though each of the members of the brief committee contributed to the substance of the statement that emerged over the summer of 1952, its actual composition fell to Kenneth Clark and two New York psychologists, Isidor Chein, director of Research for the Commission on Community Interrelations of the American Jewish Congress, and Stuart W. Cook, chairman of New York University's Department of Psychology. The final draft of the brief, titled "The Effects of Segregation and the Consequences of Desegregation: A Social Science Statement," consisted of eighteen typewritten pages with a total of thirty-five footnotes citing primarily experimental psychological studies and several sociological works. Clark submitted the statement to the NAACP-LDEF on September 22, 1952, and it was soon appended to the NAACP's brief, which the Supreme Court solicited when it agreed to hear the school cases in the October 1952 term.

"The statement was a huge success," according to one historian, offering the Court the "authority" of modern psychological knowledge on the damage done by segregation. In the Court's opinion issued on May 17, 1954, Chief Justice Earl Warren made ample use of the statement to explain the unanimous decision overturning *Plessy* and "separate but equal": "To separate [black students] from others of similar age and qualifications solely because of their race generates a feeling of inferiority as to their status in the community that may affect their hearts and minds in a way unlikely ever to be undone. . . . Whatever may have been the extent of psychological knowledge at the time of *Plessy v. Ferguson*, this finding is amply supported by modern authority."[62] Warren would later claim that the *Brown* decision was not founded on the social scientific evidence, insisting that segregation was inherently unequal, and thus a violation of the Fourteenth Amendment. He downplayed the famous eleventh footnote in the court's decision, which cited the works of Clark, Myrdal, and other social scientists. Most subsequent scholars have reaffirmed Warren's contention.[63]

But one scholar has effectively challenged the orthodoxy. Legal historian Paul L. Rosen shows that the *Brown* decision represented a ratification of sociological jurisprudence that incorporated empirical social science into its legal decision-making process. In other words, the social science evidence was not merely supplemental to the legal reasoning in ruling segregation to be a violation of the equal protection clause, but was integral to it. "The basic fact," writes Rosen, "is that the Court's pronounced interest in fact-finding represented a long trend in judicial interpretation; empirically defined facts gradually became more important or superseded facts drawn from judicial introspection."[64]

The Supreme Court's acknowledgment of the psychological harm done by segregation represented the crowning achievement of postwar antiracist social science. But Wertham's signal contribution to the scientific campaign disappeared almost immediately from both academic and public conversation about *Brown v. Board of Education* and its significance. What seemed to be a personal slight to Wertham effected a peculiar silencing of an important contribution to scientific thought on the effects of racism. One can only conclude that this was deliberate.[65]

The contributions of Wertham and the Lafargue Clinic to the fundamental arguments of the scientific case against school segregation permeated the social science statement, but they appear without any attribution. Clark and his colleagues appear to have borrowed freely Wertham's argument about the role of the state as a source of authority that produced emotional conflict and anxiety in children: "The child who, for example, is compelled to attend a segregated school may be able to cope with ordinary expressions of prejudice by regarding the prejudiced person as evil or misguided; but he cannot readily cope with symbols of authority, the full force of the authority of the State . . . in the same manner."[66] This erasure symbolized the general marginalization of Wertham's contributions to antiracist social and medical science in the 1950s and left the Lafargue Clinic in very much the same marginal position in the field of mental health care in New York City that it had occupied before *Brown*.

While Wertham's exclusion from the drafting committee might have been understandable, why the committee never asked him to sign the final statement remains a mystery. One historian notes that the criteria for selecting the signatories were professional standing and geography, as the list would need to comprise representatives from each region of the country. Yet, of the thirty-five men and women who signed the statement, fifteen were from New York City. Concern for geographical distribution was less important than suggested.[67]

It is safe to say that the social science brief committee excluded Wertham for personal, professional/methodological, and likely political reasons. He persistently advocated the preeminence of clinical evidence in matters of psychology and emphasized the connection between socioeconomic oppression, racism, and mental health. He believed that experimental studies involving lab-like tests of children and adults merely supplemented the total picture of human psychology. This stance surely alienated psychologists such as Clark who staked their claims to science on the validity and import of experiments using projective methods. It was not that Wertham wholly rejected the usefulness of experimental psychology. Rather, he suggested both at the Delaware trial and in his written work before and after Wilmington that the clinical setting and method established the conditions for the "spontaneous expression" of an individual's thoughts and emotions. In the instance of the Lafargue Clinic's examinations of the Delaware children, for example, it was the openness of the dialogues that revealed the most substantive aspects of segregation's negative effects on the youngsters.

The problem for Wertham was that the virtues of the clinical method also proved to be defects in the context of efforts to make psychological knowledge approximate the physical sciences. Where experimental psychology established its claims to accuracy on representative sampling of test subjects and procedural uniformity in the accumulation of data, clinical psychiatry relied upon narrative information from the subject under examination and the ability of the individual psychiatrist to interpret both spoken and unspoken data. Referring to Wertham's testimony during the *Brown* hearings, Supreme Court Justice Felix Frankfurter himself captured the limits of clinical psychiatric evidence: "If a man says three yards, and I have measured it, and it is three yards, there it is. But if a man tells you the inside of your brain and mine, and how we function, that is not a measurement, and there you are. . . . We are dealing here with very subtle things, very subtle testimony."[68]

Countering Psychic Violence

Wertham's work in the Delaware case demonstrating the negative public health aspects of state-imposed segregation was part of a broad effort to harness social psychiatry to the alleviation of major problems in American society. The Lafargue Clinic itself had emerged from the concern shared among Wertham, Richard Wright, and St. Philip's Episcopal's Rev. Shelton Hale Bishop that black New Yorkers' encounters with racism in the hostile atmosphere of the city engendered psychic strains that led to violence. Wertham argued vigorously that racial segregation, both de jure and de facto, and crime comic books enacted forms of social and cultural violence upon the most vulnerable members of American society.

At one point in his Delaware testimony, he made this association explicit—much to the annoyance of Jack Greenberg, who wanted Wertham simply to stick to the case against school segregation. Prior to Wilmington, "[as] we discussed his testimony," recalled Greenberg, "Wertham kept veering off into denouncing the malignant influence of comic books, and I kept trying to steer him back . . . thinking the comic book issue irrelevant and distracting." In the middle of his testimony, though, Wertham pulled out a copy of a comic book to illustrate the social context in which children receive antiblack messages. It was a copy of *Jumbo Comics* in which a group of black people were placed in a cage suspended from a tree in the jungle. Wertham read the caption aloud: "Helpless natives left to starve or be prey to any prowling beast." Greenberg was forced as a matter of procedure to introduce the comic book into evidence, and tried immediately to bring Wertham back to the matter at hand. He was soon successful, but Wertham first wanted simply to show that images of black people being degraded were connected to segregation. "The children read that, and they are there indoctrinated with the fact that you can do all kinds of things to colored races." He still concluded that "segregation in schools assumes very much greater importance in these children's minds than" the racism depicted in the comic books. Nevertheless, Wertham alerted the court to the continuity between state action and mass culture as the social sources of emotional and psychic strain upon children.[69]

Wertham's central argument in both his testimony against segregation and his attack upon comic books was that both contributed to a hostile climate that interfered with the emotional and mental health of young people. Moreover, the argument was founded on evidence derived from the clinical methods of social psychiatry practiced at Lafargue. And Wertham's stance on both issues derived from a belief fundamental to his public advocacy in the 1950s: phenomena that occurred in society, such as racism and juvenile delinquency, may have resulted from multiple factors, but it was both scientifically and politically legitimate to isolate and address discrete individual factors that took on preeminent, determining importance—state-sanctioned school segregation and crime comic books, respectively.[70]

In the spring of 1974, on the twentieth anniversary of the *Brown v. Board of Education* school desegregation ruling by the U.S. Supreme Court, Jack Greenberg, by then director of the NAACP-LDEF, wrote to ask Fredric Wertham if he would participate in a dinner commemoration of *Brown*. Wertham rejected the invitation, expressing a frank bitterness about the erasure of the Lafargue Clinic from the historical narrative of *Brown*:

> Under no circumstances would my conscience permit me to contribute to nor endorse the completely false monolithic legend that has been built up skillfully over the years with regard to the basic scientific foundation of the Supreme Court decision. It was not based on primitive insignificant dolls play, but on careful lifelike clinical studies by the Lafargue Clinic group of black and white psychiatrists, psychologists, teachers and social workers. The Clinic for the first time presented segregation as a public health problem, affecting white children as well as black children, using clinical psychiatric methods, and as a question of what the Lafargue group called "positive mental health."

Wertham's letter clearly left an impression on Greenberg. When Wertham died in November 1981, the *New York Times* obituary described only his early career as a forensic psychiatrist and highlighted his role in the anti-comic furor of the 1950s, most especially his 1954 study *Seduction of the Innocent*. In a letter to the editor published ten days after the obituary, Greenberg noted that the *Times* had omitted any reference to Wertham's "important role in the school segregation cases." Full of quotations from Chancellor Seitz's opinion recognizing the importance of Wertham's testimony, the letter was one small bit of recompense for a hard-fought life.[71]

Epilogue

"An Experiment in the Social Basis of Psychotherapy"

> The black man's is a strange situation; it is a perspective, an angle of vision held by oppressed people; it is an outlook of people looking upward from below. It is what Nietzsche once called a "frog's perspective." Oppression oppresses, and this is the consciousness of black men who have been oppressed for centuries,—oppressed so long that their oppression has become a tradition, in fact, a kind of culture.
>
> RICHARD WRIGHT, FOREWORD TO GEORGE PADMORE'S *PAN-AFRICANISM OR COMMUNISM*, 1955

> Maybe the history of the Clinic is a more important experiment than the Clinic itself.
>
> DR. FREDRIC WERTHAM TO RICHARD WRIGHT, MAY 12, 1953

Fredric Wertham and his colleagues at Lafargue not only fashioned a conceptual framework for addressing the social basis of mental illness among an oppressed people, but also institutionalized that framework and applied this social psychiatry therapeutically in a way that touched the lives of thousands of everyday people. This book has shown how this intervention distinguished the Lafargue Clinic in the history of American psychiatry. Lafargue's emergence was of course the product of a widespread American concern with the mental health of its citizens, but it went further than any other therapeutic institution by linking race and class oppression as a source of mental disorder and personality problems. Moreover, the clinic's founders and supporters argued that mental health care for African Americans was an extension of democracy into the fundamental institutional life of the nation. The Lafargue Clinic became a key site in the battle for the desegregation of American society.[1]

The social context of New York City at midcentury was ripe for producing in African Americans a considerable degree of anxiety about their basic survival in a constricted ambit characterized by hostile competition for living space, jobs, health, recreation. Extraordinary measures were required of black people just to attain the material necessities and those intangible human needs of status and recognition and feelings of personal safety.[2] This book has sought to provide a window onto a world in which the mental health of African Americans was either an invisible, underground absence or something over which many professionals in the human sciences obsessed. This is the striking paradox at work in the research and thinking of early post–World War II social scientists, government officials, and mental health professionals. In this context, the Lafargue Clinic was indeed unique, even exceptional. But its work—Wertham called it "an experiment in the social basis of psychotherapy"—was part of something larger than itself. The clinic sat at the intersection of major intellectual, political, and institutional developments in the early postwar period: the social scientific study of the effects of discrimination on minority groups; liberal antiracist social policy; and the push to move mental health care "from asylum to community."[3] Most important, though, the clinic addressed the vital issue of what healthy African American minds should look like, in practical terms, through practical means.

In his 1952 classic study, *Black Skin, White Masks*, which blurred the genres of scientific analysis, autobiography, and philosophical treatise, Martinican psychiatrist Frantz Fanon argued for a sociogenic approach to the origin of psychological structures of "the black living in an anti-black world." Fanon noted that Freud, "reacting to the constitutionalist tendency of the late nineteenth century," introduced the ontogenetic (individual) as a substitute for the phylogenetic (group/family) theory of human psychology. "It will be seen," declared Fanon, "that the black man's alienation is not an individual question. Beside phylogeny and ontogeny stands sociogeny."[4]

Fanon's work was contemporaneous with Wertham's attempts to fashion a social psychiatry whose basic orientation was sociogenic. This psychiatry considered the lives and thoughts of the patient within a social context, within the quotidian experience of modern society. In a December 1946 lecture, Wertham explained that "in every mental disorder social factors are operative. It has to be determined if they are etiologically predominant, in which case we speak of *sociogenic*; or if they merely color the symptomatic manifestations in form or content, in which case we use the term *socioplastic*."[5] Wertham was convinced that psychiatry had to move beyond its binary emphasis on *either* somatic/constitutional determinants *or* individual psychopathology rooted in childhood trauma. Like Fanon, Wertham was a practicing psychoanalyst, someone whose critique of what he called "old-style conservative" psychoanalysis was an internal argument for transforming the field both philosophically and scientifically.

Race sat at the center of both Fanon's and Wertham's projects as the exemplary variable in the sociogenesis of mental disorders among modern "Negroes." And while Richard Wright himself was no clinician, he too argued that the psychosocial alienation that blacks experienced, especially in the urban North, engendered among many a type of free-floating anxiety that threatened their mental health. Wertham never produced an extended study on what constituted mental health, but he persistently referred to the notion of the "will to survive in a hostile world" as the ideal state of mind for his patients who came to the Lafargue Clinic. Coming from Wertham this was of course an idea that moved beyond individual survival to consider the survival of a whole community. Thus the mental health, the psychic health of black people or any other human population, could be gauged by the presence or absence of thoughts and/ or behavior directed to self-harm or violence against other community members.

The key issue here is that of irrationality or loss of control. While the notion of rationality is of course fraught with issues of racialized normativity, as generations of antiracist writers have demonstrated, the concept is useful here as a distinguishing feature of individual thought and action that threaten one's or another's survival.[6] Wertham had a progressive faith in reason as both faculty and mechanism for helping everyday people identify the sources of mental conflict, such as anxiety or disorganized thinking. This notion becomes relevant when applied to black people living under the pressures of racism and class subjugation. The aim of Wertham's approach was not to mold African Americans into embodiments of normative rationality. Rather, Wertham's goal was to direct his patients toward the roots of their mental conflicts that connected deep into the social order of *racial capitalism*, as Cedric Robinson would later term the articulation of white supremacy and the capitalist mode of production.[7]

Cultural Competency and the Lafargue Clinic

It helps to place the antiracist work of Lafargue in conversation with the push for *cultural competency* in contemporary mental health care. The Lafargue Clinic's emphasis on its Harlem patients' *intersecting* statuses as black, largely poor, and disempowered, rather than on their "culture," in treating mental disorders or problems of everyday living eschewed the framework of culture as a psychic determinant and offered a model of psychotherapy that was "radical" in the etymological sense: that is, of seeking answers and interventions in the *roots*—the social origins—of anxiety and other mental health problems.

We are in a moment in the West where scholars and laypeople alike explain human behavior, that of both individuals and collectives, through the language of "hard wiring," of "evolutionary foundations," of "Darwinian adaptations." It is a return to the constitutionalism of a century ago that was thought by many to be defeated with the fall of eugenic ideology in the Allied-Axis war. What is lost in this deference to the gene, to hereditarian fixity, is the *social*—the world of human activity and thus contingency. The neglect of the social, of sociality as such, in the "normal science" of research in a wide array of fields enshrines matter/bodies at the expense of understanding complex causality in the shaping of human substance.[8]

Yet it has also become a commonplace within academia to proclaim *race* to be a social construction. In this formulation, *race* is really just a misguiding shorthand for explaining human difference based upon symbolic cues, read contextually, which have no fundamental bases in verifiable biological entities such as genes. And yet, the commonplace claim of *race as social construction* has hardly permeated the commonsense institutional life of so many spheres of contemporary activity, including that of psychotherapy. As historian and psychiatrist Jonathan Metzl has recently argued, "To a remarkable extent, anxieties about racial difference shape diagnostic criteria, health-care policies, medical and popular attitudes about mentally ill persons, the structures of treatment facilities, and, ultimately, the conversations that take place there within."[9]

These anxieties about racial difference intersect with entrenched social-structural inequities in modern U.S. society to generate a range of racialized disparities in the access to care, diagnosis, treatment, and outcome in the area of mental health care.[10] Changing the fundamental structure of an unequal social order is difficult, to say the least. So contemporary workers in the mental health care field turn to culture, to the culture of their patients and, to a lesser degree, the culture of the fields within which they work. Many practitioners and policy makers propose a concept and practice of *cultural competency* as a remedy to both the anxiety of encounter and the disparity in care.

From the office receptionist to the chief executive, the attainment of cultural competency has become imperative among clinical staff at all levels. Promoters of cultural competency argue that an important step in reducing disparities is for health care systems and providers to become not only aware of cultural differences among their clients and patients, but to adopt strategies for incorporating that difference into their diagnostic and treatment protocols. Professional organizations, including the American Psychiatric Association, along with individual hospitals and clinics, have devised specific guidelines that signal to their members what to be aware of when treating members of different "ethnic" and "cultural" groups, that is, what to know about "African Americans," "Asians," "Latinos," and "Native Americans."[11] In their best versions, cultural competency guidelines promote awareness among the caregivers of their own possession of a culture, as well as the distinct culture of the treatment environment—the clinic, hospital, or office, for example. What cultural competency advocates hope to emerge from this stew of "cross-cultural" awareness is a reduction in miscommunication, misunderstanding, and ultimately misdiagnosis and mistreatment.

Culture, as word and concept, emerged over the last century as a placeholder for mental health professionals, policy makers, and socio-behavioral scientists for that which used to evoke or be applied to race—race as those embodied, intrinsic, fixed, and heritable traits/qualities within a population group and each one of its members.[12] In contemporary discourse seeking to address disparities in the context of psychotherapy as it relates to the wider field of mental health care, cultural difference has emerged as a proxy—a stand-in for racial difference. Race becomes culture becomes race in a reflexive, circular interaction through the demand that the psychotherapist *read* and *interpret* the visible and aural signs of difference that are indeed marked by embodied difference—reading culture becomes reading race, and that process of reading is governed by a fundamental, long-embedded ensemble of associations and expectations of what it means to be X type of person.

Within the clinical encounter, the shift from race to culture has historically been a well-intentioned, often antiracist, attempt to address problems of alterity. Yet the consequences of this well-intentioned shift from race to culture are profound evasions of the persistent significance not only of racial identification and identity, but of *racism* as a determining force in constituting psychic health. And what is at stake in these evasions is nothing less than the very meaning of health and pathology, questions that will shape—that are no doubt shaping—the contours and substance of modern therapeutic cultures.

In highlighting the efforts of cultural competency to confront the significance of racial and ethnic difference in the clinical setting, I wish to suggest that the emphasis on the patient's "culture" and the clinician's capacity to read and accommodate that patient's difference tends to elide the larger structures of inequity that perpetuate not race, but racism. And beyond that I wish to suggest that the focus on cultural competency evades the very fundamental issue of how racial difference structures how pathology is recognized, diagnosed, and treated.[13]

By contrast, Lafargue was a modestly radical, local effort to confront directly the individual and social effects of intersecting racial and class oppressions in the mid-twentieth-century United States. By taking concrete, institutional measures to address the anxiety of the black individuals and communities living in New York, Lafargue had chipped away at the edifice of Jim Crow in the North. While it anticipated the community mental health movement of the 1960s, the clinic did not shake up the entire system of mental health care in America, or even New York City, for that matter. Yet the very existence of Lafargue forced city officials, and at least some psychiatrists, to take seriously black people's need for humane and accessible psychiatric services.

The End of an Experiment

In 1954, the same year that *Seduction of the Innocent* was published and the Supreme Court overturned "separate but equal," the State of New York passed a law that seemed to bode well for the future of the Lafargue

Clinic. The Community Mental Health Services Act represented the post-war shift in mental health care policy toward public health measures based on localized efforts to prevent serious mental illness. The act established community mental health boards in cities and counties of fifty thousand or more residents. Each local board would now be responsible for dispensing considerable funds allocated by the state to licensed providers of mental health care. Some of the clinic staff had always hoped they might be able to operate on a full-time, all-day basis, and the new law rekindled that hope. In its first eighteen months, the seventeen mental health boards across New York State dispensed approximately $4 million to outpatient clinics, inpatient general hospital psychiatric services, and a variety of psychiatric rehabilitation and remedial education programs. Kenneth and Mamie Clark's Northside Center received over $72,000 of the New York City Community Mental Health Board's total allotment of $436,000.[14]

The Lafargue Clinic applied to the state and city for funding under the 1954 act but was summarily denied. In letters to the state commissioner of mental hygiene and to New York City's director of mental health services, Lafargue physician-in-charge Hilde L. Mosse appealed the rejection for funding. She challenged the mental health board's finding that Lafargue did not qualify under the new law. She characterized the clinic as fulfilling a community need that no other mental hygiene clinic in Harlem had done. "As you know," Mosse wrote to the state commissioner, "the Northside Center restricts it cases to children, and Harlem Hospital is not able to take care of the needs of the community. Our long waiting list proves this conclusively." Moreover, the Lafargue Clinic's contribution to pioneering clinical research had already far exceeded anything one might expect from an institution subsisting on low fees and piecemeal donations. Citing a list of studies conducted at the clinic, Mosse concluded her letter: "It is my feeling therefore that our research work also qualifies us for inclusion in the Mental Health Act." Lafargue fit the model perfectly of locally based outpatient mental health services imagined under the 1954 act. But clearly the die had been cast long before the new legislation; no amount of persuasion or pleading could undo the calumny Wertham had directed against the psychiatric establishment or his reputation as a self-important nuisance. And so the Lafargue Clinic, Wertham's "experiment in the social basis of psychotherapy," never received any of the new money for community mental health care.[15]

The Lafargue Clinic's failure to secure government funding coincided with the impending retirement of its most important supporter, Rev. Shelton Hale Bishop. In 1957, Bishop announced his retirement, and the board of St. Philip's Episcopal Church announced its selection of Rev. Dr. M. Moran Weston, a graduate of Columbia University and Union Theological Seminary in New York City, to replace him. Like Bishop, Weston was committed to the mental health care needs of the Harlem community, but his opinion of Wertham and the Lafargue Clinic's approach to social and psychological problems remains unknown. In the first year of his rectorship, Weston transformed the St. Philip's community center and parish house, where the Lafargue Clinic had been housed since its opening, into a clearinghouse for community services and new health programs directed by a doctors' committee he appointed. The men and women who executed the new programming represented medical professionals drawn from the St. Philip's congregation.

Weston's health initiative was not a slight directed at Wertham and the Lafargue Clinic. Rather it reflected a changing of the guard and perhaps the desire to place the health needs of the central Harlem community in the hands of black professionals. As if the leadership change at St. Philip's were not enough to affect the Lafargue Clinic's survival, several members of the clinic staff had died in the past year, and a few others were suffering from severe illnesses. And so, on November 1, 1958, the Lafargue Clinic staff held their last therapy and counseling sessions with thirty or so men, women, and children who represented the thousands that over the past twelve years had descended into the parish house basement.[16]

Notes

Introduction

1. *Time*, July 28, 1941.

2. Michel Fabre, *The Unfinished Quest of Richard Wright*, trans. Isabel Barzun (New York: William Morrow & Co., 1973), 236.

3. "Murder Is Admitted by Negro Musician," *New York Times*, December 3, 1941, 52.

4. Frederic Wertham, *Dark Legend: A Study in Murder* (New York: Duell, Sloan and Pearce, 1941). At some point in the mid-1940s Wertham dropped the second *e* from the spelling of his first name.

5. David Park, "The Couch and the Clinic: The Cultural Authority of Popular Psychiatry and Psychoanalysis," *Cultural Studies* 18, no. 1 (January 2004): 109–33.

6. James E. Reibman, "The Life of Dr. Fredric Wertham," in *The Fredric Wertham Collection: Gift of His Wife Hesketh* (Cambridge, MA: Busch-Reisinger Museum, Harvard University, 1990), 11–22. Ella Winter was married to the writer Lincoln Steffens, with whom she joined the League of American Writers, "an affiliate of the International Union of Revolutionary Writers," in 1935; see Constance Webb, *Richard Wright: A Biography* (New York; G. P. Putnam's Sons, 1968), 134. Wright describes his involvement with the League of American Writers in a memorable section of *Black Boy (American Hunger): A Record of Childhood and Youth* (New York: Perennial Classics, Harper Collins, 1998), 346–50.

7. Richard Wright to Frederic Wertham, October 24, 1941. Quoted in *Richard Wright: Books and Writers*, ed. Michel Fabre (Jackson: University Press of Mississippi, 1990), 171.

8. Fredric Wertham to Richard Wright, November 9, 1941, box 108, folder 1677, Richard Wright Papers, James Weldon Johnson Collection MSS 3, Beinecke Library, Yale University, New Haven, CT (hereafter cited as Wright Papers).

9. "Mental hygiene" was both a generic term and a specific movement to institute preventive mental health care throughout the United States. In the first half of the twentieth century, many people used "mental hygiene" simply as substitute for saying "psychiatry." See Gerald N. Grob, *Mental Illness and American Society, 1875–1940* (Princeton, NJ: Princeton University Press, 1983).

10. Reibman, "Life of Dr. Fredric Wertham," 12; Sidney M. Katz, "Jim Crow Is Barred from Wertham's Clinic," *Magazine Digest*, September 1946, and Therese Pol, "Psychiatry in Harlem," *Protestant*, June–July 1947, 28–30, reprint in "Publicity," box 3, folder 1, Lafargue Clinic Records, Schomburg Center for Research in Black Culture, New York Public Library (hereafter cited as Lafargue Clinic Records). Clarence Darrow's relationship with African American clients is discussed in Kevin Boyle's excellent history of the Ossian Sweet case in Detroit, *The Arc of Justice*.

11. Jacques Cattell, ed., *American Men of Science: A Biographical Directory* (Lancaster, PA: Science Press, 1944), 1908.

12. Historian Matthew Frye Jacobson documents the pre–World War II complexity of American whiteness by exploring how scientists and everyday people developed systems of racialized differentiation *among* varieties of white populations that are now referred to as ethnicities or nationalities. See Jacobson's *Whiteness of a Different Color: European Immigrants and the Alchemy of Race* (Cambridge, MA: Harvard University Press, 1998).

13. Lorraine Maynard (in collaboration with Laurence Miscall), *Bellevue* (New York: Julian Messner, 1940), 61, 139–40, italics in original; see also Cheryl Lynn Greenberg *"Or Does It Explode?": Black Harlem in the Great Depression* (New York: Oxford University Press, 1991), 86–91; and see also Dennis Doyle, " 'Racial Differences Have to Be Considered': Lauretta Bender, Bellevue Hospital, and the African American Psyche, 1936–52," *History of Psychiatry* 21, no. 2 (2010): 206–23.

14. "Harlem Pioneers with Mental Clinic," *Headlines and Pictures*, July 1946, reprint in "Publicity," box 3, folder 1, Lafargue Clinic Records.

15. In 1949, the Democratic, Republican, and Liberal Parties formed in New York City and drafted Brown to defeat the Communist city councilman Benjamin J. Davis Jr. The repeal of proportional representation in 1947 enabled Davis's defeat. According to a *New York Times* editorial, "The 'bullet' voting of PR was an ideal weapon of the Communists in putting Mr. Davis into office and keeping him there." See *New York Times*, July 22, 1949, 38; November 9, 1949, 26.

16. Katz, "Jim Crow Is Barred," no pagination; Richard Wright, "Psychiatry Comes to Harlem," *Free World*, September 1946, reprint, p. 3, box 3, folder 1, Lafargue Clinic Records.

17. Ralph G. Martin, "Doctor's Dream in Harlem," *New Republic*, June 3, 1946, 799. At the time the clinic opened African Americans were only 6.5 percent of New York City's population; in 1940 there were 458,000 blacks out of a total population of 7,455,000, and in 1950 they were 748,000 out of a total 7,892,000. Yet in the early 1940s black people were five times as likely to be in jail and were one-third of the city's prison population. Black youth were reported to be 53 percent of all juvenile delinquency cases in Manhattan. See Ira Rosenwaike, *Population History of New York City* (Syracuse, NY: Syracuse University Press, 1972), chap. 6.

18. Bishop was not completely alone at the time among Harlem pastors who sought rapprochement between the ministry and psychiatry. In his autobiography the Reverend James H. Robinson wrote: "I dreamed of a minister and a psychiatrist working together in an experiment in spiritual psychiatry. It would be no trick at all if two such persons of equal stature and mutual confidence and respect for one another's respective fields could be found who would deal with people both as moral and physical beings." James H. Robinson, *Road without Turning: The Story of Rev. James H. Robinson; An Autobiography* (New York: Farrar, Straus and Giroux, 1950), 253. Lawrence Jackson, *Ralph Ellison: Emergence of Genius* (New York: John Wiley & Sons, 2002),

300–336; Shelton H. Bishop, "A History of St. Philip's Church," *Historical Magazine of the Protestant Episcopal Church*, 1946, 298; "Biggest Episcopal Church: Harlem's St. Philip's Tops in U.S. Membership," *Ebony*, November 1952, 58–66.

19. Lafargue Clinic pamphlet, box 2, folder 1, Lafargue Clinic Records.

20. Florence Hesketh Wertham to Richard Wright, no date, approximately late 1946, box 108, folder 1677, Wright Papers.

21. The "Lafargue Clinic Statistics" report dated March 6, 1956, explains that for records of correspondence between the clinic and city, state, and private funding agencies, "all data in Dr. Wertham's file Official Papers." Box 1, folder 9, Lafargue Clinic Records. Just several blocks away in the very same month, Kenneth and Mamie Clark opened the famed Northside Center for Child Development, where their doll tests with black children were used as evidence in *Brown v. Board of Education of Topeka*. See Gerald Markowitz and David Rosner, *Children, Race, and Power: Kenneth and Mamie Clark's Northside Center* (New York: Routledge, 2000) and chapters 3 and 4 for a discussion of the Clarks and the Northside Center in relation to the Lafargue Clinic's history.

22. Lafargue clinic pamphlet, box 2, folder 1, Lafargue Clinic Records, http://www.marxists.org/archive/lafargue/1883/lazy/preface.htm. For recent exploration of Lafargue's thought see Tom Lutz, *Doing Nothing: A History of Loafers, Loungers, Slackers, and Bums in America* (New York: Farrar, Straus and Giroux, 2006), 103–9.

23. For a broad, interdisciplinary exploration of psychiatric representations of African American madness and black mental illness as a mark of distinctly racial proclivities toward irrationality and psychopathology see Sander Gilman's "On the Nexus of Blackness and Madness," in *Difference and Pathology: Stereotypes of Sexuality, Race, and Madness* (Ithaca, NY: Cornell University Press, 1985), 131–49. See also Markowitz and Rosner, *Children, Race, and Power*; Matthew Gambino, "'These Strangers within Our Gates': Race, Psychiatry, and Mental Illness among Black Americans at St. Elizabeths Hospital in Washington, D.C., 1900–1940," *History of Psychiatry* 19, no. 4 (2008): 387–408; Jonathan Metzl, *The Protest Psychosis: How Schizophrenia Became a Black Disease* (Boston: Beacon Press, 2009); Martin Summers, "'Suitable Care of the African When Afflicted with Insanity': Race, Madness, and Social Order in Comparative Perspective," *Bulletin of the History of Medicine* 84, no. 1 (2010).

24. See Jay Garcia, *Psychology Comes to Harlem: Rethinking the Race Question in Twentieth-Century America* (Baltimore: Johns Hopkins University Press, 2012), and Jonathan C. Hagel, "In Search of the 'Racist White Psyche': Racism and the Psychology of Prejudice in American Social Thought, 1930–1960" (PhD diss., Brown University, 2012) and my discussion below of the literature of *race* and the human sciences in postwar American society. In his book *Madness Is Civilization: When the Diagnosis Was Social, 1948–1980* (Chicago: University of Chicago Press, 2011), Michael Staub shows that in the three decades following World War II, psychiatry developed a turn toward "environmental" factors in mental life and toward "social analyses of individual problems," reflecting "beliefs that analyzing interpersonal relations and environmental conditions offered an exciting key for the curing of individual psychological difficulties," 4. See also Martin Halliwell, *Therapeutic Revolutions: Medicine, Psychiatry, and American Culture, 1945–1970* (New Brunswick, NJ: Rutgers University Press, 2013), and Trysh Travis and Timothy Aubry, eds., *Rethinking Therapeutic Culture* (Chicago: University of Chicago Press, forthcoming).

25. See Abram Kardiner and Lionel Ovesey, *The Mark of Oppression: A Psychosocial Study of the American Negro* (New York: W. W. Norton & Co., 1951). Albert Murray's writing has been an invaluable guide for thinking about social scientific explorations of black personality. See his self-admittedly polemical *The Omni-Americans: Some Alternatives to the Folklore of White Supremacy* (New York: Vintage, 1983), published originally in 1970. Ruth Feldstein's *Motherhood in Black and White: Race and Sex in American Liberalism* (Ithaca, NY: Cornell University Press, 2000) is particularly helpful for considering the gendered dimensions of the mid-twentieth-century

pathologizing of African Americans in the human sciences. See also Anna Creadick, *Perfectly Average: The Pursuit of Normality in Postwar America* (Amherst: University of Massachusetts Press, 2010), and Deborah Weinstein, *The Pathological Family: Postwar America and the Rise of Family Therapy* (Ithaca, NY: Cornell University Press, 2013).

26. Historian James T. Patterson writes that "roughly a million blacks (along with even more whites) moved from the South during the 1940s. Another 1.5 million Negroes left the South in the 1950s." Patterson, *Grand Expectations: The United States, 1945–1974* (New York: Oxford University Press, 1996), 19.

27. See Robert Gregg, *Sparks from the Anvil of Oppression: Philadelphia's African Methodists and Southern Migrants, 1890–1940* (Philadelphia: Temple University Press, 1993).

28. See David Park, "Putting the World on the Couch: Cultural Authority as a Dimension of Mid-20th Century Popular Psychiatry and Psychoanalysis" (PhD diss., University of Pennsylvania, 2001).

29. See Lee D. Baker, *From Savage to Negro: Anthropology and the Construction of Race, 1896–1954* (Berkeley: University of California Press, 1998), and Daryl Michael Scott, *Contempt and Pity: Social Policy and the Image of the Damaged Black Psyche, 1880–1996* (Chapel Hill: University of North Carolina Press, 1997). Historian Dennis Doyle convincingly shows, though, that some psychiatrists and social scientists continued to entertain bio-racial explanations for supposed differences in white and black behavior and culture; see Doyle, "'Racial Differences.'"

30. See Walter Jackson, *Gunnar Myrdal and America's Conscience: Social Engineering and Racial Liberalism, 1938–1987* (Chapel Hill: University of North Carolina Press, 1990), 272–93, and Ellen Herman, *The Romance of American Psychology: Political Culture in the Age of Experts* (Berkeley: University of California Press, 1995), 174–207.

31. The phrase "psychological reworking of race" comes from Jay Garcia's "Psychology Comes to Harlem: Race, Intellectuals, and Culture in the Mid-Twentieth Century U.S." (PhD diss., Yale University, 2003). See also Anne C. Rose, "Putting the South on the Psychological Map: The Impact of Region and Race on the Human Sciences during the 1930s," *Journal of Southern History* 71, no. 2 (May 2005): 321–35; Jackson, *Gunnar Myrdal*; Ruth Feldstein, *Motherhood in Black and White: Race and Sex in American Liberalism* (Ithaca, NY: Cornell University Press, 2000), 40–61; Herman, *Romance of American Psychology*; Scott, *Contempt and Pity*; Leah Gordon, "The Question of Prejudice: Social Science, Education, and the Struggle to Define 'the Race Problem' in Mid-Century America, 1935–1965" (PhD diss., University of Pennsylvania, 2008); Hagel, "In Search of the 'Racist White Psyche.'" The most prominent exponent of the theory of frustration and aggression in race relations was social psychologist John Dollard; see his "Hostility and Fear in Social Life," *Social Forces* 17, no. 1 (October 1938): 15–26; see also Hortense Powdermaker, "The Channeling of Negro Aggression by the Cultural Process," in *Personality in Nature, Society, and Culture*, ed. Clyde Kluckhohn and Henry A. Murray (New York: Alfred A. Knopf, 1948), 473–84.

32. See the U.S. Army Medical Department, *Neuropsychiatry in World War II*, 2 vols. (Washington, DC: Government Printing Office, 1966–73); Roy R. Grinker and John P. Siegel, *War Neuroses* (Philadelphia: Blakiston Co., 1945); Grob, *Mental Illness and American Society*, 5–23; and Nathan G. Hale Jr., *The Rise and Crisis of Psychoanalysis in the United States: Freud and the Americans, 1917–1985* (Oxford: Oxford University Press, 1995), 187–210; Herman, *Romance of American Psychology*, esp. chaps. 2–4.

33. Karl A. Menninger, *A Psychiatrist's World: The Selected Papers of Karl Menninger* (New York: Viking, 1959), 526–28, quoted in Gerald Grob, *From Asylum to Community: Mental Health Policy in Modern America* (Princeton, NJ: Princeton University Press, 1991), 7.

34. See Guy B. Johnson, "The Stereotype of the American Negro," in *Characteristics of the American Negro*, ed. Otto Klineberg (New York: Harper & Bros., 1944), 4–22. For an excellent historical study of black encounters with psychiatry in the World War II U.S. armed forces see

Ellen Dwyer, "Psychiatry and Race during World War II," *Journal of the History of Medicine and Allied Sciences* 61, no. 2 (2006): 117–43.

35. Kay Cremin, "Brown Breakdown: Negro Mental Patients Increase as Race Hate Takes Its Toll," *Negro Digest*, March 1947, 51. See also E. Franklin Frazier, "Mental Deficiency and Insanity," in his textbook *The Negro in the United States* (New York: Macmillan Co., 1949); Park, "Couch and the Clinic," 109–33.

36. Grob, *From Asylum to Community*; Gerald Grob, *The Mad among Us: A History of the Care of America's Mentally Ill* (New York: Free Press, 1994).

37. Robert Bendiner, "Psychiatry for the Needy," *Tomorrow*, May 1946, 24.

38. See Steven F. Lawson, ed., *To Secure These Rights: The Report of Harry S. Truman's Committee on Civil Rights* (1947; Boston: Bedford / St. Martin's, 2004).

39. Kenneth Spencer, "Sans Funds, LaFarge [*sic*] Clinic Lives," *The People's Voice*, July 13, 1946, reprint in "Publicity," box 3, folder 1, Lafargue Clinic Records.

40. While there are several chapter and article-length examinations of the Lafargue Clinic that provide a wealth of insight into what distinguished it on the intellectual and social landscape of mid-twentieth-century psychiatry and racial knowledge, *Under the Strain of Color* offers a comprehensive exposition of the story and significance of Lafargue. It does so by using both widely known published and unpublished sources and heretofore untapped archival material to position the clinic in a set of distinct yet convergent discursive, institutional, and geographical contexts that reveal histories of African American migration and urbanization, dramatic developments in psychiatric science and practice in both Western Europe and the United States, as well as interracial networks of collaboration among the noncommunist radical Left in postwar America. Shelly Eversley, "The Lunatic's Fancy and the Work of Art," *American Literary History* 13, no. 3 (2001): 445–68; David Marriot, "The Derived Life of Fiction: Race, Childhood, and Culture," in *Haunted Life: Visual Culture and Black Modernity* (New Brunswick, NJ: Rutgers University Press, 2007); Dennis Doyle, "'A Fine New Child': The Lafargue Mental Hygiene Clinic and Harlem's African American Communities, 1946–1958," *Journal of the History of Medicine and Allied Sciences* 64, no. 2 (2009); Dennis A. Doyle, "'Where the Need Is Greatest': Social Psychiatry and Race-Blind Universalism in Harlem's Lafargue Clinic, 1946–1958," *Bulletin of the History of Medicine* 83, no. 4 (Winter 2009): 746–74; Badia Sahar Ahad, "'A Genuine Cooperation': Richard Wright's and Ralph Ellison's Psychoanalytic Conversations," in *Freud Upside Down: African American Literature and Psychoanalytic Culture* (Urbana: University of Illinois Press, 2010); J. Bradford Campbell, "The Schizophrenic Solution: Dialectics of Neurosis and Anti-Psychiatric Animus in Ralph Ellison's *Invisible Man*," *Novel: A Forum for Fiction* 43, no. 3 (2010): 443–65; and Catherine Stewart, "'Crazy for This Democracy': Postwar Psychoanalysis, African American Blues Narratives, and the Lafargue Clinic," *American Quarterly* 65, no. 2 (June 2013): 371–95, which is an extraordinarily capacious and well-crafted synthesis of both literary studies and institutional history that makes creative use of the Lafargue patient files to situate the clinic's work within a compelling cultural frame, namely African American blues narratives.

41. Keith Wailoo, *Dying in the City of the Blues: Sickle Cell Anemia and the Politics of Race and Health* (Chapel Hill: University of North Carolina Press, 2000); Nayan Shah, *Contagious Divides: Epidemics and Race in San Francisco's Chinatown* (Berkeley: University of California Press, 2001); Natalia Molina, *Fit to Be Citizens: Public Health and Race in Los Angeles, 1879–1939* (Berkeley: University of California Press, 2006); Gambino, "'These Strangers within Our Gates'"; Samuel K. Roberts, *Infectious Fear: Politics, Disease, and the Health Effects of Segregation* (Chapel Hill: University of North Carolina Press, 2009); Metzl, *Protest Psychosis*; and Alondra Nelson, *Body and Soul: The Black Panther Party and the Fight against Medical Discrimination* (Minneapolis: University of Minnesota Press, 2011); Jenna Lloyd, *Health Rights Are Civil Rights: Peace and Justice Activism in Los Angeles, 1963–1978* (Minneapolis: University of Minnesota Press, 2014).

42. T. H. Marshall, *Citizenship and Social Class, and Other Essays* (Cambridge: Cambridge University Press, 1950). In addition to the works referenced in this paragraph, historian Andrea Friedman uses Marshall's "social citizenship" to analyze Wertham's efforts "to redefine national security for those left behind by democracy." See *Citizenship in Cold War America: The National Security State and the Possibilities of Dissent* (Amherst: University of Massachusetts Press, 2014). Unfortunately, I encountered Friedman's book too late in the production of this book for me to engage her insights in any sustained, substantive manner.

43. Nelson, *Body and Soul*, 9–11.

44. John Stanfield, *Philanthropy and Jim Crow in American Social Science* (Westport, CT: Greenwood Press, 1985); Jackson, *Gunnar Myrdal*; Patricia Morton, *Disfigured Images: The Historical Assault on Afro-American Women* (New York: Greenwood Press, 1991); James B. McKee, *Sociology and the Race Problem: The Failure of a Perspective* (Urbana: University of Illinois Press, 1993); Herman, *Romance of American Psychology*; Ben Keppel, *The Work of Democracy: Ralph Bunche, Kenneth B. Clark, Lorraine Hansberry, and the Cultural Politics of Race* (Cambridge, MA: Harvard University Press, 1995); Scott, *Contempt and Pity*; Feldstein, *Motherhood in Black and White*; John Jackson, *Social Scientists for Social Justice: Making the Case against Segregation* (New York: NYU Press, 2001); Alice O'Connor, *Poverty Knowledge: Social Science, Social Policy, and the Poor in Twentieth-Century U.S. History* (Princeton, NJ: Princeton University Press, 2001); Jonathan Scott Holloway, *Confronting the Veil : Abram Harris, Jr., E. Franklin Frazier, and Ralph Bunche, 1919–1941* (Chapel Hill: University of North Carolina Press, 2002); Roderick Ferguson, *Aberrations in Black: Toward a Queer of Color Critique* (Minneapolis: University of Minnesota Press, 2004); Rose, "Putting the South on the Psychological Map"; Jodi Melamed, *Represent and Destroy: Rationalizing Violence in the New Racial Capitalism* (Minneapolis: University of Minnesota Press, 2011); Garcia, *Psychology Comes to Harlem*.

45. Scott, *Contempt and Pity*, xix. Alongside Scott's, the works most critical of the reifying normativity and constricting, neutralizing liberalism of postwar human sciences are Feldstein, *Motherhood in Black and White*; Ferguson, *Aberrations in Black*; and Melamed, *Represent and Destroy*.

46. Richard Wright, "Urban Misery in an American City: Juvenile Delinquency in Harlem," *Twice a Year* 14–15 (Fall 1946–Winter 1947): 339–46, and Wright's 1945 private journal, box 117, folder 1860, Wright Papers. Just as insightful is Garcia's contention that scholars today who seek to locate traditions of black radicalism need to pay more attention to the ways in which black writers and activists in the twentieth century articulated together analyses and critiques of political economy, psychology inquiry, and cultural commentary; Garcia, *Psychology Comes to Harlem*, 12–18.

47. Fredric Wertham, "What Is Social Psychiatry?," lecture read at the Brooklyn State Hospital Psychiatric Forum on December 5, 1946, 16–17, box 85, folder 8, Fredric Wertham Papers, Manuscript Division, Library of Congress (hereafter cited as Wertham Papers).

48. Bart Beaty's *Fredric Wertham and the Critique of Mass Culture* (Jackson: University of Mississippi Press, 2005) is a vital exception within the historiography.

1. "This Burden of Consciousness"

1. Michel Fabre, *The Unfinished Quest of Richard Wright*, trans. Isabel Barzun (New York: William Morrow & Co., 1973), 179. For more on the significance of inclusion in the Book-of-the-Month Club see Janice A. Radway, *A Feeling for Books: The Book-of-the-Month Club, Literary Taste, and Middle-Class Desire* (Chapel Hill: University of North Carolina Press, 1997).

2. FBI File No. 100-41674, "Richard Nathaniel Wright," July 8, 1944, 2–3, http://vault.fbi.gov/Richard%20Nathaniel%20Wright. See also Fabre, *Unfinished Quest*, 245–46, and Hazel Rowley, *Richard Wright: The Life and Times* (New York: Henry Holt and Co., 2001), 285–86.

3. See also Jay Garcia, *Psychology Comes to Harlem: Rethinking the Race Question in Twentieth-Century America* (Baltimore: Johns Hopkins University Press, 2012).

4. See Ellen Herman, *The Romance of American Psychology: Political Culture in the Age of Experts* (Berkeley: University of California Press, 1995); Daryl Michael Scott, *Contempt and Pity: Social Policy and the Image of the Damaged Black Psyche, 1880–1996* (Chapel Hill: University of North Carolina Press, 1997); Ruth Feldstein, *Motherhood in Black and White: Race and Sex in American Liberalism* (Ithaca, NY: Cornell University Press, 2000); John Jackson, *Social Scientists for Social Justice: Making the Case against Segregation* (New York: NYU Press, 2001); Jodi Melamed, *Represent and Destroy: Rationalizing Violence in the New Racial Capitalism* (Minneapolis: University of Minnesota Press, 2011); Garcia, *Psychology Comes to Harlem.*

5. See James T. Campbell, *Middle Passages: African American Journeys to Africa, 1787–2005* (New York: Penguin Press, 2006).

6. Wright Journal, January 6, 1945, box 117, folder 1860, Richard Wright Papers.

7. At the time the population was approximately three million people, of which around three hundred thousand were African American. The Black Belt, that strip of land on which blacks were forced to settle, "was seven miles in length and one and one-half miles of width." See St. Clair Drake and Horace R. Cayton, *Black Metropolis: A Study of Negro Life in a Northern City*, vol. 1, rev. and enlarged ed. (1945; New York: Harper Torchbooks, 1962), 8.

8. Richard Wright, *Black Boy (American Hunger): A Record of Childhood and Youth*, restored text established by the Library of America (New York: Harper Perennial, 1993), 261.

9. Ibid., 284.

10. See Fred H. Matthews, *Quest for an American Sociology: Robert E. Park and the Chicago School* (Montreal: McGill–Queen's University Press, 1977), and Carla Cappetti, *Writing Chicago: Modernism, Ethnography, and the Novel* (New York: Columbia University Press, 1993).

11. James F. Short, ed., *The Social Fabric of the Metropolis: Contributions of the Chicago School of Urban Sociology* (Chicago: University of Chicago Press, 1971), xix.

12. Robert E. Park, Ernest W. Burgess, and Roderick D. McKenzie, *The City* (1925; Chicago: University of Chicago Press, 1967), 2.

13. "Reflections on Richard Wright: A Symposium on an Exiled Native Son," in *Anger and Beyond: The Negro Writer in the United States*, ed. Herbert Hill (New York: Harper & Row, 1965), 196–97. Cayton would confess in his 1965 autobiography, *Long Old Road*, that Wright had to remind him they had met previously and that Wright described their meeting in the way Cayton claimed to remember at the Berkeley symposium; see Cayton, *Long Old Road* (New York: Trident Press, 1965), 247–48. See also Rowley, *Richard Wright*, 81–82.

14. Alice O'Connor, *Poverty Knowledge: Social Science, Social Policy, and the Poor in Twentieth-Century U.S. History* (Princeton, NJ: Princeton University Press, 2001), 46. See also Cappetti, *Writing Chicago.*

15. Wright was drawing on the concepts of German sociologist Ferdinand Tonnies as distilled through the Chicago School. See Louis Wirth, "The Sociology of Ferdinand Tonnies," *American Journal of Sociology* 32, no. 3 (November 1926), and Louis Wirth, "Urbanism as a Way of Life," *American Journal of Sociology* 44, no. 1 (July 1938): 3, 20–21; Wright, *Black Boy*, 284.

16. Quoted in Campbell, *Middle Passages*, 275.

17. Book-of-the-Month *Bulletin*, February 1942, quoted in Fabre, *Unfinished Quest*, 572, n.41.

18. Wright, *Black Boy*, 297–98.

19. See Cedric Robinson, "The Emergent Marxism of Richard Wright's Ideology," *Race and Class* 19, no. 3 (1978): 221–37.

20. See "How Bigger Was Born," in Richard Wright, *Native Son*, restored ed. by Library of America (New York: Harper Collins, 1998), 443. The story of Wright's experiences within the Chicago Communist Party is well-known and remains a subject of discussion and debate. See Paul Gilroy, *The Black Atlantic: Modernity and Double Consciousness* (Cambridge, MA: Harvard University Press, 1993), and William J. Maxwell, *New Negro, Old Left: African-American Writing and Communism between the Wars* (New York: Columbia University Press, 1999).

21. Wright, *Black Boy*, 318.

22. Daniel Aaron, "Richard Wright and the Communist Party," in *Richard Wright: Impressions and Perspectives*, ed. David Ray and Robert M. Farnsworth (Ann Arbor: University of Michigan Press, 1971), 41–42; see also St. Clair Drake and Cayton, *Black Metropolis*, 734–37; and Jacquelyn Dowd Hall, "The Long Civil Rights Movement and the Political Uses of the Past," *Journal of American History* 91, no. 4 (March 2005): 1233–63.

23. Wright, *Black Boy*, 319–20; Fabre, *Unfinished Quest*, 105.

24. See Cedric Robinson, *Black Marxism: The Making of the Black Radical Tradition* (1983; Chapel Hill: University of North Carolina Press, 2000), 287–305.

25. Wright, *Black Boy*, 333, 352–58; Rowley, *Richard Wright*, 88–101.

26. Fabre, *Unfinished Quest*, 105.

27. Wright, *Black Boy*, 332; for more on Poindexter see Addison Gayle, *Richard Wright: Ordeal of a Native Son* (Garden City, NY: Anchor Press / Doubleday, 1980), 73–78.

28. Robert Park, "Human Migration and the Marginal Man," *American Journal of Sociology* 33, no. 6 (1928): 881; Wright, *Black Boy*, 332.

29. Wright, *Black Boy*, 341; Wright, "How Bigger Was Born," in *Native Son*, 453–54.

30. "The Negro Boy Problem and the South Side Boy's [*sic*] Club Foundation," n.d., n.p., Chicago Historical Society, quoted in Thomas Lee Philpott, *The Slum and the Ghetto: Neighborhood Deterioration and Middle-Class Reform, Chicago, 1880–1930* (New York: Oxford University Press, 1978).

31. Wright, *Black Boy*, 341.

32. Wright, "How Bigger Was Born," in *Native Son*, 454.

33. Wright, *Native Son*, 294.

34. Wright Journal, February 5, 1945, box 117, folder 1860, Wright Papers.

35. Wright, *Black Boy*, 382. This passage does not appear in the 1944 essay "I Tried to Be a Communist," a long excerpt from *American Hunger*, the second part of Wright's autobiography. See Richard Crossman, ed., *The God That Failed* (New York: Bantam Books, 1950), 103–46. See "Note on the Text," in Wright, *Black Boy*, 409–10.

36. Rowley, *Richard Wright*, 123; Margaret Walker, "Richard Wright," in Ray and Farnsworth, *Richard Wright: Impressions and Perspectives*, 57.

37. Rowley, *Richard Wright*, 128–29; Wright to Ellison, November 2, 1937, quoted ibid., 129.

38. When asked by his lawyer Max whether the South Side Boys' Club kept him out of trouble, Bigger replies, "Kept me out of trouble? Naw; that's where we planned most of our jobs": Wright, *Native Son*, 355.

39. Wright, "How Bigger Was Born," in *Native Son*, 450, 452.

40. Fredric Wertham, "An Unconscious Determinant in *Native Son*," *Journal of Clinical Psychopathology and Psychotherapy* 6 (July 1944): 111–15.

41. Frederic Wertham, introduction to *The World Within: Fiction Illuminating the Neuroses of Our Time*, ed. Mary Louis Aswell (New York: Whittlesey House, McGraw-Hill, 1947), xxi.

42. Wertham, "Unconscious Determinant," 111–15.

43. For a detailed study of the intersections of literature, psychoanalysis, and race within the Wright/Wertham relationship, which uses "An Unconscious Determinant" as a prism, see David Marriot, "The Derived Life of Fiction," in his *Haunted Life: Visual Culture and Black Modernity* (New Brunswick, NJ: Rutgers University Press, 2007), 69–105, and Claudia Tate, *Psychoanalysis and Black Novels: Desire and the Protocols of Race* (New York: Oxford University Press, 1998).

44. Richard Wright Journal, January 25, 1945, box 117, folder 1860, Wright Papers.

45. See Herman, *Romance of American Psychology*; Eli Zaretsky, *Secrets of the Soul: A Social and Cultural History of Psychoanalysis* (New York: Alfred A. Knopf, 2004); Mari Jo Buhle, *Feminism and Its Discontents: A Century of Struggle with Psychoanalysis* (Cambridge, MA: Harvard University Press, 1998); David Park, "The Couch and the Clinic: The Cultural Authority of Popular Psychiatry and Psychoanalysis," *Cultural Studies* 18, no. 1 (January 2004): 109–33.

46. Fabre, *Unfinished Quest*, 228–29.

47. Quoted ibid., 230–31.

48. Ray and Farnsworth, *Richard Wright: Impressions and Perspectives*.

49. Richard Wright Journal, January 20–21, 1945, box 117, folder 1860, Wright Papers.

50. Wright, "Towards the Conquest of Ourselves," n.d., n.p., box 6, folder 148, Wright Papers.

51. Ibid.

52. Cayton to Wright, October 22, 1944, box 95, folder 1254, Wright Papers.

53. Rowley, *Richard Wright*, 298–300.

54. Wright's interest in the utility of psychological readings of the race problem applied to all people, but his emphasis was decidedly on the psychic health of black boys and men. The literature on the masculinist character of Wright's thought and fiction is voluminous. A good starting point is Paul Gilroy's discussion of this issue in *The Black Atlantic: Modernity and Double Consciousness* (Cambridge, MA: Harvard University Press, 1993), 173–86.

55. Cayton to Wright, April 2, 1945, box 95, folder 1254, Wright Papers.

56. See Cayton, *Long Old Road*, 249; Rowley, *Richard Wright*, 277–78; Fabre, *Unfinished Quest*, 249–52; and Scott, *Contempt and Pity*, 100–102, 231. There is no extant copy of the lecture Wright delivered at the Chicago Institute for Psychoanalysis.

57. Fabre, *Unfinished Quest*, 249.

58. See Ralph Ellison's treatment of this topic in his classic review of *Black Boy* titled "Richard Wright's Blues," in *Shadow and Act* (New York: Quality Paper Back Book Club, 1994), 77–94.

59. Cayton, *Long Old Road*, 260.

60. Horace Cayton, "Frightened Children of Frightened Parents," *Twice a Year* 12–13 (Spring–Summer and Fall–Winter 1945): 262–65.

61. Ibid., 266.

62. Horace Cayton, "A Psychological Approach to Race Relations," *Reed College Bulletin* 25 (November 1946): 8.

63. Ibid., 6.

64. Earlier in the essay, Cayton applied the term "oppression psychosis" to the Negro. He was borrowing the concept from Herbert A. Miller's *Races, Nations and Classes: The Psychology of Domination and Freedom* (Philadelphia: J. B. Lippincott Co., 1924). It is worth noting that Cayton never made reference, in either his letters to Wright or the essays discussed here, to the published research of John Dollard, Hortense Powdermaker, or Allison Davis, each of whom made use of psychoanalysis to explain the psychic dimension of whites' oppression of blacks and its impact on the personalities of both blacks and whites in the Jim Crow South. See Anne C. Rose, "Putting the South on the Psychological Map: The Impact of Region and Race on the Human Sciences during the 1930s," *Journal of Southern History* 71, no. 2 (May 2005): 321–56.

65. Cayton, *Long Old Road*; Cayton to Wright, April 2, 1945, box 95, folder 1254, Wright Papers.

66. On the distinction among sociogeny, ontogeny, and phylogeny to which I refer see Frantz Fanon, *Black Skin, White Masks*, trans. Charles Lam Markmann (1952; New York: Grove Press, 1967). Also see Wertham's unpublished lecture "What Is Social Psychiatry," December 5, 1946, box 186, Fredric Wertham Papers, Manuscript Division, Library of Congress (hereafter cited as Wertham Papers).

67. Richard Wright, "A World View of the American Negro," *Twice a Year* 14–15 (1946–47): 346–47.

68. See Dorothy Norman, *Encounters: A Memoir* (San Diego: Harcourt Brace Jovanovich, 1987), 181–201; Simone de Beauvoir, *America Day by Day*, trans. Carol Cosman (1953; Berkeley: University of California Press, 1999); Fabre, *Unfinished Quest*, 276.

69. See the anthology Bernard Sternsher, ed., *The Negro in Depression and War: Prelude to Revolution, 1930–1945* (Chicago: Quadrangle Books, 1969), esp. "The 'Forgotten Years' of the

Negro Revolution" by Richard M. Dalfiume, 298–316; see also Kenneth B. Clark on "Morale among Negroes," in *Civilian Morale: Second Yearbook of the Society for the Psychological Study of Social Issues*, ed. Goodwin Watson (Boston: Reynal & Hitchcock, Houghton Mifflin Co., 1942).

70. "The Story of the City-Wide Citizens' Committee on Harlem," May 23, 1943, box 338, folder 5, series 14.9, Viola W. Bernard Papers, Columbia University Health Sciences Library Archives and Special Collections, New York. See also Gerald Markowitz and Mark Rosner, *Children, Race, and Power: Kenneth and Mamie Clark's Northside Center* (New York: Routledge, 2000), 6–12.

71. Report of the Exploratory Committee on Negro Welfare, 1939, quoted in Justine Wise Polier, *Everyone's Children, Nobody's Child: A Judge Looks at Underprivileged Children in the United States* (New York: Charles Scribner's Sons, 1941), 241. See also Markowitz and Rosner, *Children, Race, and Power*, 1–17.

72. See Dorothy Norman's *New York Post* column "A World to Live In," June 26, 1944, as well as Markowitz and Rosner, *Children, Race, and Power*, 7–12.

73. Wright Journal, February 6, 1945, box 117, folder 1860, Wright Papers.

74. Ibid.

75. For a critical examination of the role of philanthropy in constituting a regime of racially liberal "official antiracism" that constrained more radical efforts to achieve racial justice in the United States see Jodi Melamed, *Represent and Destroy: Rationalizing Violence in the New Racial Capitalism* (Minneapolis: University of Minnesota Press, 2011). Oddly, Melamed fails to cite vital precursors to her argument on the topic, namely Ralph Ellison, "*An American Dilemma: A Review*" (1944), in *Shadow and Act* (1953; New York: Vintage Books, 1964) and John Stanfield, *Philanthropy and Jim Crow in American Social Science* (Westport, CT: Greenwood Press, 1985).

76. Richard Wright, "The Children of Harlem," 22–23, n.d., box 7, folder 150, Wright Papers.

77. Ibid., 41.

78. Wright Journal, February 12, 1945, box 117, folder 1860, Wright Papers.

2. "Intangible Difficulties"

1. F. I. Wertham Correspondence, series 4000 / folder 9, Adolf Meyer Papers, Alan Mason Chesney Medical Archives, Johns Hopkins University, Baltimore (hereafter cited as Meyer Papers). Wertham changed his name from Friedrich Ignanz Wertheimer to Frederick Wertham in 1928 and later dropped the *k*, then the second *e*, from his first name sometime in the 1930s and the 1940s, respectively.

2. Dr. Adolf Meyer to Dr. H. Gideon Wells, University of Chicago, November 12, 1931, series 4000 / folder 18, Meyer Papers.

3. Adolf Meyer to Dr. F. I. Wertham, January 5, 1931, series 4000 / folder 16, Meyer Papers.

4. See Bart Beaty, *Fredric Wertham and the Critique of Mass Culture* (Oxford: University Press of Mississippi, 2005).

5. Wertham's major book publications include *The Brain as an Organ: Its Postmortem Study and Interpretation*, introduction by Adolf Meyer, MD (New York: Macmillan Co., 1934); *Dark Legend: A Study in Murder* (New York: Duell, Sloan and Pearce, 1941); *The Show of Violence* (Garden City, NY: Doubleday, 1949); *Seduction of the Innocent* (New York: Rinehart & Co., 1954); *The Circle of Guilt* (New York: Rinehart & Co., 1956); *A Sign for Cain: An Exploration of Human Violence* (New York: Macmillan Co., 1966); *The World of Fanzines: A Special Form of Communication* (Carbondale: Southern Illinois University Press, 1973).

6. Medical psychology refers to the study and treatment of mental or psychic functions in relation to medical approaches to health and illness. Medical psychology is to be distinguished from experimental or academic psychology; see Fredric Wertham, "The Social Basis of Psychotherapy," lecture presented at Columbia University, November 13, 1947, 7, box 186, Fredric

Wertham Papers, Manuscript Division, Library of Congress, Washington, DC (hereafter cited as Wertham Papers).

7. Robert Park, "Human Migration and the Marginal Man," *American Journal of Sociology* 33 (1928): 881–93.

8. See Hazel Rowley, *Richard Wright: The Life and Times* (New York: Henry Holt and Co., 2001), 286, 294–95.

9. In 1895 the population of Nuremberg was 142,500, of which 4,737 (3.3 percent) were Jews. Anthony Kauders, *German Politics and the Jews: Dusseldorf and Nuremberg, 1910–1933* (Oxford: Clarendon Press, 1996), 14. Nuremberg would later become known as fertile soil for anti-Jewish sentiments and politics—as the city's name would be attached to the laws stripping Jews of their civil rights. And anyone who has seen Leni Riefenstahl's *Triumph of the Will* must have an image of the Nuremberg rallies for the Nazi Party in the mid-1930s.

10. Ella Winter, *And Not to Yield* (New York: Harcourt, Brace & World, 1963), chap. 1; James E. Reibman, "The Life of Dr. Fredric Wertham," in *The Fredric Wertham Collection: Gift of His Wife Hesketh* (Cambridge, MA: Busch-Reisinger Museum, Harvard University, 1990), 11–13. Wertham's sister Ida Macalpine coauthored several major studies with her son Richard Hunter, including *Three Hundred Years of Psychiatry: 1535–1860* and *George III and the Mad Business*.

11. Ella Winter would later become a prominent Communist activist and writer married first to the famed muckraking journalist Lincoln Steffens and then to screenwriter Donald Ogden Stewart, later a victim of the McCarthyite blacklist. It was she who first introduced Richard Wright and Fredric Wertham in 1941. Winter, *And Not to Yield*, 1963.

12. Paul Cohen-Portheim, *Time Stood Still, 1914–1918* (New York: E. P. Dutton & Co., 1932), 65; see also Panikos Panayi, *The Enemy in Our Midst: Germans in Britain during the First World War* (New York: Berg Publishers, 1991), esp. 99–131.

13. "Medical Career of Mr. Friedel Wertheimer," ca. 1920, series 4000/1, Meyer Papers.

14. See Deborah Cohen, *The War Come Home: Disabled Veterans in Britain and Germany, 1914–1939* (Berkeley: University of California Press, 2001), and Paul F. Lerner, *Hysterical Men: War, Psychiatry, and the Politics of Trauma in Germany, 1890–1930* (Ithaca, NY: Cornell University Press, 2003).

15. There were of course many important workers in medical psychology in European countries other than Germany and Switzerland, as well as in the United States, but my emphasis here is on the institutional and scientific context of Wertham's initial encounters with clinical psychiatry in German-speaking Central Europe. See Eric Engstrom, *Clinical Psychiatry in Imperial Germany: A History of Psychiatric Practice* (Ithaca, NY: Cornell University Press, 2003); for the U.S. context see Nathan G. Hale Jr., *Freud and the Americans: The Beginnings of Psychoanalysis in the United States, 1876–1917* (New York: Oxford University Press, 1971), esp. parts 1 and 2.

16. Engstrom, *Clinical Psychiatry in Imperial Germany*, 4.

17. Fredric Wertham, "Episodes: From the Life of a Psychiatrist," 31, box 108, Wertham Papers (hereafter cited as Wertham, "Episodes").

18. Norman Cameron, "The Functional Psychoses," in *Personality and the Behavior Disorders*, vol. 2, ed. J. McV. Hunt (New York: Ronald Press Co., 1944), 874. Cameron's essay provides an invaluable digest of the state of knowledge on the psychoses during the period under discussion.

19. Engstrom, *Clinical Psychiatry in Imperial Germany*. The eminent historian of the unconscious Henri Ellenberger counters the myth surrounding Kraepelin's work: "Kraepelin has become the whipping boy of many present-day psychiatrists who claim that his only concern for his patients was to place diagnostic labels on them, after which nothing more was done to help them. In fact, however, he took the greatest care that every one of his patients should receive the best treatment available in his time, and he was an extremely human person." See Ellenberger, *The Discovery of the Unconscious: The History and Evolution of Dynamic Psychiatry* (New York: Basic Books, 1970), 285.

20. Wertham, "Episodes," 30.

21. Eugen Kahn, "Emil Kraepelin Memorial Lecture," in *Epidemiology of Mental Disorder*, ed. Benjamin Pasamanick (Washington DC: American Association for the Advancement of Science, Publication No. 60), 24–25; Emil Kraepelin, *Memoirs*, ed. H. Hippius, G. Peters, and D. Ploog, in collaboration with P. Hoff and A. Kreuter, trans. Cheryl Wooding-Deane (Berlin: Springer-Verlag, 1987), 180; see especially Wertham's *Brain as an Organ*. The relationship between neurology and psychiatry during the formative years of modern mental science in the later nineteenth and early twentieth centuries consisted of a complex (international) debate over the scientific understanding of the mind-brain problem in medicine. See Hale, "The Somatic Style," in his *Freud and the Americans*, 47–97; and Engstrom, *Clinical Psychiatry in Imperial Germany*, esp. 98–127.

22. Ian Kershaw, *Hitler: A Biography* (London: Longman Press, 1991), 112.

23. Anthony Nicholls, "Hitler and the Bavarian Background to National Socialism," in *German Democracy and the Triumph of Hitler*, ed. Anthony Nicholls and Erich Matthias (London: George Allen & Unwin, 1971), 109.

24. Hermann Oppenheim, "Seelenstorung und Volksbewegung," *Berliner Tageblatt*, April 16, 1919, 1–2, quoted in Lerner, *Hysterical Men*, 2003, 217

25. Emil Kraepelin, "Psychiatrische Randbemerkungen zur Zeitgeschicte," *Süddeutsche Monatshefte* 16 (1919): 171–83, quoted in Lerner, *Hysterical Men*, 215–16. In an analysis of sixty-six Bavarian revolutionists, one of Kraepelin's underlings, Eugen Kahn, concluded that "scarcely one of the sixty six can in any way be viewed as completely psychically in tact." Kahn, "Psychopathen als revolutionäre Führer," *ZgNP* 52 (1919): 90–106, quoted in Lerner, *Hysterical Men*, 215.

26. See Lerner, *Hysterical Men*, 214–17; Detlev J. K. Peukert, *The Weimar Republic: The Crisis of Classical Modernity*, trans. Richard Deveson (1987; New York: Hill & Wang, 1992), 139. See also Paul Weindling, *Health, Race, and German Politics between National Unification and Nazism, 1870–1945* (New York: Cambridge University Press, 1989).

27. Kraepelin, *Memoirs*, 190.

28. Wertham, *Show of Violence*, 246; Peter Pulzer, *Jews and the German State: The Political History of a Minority, 1848–1933* (Oxford: Blackwell, 1992), 210. For the history of interwar politics in Germany see Ian Kershaw, ed., *Weimar: Why Did German Democracy Fail?* (London: Weidenfeld & Nicolson, 1990); for the relationship between German politics and public health issues, including mental health, see Weindling, *Health, Race, and German Politics*.

29. Dr. Alfred E. Cohn to Dr. Adolf Meyer, December 16, 1920; Dr. Bernard Sachs to Dr. Adolf Meyer, November 28, 1921; Dr. F. I. Wertheimer to Dr. Adolf Meyer, January 15, 1922, series 4000/1, Meyer Papers.

30. Richard Wright, *Black Boy (American Hunger): A Record of Childhood and Youth*, restored text established by the Library of America (New York: Harper Perennial, 1993), 244–57.

31. Gerald Grob, *The Mad among Us: A History of the Care of America's Mentally Ill* (New York: Free Press, 1994), 141–49.

32. Eli Zaretsky, *Secrets of the Soul: A Social and Cultural History of Psychoanalysis* (New York: Alfred A. Knopf, 2004), 79–80.

33. Grob, *Mad among Us*, 129–64; Hale, *Freud and the Americans*, 434–61.

34. See Ruth Leys, "Adolf Meyer: A Biographical Note," in *Defining American Psychology: The Correspondence between Adolf Meyer and Edward Bradford Titchener*, ed. Leys and Rand B. Evans (Baltimore: Johns Hopkins University Press, 1990).

35. Hale, *Freud and the Americans*, 446–47.

36. For an overview of the historiography on Progressivism see Daniel T. Rodgers, "In Search of Progressivism," *Reviews in American History* 10, no. 4 (December 1982): 113–32. On the mental hygiene movement see John Chynoweth Burnham, "Psychiatry, Psychology and the Progressive Movement," *American Quarterly* 12, no. 4 (Winter 1960), 457–65; Theresa R. Richardson,

The Century of the Child: The Mental Hygiene Movement and Social Policy in the United States and Canada (Albany: SUNY Press, 1989), esp. chaps. 7 and 8; Gerald Grob, *Mental Illness and American Society, 1875–1940* (Princeton, NJ: Princeton University Press, 1983), esp. chap. 6. Fred Matthews offers perhaps the most erudite and suggestive assessment of the mental hygiene movement in his essay "In Defense of Common Sense: Mental Hygiene as Ideology and Mentality in Twentieth-Century America," *Prospects: An Annual of American Cultural Studies* 4 (1979): 459–516.

37. Sol Cohen, "The Mental Hygiene Movement, the Development of Personality and the School: The Medicalization of American Education," *History of Education Quarterly* 23, no. 2 (Summer 1983): 140.

38. For a discussion of psychophysical parallelism see P. Hoff, "Kraepelin," in *A History of Clinical Psychiatry: The Origins and History of Psychiatric Disorders*, ed. German E. Berrios and Roy Porter (New York: NYU Press, 1995), 261–79.

39. Adolf Meyer, "Psychobiological Point of View," in *The Problem of Mental Disorder*, ed. Madison Bentley and E. V. Cowdry (New York: McGraw-Hill, 1934), 70.

40. See the glossary of Meyerian psychobiology in Alfred Lief, ed., *The Commonsense Psychiatry of Dr. Adolf Meyer* (New York: McGraw-Hill, 1948), 641–52.

41. Adolf Meyer, "Substitutive Activity and Reaction-Types," in Lief, *Commonsense Psychiatry of Dr. Adolf Meyer*, 203. For more on Meyer's views of Kraepelinian, or German, nosology, as he referred to it during World War I, see his "The Aims and Meaning of Psychiatric Diagnosis," *American Journal of Insanity* 74 (1917): 163–67.

42. Leys, "Adolf Meyer: A Biographical Note," 46.

43. Morton White, *Social Thought in America: The Revolt against Formalism* (1949; Boston: Beacon Press, 1957); see also Cornel West, *The American Evasion of Philosophy: A Genealogy of Pragmatism* (Madison: University of Wisconsin Press, 1989).

44. Leys, "Adolf Meyer: A Biographical Note," 44–45.

45. See Paul R. McHugh, "Commentary on 'Inpatient Diagnoses' during Adolf Meyer's Tenure as Director of the Henry Phipps Psychiatric Clinic, 1913–1940,'" *Journal of Nervous and Mental Disease* 174, no. 12 (1986): 752–53.

46. F. I. Wertheimer, "A Brief Survey of American Psychiatry, 1914–1924," *State Hospital Quarterly* 11, no. 2 (February 1926): 167–80, trans. reprint from *Allgemeine Zeitschrift für Psychiatrie* 81 (1925): 442–55. For general histories of American psychiatry during this period see Grob, *Mental Illness and American Society*, and Nathan G. Hale Jr., *The Rise and Crisis of Psychoanalysis in the United States: Freud and the Americans, 1917–1985* (Oxford: Oxford University Press, 1995).

47. F. I. Wertheimer and Florence E. Hesketh, *The Significance of the Physical Constitution in Mental Disease* (Baltimore: Williams & Wilkins Co., 1926), 69. Florence Hesketh, who would soon marry Wertham, was a young woman visiting Johns Hopkins as a Charlton Fellow in Medicine. She illustrated all the images of subjects of the study.

48. Ibid., 8–9.

49. Wertham was referring to the work of Ales Hrdlicka; see Hrdlicka's *Anthropometry* (Philadelphia: Wistar Institute of Anatomy and Biology, 1925).

50. Wertham and Hesketh, *Significance of the Physical Constitution*, 5–7.

51. Ibid., 17.

52. See C. Macfie Campbell, "The Mental Health of the Community and the Work of the Psychiatric Dispensary," *Mental Hygiene* 1, no. 4 (October 1917): 1–13.

53. Wertheimer to Dr. Richards, December 22, 1927, and January 4, 1928, series 4000/8, Meyer Papers.

54. Untitled and undated four-page report in series 4000/9, Meyer Papers.

55. Dr. Franklin C. McLean to Dr. Adolf Meyer, April 4, 1929, series 4000/10, Meyer Papers.

56. Dr. Adolf Meyer to Dr. Franklin C. McLean, April 11, 1929, series 4000/10, Meyer Papers.

57. Untitled and undated memorandum (ca. April 1929), series 4000/10, Meyer Papers.

58. Wertham to Adolf Meyer, August 28, 1929, series 4000/11, Meyer Papers; Adolf Meyer to Dr. G. C. Huber, September 25, 1929, series 4000/12, Meyer Papers; G. Carl Huber to Adolf Meyer, November 2, 1929, series 4000/13, Meyer Papers. Wertham published the results of his studies in Munich as *The Brain as an Organ: Its Postmortem Study and Interpretation* (1934).

59. Hans Jakob Ritter and Volker Roelcke, "Psychiatric Genetics in Munich and Basel between 1925 and 1945," *Osiris* 20 (2005): 267.

60. See Paul Weindling's excellent history of the science and politics of German racial hygiene during this era, *Health, Race, and German Politics between National Unification and Nazism, 1870–1945*, 1989. For mention of the role of eugenics in American psychiatry in the first decades of the twentieth century see Grob, *Mental Illness and American Society*, 167–78.

61. Dr. Walther Spielmeyer to Adolf Meyer, February 21, 1930, and December 13, 1930, series 4000/15, Meyer Papers. For biographical information on Spielmeyer see Webb Haymaker and Francis Schiller, eds., *The Founders of Neurology: One Hundred and Forty-Six Biographical Sketches by Eighty-Eight Authors*, 2nd ed. (Springfield, IL: Thomas Publishers, 1970), 377.

62. F. I. Wertham to Adolf Meyer, December 6, 1930, series 4000/15, Meyer Papers; Adolf Meyer to F. I. Wertham, January 5, 1931, series 4000/16, Meyer Papers.

63. F. I. Wertham to Adolf Meyer, December 6, 1930, series 4000/15, Meyer Papers; Adolf Meyer to F. I. Wertham, January 5, 1931, series 4000/16, Meyer Papers. See John Higham's classic study, *Strangers in the Land: Patterns of American Nativism, 1860–1925* (New Brunswick, NJ: Rutgers University Press, 1955); see also Frederick Lewis Allen, *Only Yesterday: An Informal History of the Nineteen-Twenties* (New York: Harper & Bros., 1931), esp. 58–69. In the early 1920s, wrote Allen, "intolerance became an American virtue." For a later period see Laura Fermi, *Illustrious Immigrants: The Intellectual Migration from Europe, 1930–1941*, 2nd ed. (Chicago: University of Chicago Press, 1971).

64. Writing in 1943, Wertham claimed that he had had an "analytic inspection" from "the man whom Freud called the best American psychoanalyst": Wertham, "While Rome Burns: Review of Gregory Zilboorg's *Mind, Medicine and Man* (1943)," *New Republic*, May 24, 1943, 707; Wertham, "A Thwarted Interview," in "Episodes," 44–47. Apart from these brief allusions to Frink, Wertham never offered an account of the process by which he became a psychoanalyst. It isn't clear whether "analytic inspection" meant that he underwent the "training analysis," which by the 1920s came to be a requirement among psychoanalytic societies in the United States. See Hale, *Freud and the Americans*, 323.

65. See Freud-Frink file, boxes 1 and 2, Wertham Papers. For the troubling history of Freud's psychoanalysis of Frink see Peter Gay, *Freud: A Life for Our Time* (New York: W. W. Norton & Co., 1988), 565–66, and Silas L. Warner, "Freud's Analysis of Horace Frink, MD: A Previously Unexplained Therapeutic Disaster," *Journal of the American Academy of Psychoanalysis* 22, no. 1 (1994): 137–52.

66. Department of Hospitals, Psychiatric Division of the Court of General Sessions, *Report for the Year 1935*, New York Public Library; Walter Bromberg, *Psychiatry between the Wars, 1918–1945: A Recollection* (Westport, CT: Greenwood Press, 1982), 110, 104; Wickersham Commission Report, quoted in Bromberg, *Psychiatry between the Wars*, 104.

67. Wertham to Adolf Meyer, January 1, 1932, series 4000/18, Meyer Papers.

68. Bromberg, *Psychiatry between the Wars*.

69. Sheldon and Eleanor Glueck, *One Thousand Juvenile Delinquents: Their Treatment by Court and Clinic*, introduction by Felix Frankfurter (Cambridge, MA: Harvard University Press, 1939); Clifford Shaw, *The Natural History of a Delinquent Career* (Chicago: University of Chicago Press, 1931).

70. Wertham, *Show of Violence*, 24–25.

71. Wertham to Adolf Meyer, May 3, 1937, series /4000/22, Meyer Papers.

72. Gerald Grob, *Mental Illness and American Society*, 224–27.

73. Wertham, *Show of Violence*, 124.

74. Differential diagnosis is the clinical process of eliminating other possible disorders to arrive at the correct diagnosis of a patient.

75. Frederic Wertham, "The Catathymic Crisis: A Clinical Entity," *Archives of Neurology and Psychiatry* 37 (1937): 974–77; Wertham, *Show of Violence*, 179.

76. Richard Wright, *Native Son*, restored ed. by Library of America (New York: Harper Collins, 1998), 85, 91; 425–30.

77. Ibid., 105, 429.

78. Wertham, *Dark Legend*, 19–20.

79. Ibid., 230.

80. See Wertham's extended discussion of the social roots of violence in *The Show of Violence* (1949) and *A Sign for Cain* (1966).

81. Wertham, "Episodes," 128–31.

82. Wertham to Adolf Meyer, September 16, 1942, series 4000/26, Meyer Papers.

3. "Between the Sewer and the Church"

The title of this chapter is drawn from Ralph Ellison's handwritten notes in preparation for writing "Harlem Is Nowhere," his 1948 essay on the Lafargue Clinic's significance to Harlem and to American democracy more broadly. "Harlem Is Nowhere," box 1:100, Ralph Ellison Papers, Manuscript Division, Library of Congress, Washington, DC.

1. Dr. Elizabeth Bishop Davis Trussell, interview by author, tape recording, New York, January 6, 2006. Shelton Hale Bishop may have been particularly attuned to the needs of those suffering from mental illness, as one of his sisters was reputedly in an insane asylum in the early 1940s. See George Hutchinson, *In Search of Nella Larsen: A Biography of the Color Line* (Cambridge, MA: Belknap Press of Harvard University Press, 2006), 457.

2. Shelton H. Bishop, "A History of St. Philip's Church New York City," *Historical Magazine of the Protestant Episcopal Church* 15 (1946): 298–317.

3. One fellow minister noted how radical the aim of bringing the church and psychiatry together was at the time; see James H. Robinson, *Road without Turning: The Story of Rev. James H. Robinson* (Farrar, Straus and Co., 1950), 253; Dr. Elizabeth Bishop Davis Trussell interview.

4. Ralph G. Martin, "Doctor's Dream in Harlem," *New Republic*, June 3, 1946, 799; Hilde L. Mosse, "Child Psychiatry and Social Action: An Integral Part of the History of American Child Psychiatry," n.d., 7, box 3, Lafargue Clinic Records, Schomburg Center for Research in Black Culture, New York Public Library (hereafter cited as Lafargue Clinic Records).

5. Oliver Cromwell Cox, *Caste, Class, and Race: A Study in Social Dynamics* (New York: Monthly Review Press, 1948); Cedric Robinson, *Black Marxism: The Making of the Black Radical Tradition* (1983; Chapel Hill: University of North Carolina Press, 2000).

6. E. Franklin Frazier, *The Negro in the United States*, rev. ed. (New York: Macmillan Co., 1957), 264.

7. David Levering Lewis, *When Harlem Was in Vogue* (New York: Alfred A. Knopf, 1981).

8. See Cheryl Greenberg, *"Or Does It Explode?": Black Harlem in the Great Depression* (New York: Oxford University Press, 1991).

9. Alain Locke, "Harlem: Dark Weather-Vane," *Survey Graphic* 25, no. 8 (August 1936): 457.

10. Historian Dominic Capeci notes that many residents of Harlem moved in for a brief time and left for opportunities elsewhere, only to be replaced by new migrants to the city; see Capeci, *The Harlem Riot of 1943* (Philadelphia: Temple University Press, 1977), 58–59.

11. Martin, "Doctor's Dream in Harlem," 799; Robert Bendiner, "Psychiatry for the Needy," *Tomorrow*, May 1946, 22.

12. Claude Brown, *Manchild in the Promised Land* (New York: Signet Books, 1965), vii.

13. See "Editorial Comment," *Negro Quarterly* 1, no. 4 (Winter–Spring 1943): 295–302, which most scholars believe to have been penned by Ralph Ellison while he served as managing editor of this short-lived journal; Nikhil Pal Singh's incisive, provocative *Black Is a Country* (Cambridge, MA: Harvard University Press, 2004) explores how, alongside such activists as A. Philip Randolph and his March on Washington movement, a small coterie of black male radical political intellectuals who had coalesced around Ellison, Wright, and Trinidadian-born C. L. R. James militantly challenged the United States' exceptionalist self-image as they reckoned with the problem of national and racial allegiance and belonging for black Americans during World War II and its immediate aftermath; see also Richard M. Dalfiume, "The 'Forgotten Years' of the Negro Revolution," in *The Negro in Depression and War: Prelude to Revolution, 1930–1945*, ed. Bernard Sternsher (Chicago: Quadrangle Books, 1969), 298–316; and Adam Clayton Powell Jr., *Marching Blacks: An Interpretive History of the Rise of the Black Common Man* (New York: Dial Press, 1945).

14. Howard Odum, *Race and Rumors of Race* (Chapel Hill: University of North Carolina Press, 1943).

15. James Baldwin, *Notes of a Native Son* (New York: Bantam Books, 1964), 82.

16. "The Story of the City-Wide Citizens' Committee on Harlem," May 23, 1943, box 338, folder 5, series 14.9, Viola W. Bernard Papers, Columbia University Health Sciences Library Archives and Special Collections, New York (hereafter cited as Bernard Papers).

17. See Dominic J. Capeci, *The Harlem Riot of 1943* (Philadelphia: Temple University Press, 1977). Also see Eduardo Obregón Pagán, *Murder at the Sleepy Lagoon: Zoot Suits, Race, and Riot in Wartime L.A.* (Chapel Hill: University of North Carolina Press, 2003), and Luis Alvarez, *The Power of the Zoot: Youth Culture and Resistance during World War II* (Berkeley: University of California Press, 2008).

18. Capeci, *Harlem Riot of 1943*, 119; Mark Schubart, "Richard Wright Feels Grip of Harlem Tension," *PM Daily*, August 3, 1943, 8, reprinted in Kenneth Kinnamon and Michel Fabre, eds., *Conversations with Richard Wright* (Jackson: University Press of Mississippi, 1993), 49–50.

19. S. I. Hayakawa, "Second Thoughts," *Chicago Defender*, January 11, 1947, reprint in box 3, folder 1, Lafargue Clinic Records.

20. "Psychiatrist Out to Prove Himself Wrong," *Chicago Defender*, November 16, 1946, 13.

21. See Fiorello H. La Guardia, "Displaced Persons," in *The Struggle for Justice as a World Force: Report of the New York Herald Tribune Annual Forum* (New York: Herald Tribune, 1946), 92–97.

22. Ralph Ellison, "Harlem Is Nowhere" (1948), in *Shadow and Act* (New York: Quality Paper Back Book Club, 1994).

23. Benjamin Malzberg, "Migration and Mental Disease among Negroes in New York State," *American Journal of Physical Anthropology* 21, no. 1 (January–March 1936): 107, 109.

24. Ellison, "Harlem Is Nowhere," 299–300.

25. Richard Wright Journal, March 26, 1945, box 117, folder 1860, Richard Wright Papers.

26. Frazier, *Negro in the United States*, 266.

27. *Population and Housing Statistics for Health Areas, New York City* (Washington, DC: Government Printing Office, 1942), 1. Central Harlem comprised Health Areas 9 through 12.

28. "Report by Sub-Committee on Psychiatry as Related to Negro Children," City-Wide Citizens' Committee on Harlem, February 15, 1942, box 338, folder 2, Bernard Papers.

29. These nonmunicipal agencies included those associated with various Protestant, Catholic, and Jewish charities. See Gerald Markowitz and David Rosner, "The Abandonment of Harlem's Children," in *Children, Race, and Power: Kenneth and Mamie Clark's Northside Center* (New York: Routledge, 2000), 1–17.

30. Constance Curtis, "Mental Hygiene Clinic Planned in Harlem Area," *New York Amsterdam News*, May 18, 1946.

31. "Story of the City-Wide Citizens' Committee on Harlem," box 338, folder 5, Bernard Papers.

32. Lorraine Maynard (in collaboration with Laurence Miscall), *Bellevue* (New York: Julian Messner Inc., 1940), 61, 139–40; for an examination of racism in New York City hospitals at this time see also Cheryl Lynn Greenberg's discussion of attempts to get black nurses on the staff of Bellevue Hospital in the mid-1930s, *"Or Does It Explode?*," 86–91. See also Dennis Doyle, "'Racial Differences Have to Be Considered': Lauretta Bender, Bellevue Hospital, and the African American Psyche, 1936–52," *History of Psychiatry* 21, no. 2: 206–23.

33. Richard Wright Journal, January 12, 1945, box 117, folder 1860, Wright Papers.

34. Wertham, "Episodes," 51–53; Richard Wright Journal, February 24, 1945, box 117, folder 1860, Wright Papers.

35. Wertham, "Episodes," 51–53. For critical examinations of race and philanthropy see John Stanfield, *Philanthropy and Jim Crow in American Social Science* (Westport, CT: Greenwood Press, 1985) and the first chapter of Jodi Melamed's *Represent and Destroy: Rationalizing Violence in the New Racial Capitalism* (Minneapolis: University of Minnesota Press, 2011).

36. Wertham to Wright, August 1, 1945, box 108, folder 1677, Wright Papers.

37. "The Committee for Mental Hygiene for Negroes," January 10, 1943, box 338, folder 2, Bernard Papers.

38. "Report of the Third Annual Meeting for the Committee for Mental Hygiene for Negroes," February 17, 1943, box 338, folder 2, Bernard Papers.

39. Markowitz and Rosner, *Children, Race, and Power*, 43–89.

40. "Group Psychotherapy and the Treatment of Minority Problems," Ninth Annual Conference, American Society of Group Psychotherapy and Psychodrama, Commodore Hotel, February 17, 1951, p. 3, notes taken by Dr. Hilde L. Mosse, box 86, folder 17, Wertham Papers.

41. Meyer to Wertham, August 1, 1946, and Wertham to Meyer, series 4000/26, Adolf Meyer Papers, Alan Mason Chesney Medical Archives, Johns Hopkins University, Baltimore (hereafter cited as Meyer Papers), Adolf Meyer Collection.

42. "The Lafargue Clinic: A Mental Hygiene Clinic in and for the Community," box 2, folder 1, Lafargue Clinic Papers.

43. See James Jones, *Bad Blood: The Tuskegee Syphilis Experiment—a Tragedy of Race and Medicine* (New York: Free Press, 1981); Harriet A. Washington, *Medical Apartheid: The Dark History of Medical Experimentation on Black Americans from Colonial Times to the Present* (New York: Doubleday, 2006). For more information on the significance of Bishop's and St. Philip's embrace of Wertham's brand of social psychiatry as practiced at Lafargue see Dennis Doyle, "'A Fine New Child': The Lafargue Mental Hygiene Clinic and Harlem's African American Communities, 1946–1958," *Journal of the History of Medicine and Allied Sciences* 64, no. 2 (April 2009): 173–212.

44. St. Philip's Church, *Newsletter* 11, no. 7 (March 15, 1946): 2–3, box 3, folder 1, Lafargue Clinic Records. There were of course other institutions and agencies providing mental hygiene services throughout Manhattan. Many of them were restrictive or prohibitive in some way for the majority of black New Yorkers. In June 1945, Wertham compiled a list of twenty hospitals, child guidance clinics, and miscellaneous under the title "Mental Hygiene Resources in or adjacent to Harlem Territory," box 52, folder 10, Wertham Papers. From June 1947 to June 1952 the Veterans Administration maintained a contract with the Lafargue Clinic to provide treatment to veterans in New York: box 1, folder 1, Lafargue Clinic Records. There is some evidence to suggest the VA suspended the contract as a result of Wertham's treating convicted spy Ethel Rosenberg while she was imprisoned awaiting execution. In a letter to Richard Wright dated May 12, 1953, Wertham noted that "the Veterans Bureau, which told me they liked our work exceptionally, cancelled its contract with the Harlem Clinic—you guess why": box 108, folder 1677, Wright Papers. For the broader context of the psychiatric treatment of African American soldiers and veterans at this

time see Ellen Dwyer, "Psychiatry and Race during World War II," *Journal of the History of Medicine and Allied Sciences* 61, no. 2 (April 2006): 117–43.

45. Sidney M. Katz, "Jim Crow Is Barred from Wertham's Clinic," *Magazine Digest*, September 1946, box 3, folder 1, Lafargue Clinic Records.

46. "Objectives of Lafargue Clinic," notes taken by Constance Karros at clinic conference January 29, 1952, box 51, folder 11, Wertham Papers.

47. "Lafargue Clinic Organization," box 1, folder 1, Lafargue Clinic Records.

48. "Lafargue Clinic Organization," September 1, 1952, box 1, folder 1, Lafargue Clinic Records; "Mrs. Zucker's suggestion for first examination," n.d., box 1, folder 1, Lafargue Clinic Records; James L. Tuck, "Here's Hope for Harlem," *This Week Magazine, New York Herald Tribune*, January 26, 1947, box 3, folder 1, Lafargue Clinic Records; Hilde L. Mosse, "Psychotherapy at the Clinic," unpublished paper presented at the Joint Committee for Mental Hygiene Services meeting, May 6, 1947, box 51, folder 11, Wertham Papers.

49. In fusing psychoanalysis with other therapeutic methods, Wertham and his colleagues were putting into practice a suggestion made by Freud himself during the later years of World War I. In his address to the Fifth International Psycho-Analytical Congress held in Budapest in September 1918, Freud urged his fellow analysts to democratize and possibly hybridize their therapy when needed: "It is very probable too that the large-scale application of our therapy will compel us to alloy the pure gold of analysis freely with the copper of direct suggestion; and hypnotic influence, too, might find a place in it again, as it has in the treatment of the war neuroses. But, whatever form this psychotherapy for the people may take, whatever the elements out of which it is compounded, its most effective and most important ingredients will assuredly remain those borrowed from strict and untendentious psycho-analysis." Lafargue physician-in-charge Mosse even quoted from this speech in her memorandum, "Psychotherapy at the Clinic," box 51, folder 11, Wertham Papers.

50. Mosse, ""Psychotherapy at the Clinic," box 51, folder 11, Wertham Papers. See also the interview with Wertham in *Contemporary Psychotherapists Examine Themselves*, ed. Werner Wolff (Springfield, IL: Thomas Publishers, 1956), 33–40.

51. Mosse, "Psychotherapy at the Clinic," box 51, folder 11, Wertham Papers. For a detailed exposition of Mosse's view of psychoanalytic principles see "Aggression and Violence in Fantasy and Fact," *American Journal of Psychotherapy* 2 (1948): 477–83.

52. Mosse, "Psychotherapy at the Clinic," box 51, folder 11, Wertham Papers.

53. Patient file 3–4–47, box 3, Lafargue Clinic Records.

54. See Helen Swick Perry's introduction to Harry Stack Sullivan's *The Fusion of Psychiatry and Social Science* (New York: W. W. Norton & Co., 1964); and Nathan G. Hale Jr., *The Rise and Crisis of Psychoanalysis: Freud and the Americans, 1917–1985* (Oxford: Oxford University Press, 1995), chap. 10.

55. See Mari Jo Buhle, *Feminism and Its Discontents: A Century of Struggle with Psychoanalysis* (Cambridge, MA: Harvard University Press, 1998), chap. 3, esp. 111–24; Hale, *Rise and Crisis of Psychoanalysis*, chap. 8.

56. Norman V. Bell and John P. Siegel, "Social Psychiatry: Vagaries of a Term," *Archives of General Psychiatry* 14 (April 1966): 345; Gerald Grob, *From Asylum to Community: Mental Health Policy in Modern America* (Princeton, NJ: Princeton University Press, 1991), 102.

57. See Grob, *From Asylum to Community*, chapters 1, 2, and 5, for a discussion of the work of psychodynamic psychiatrists such as the Menninger brothers Karl and William.

58. Grob, *From Asylum to Community*, 7; Thomas A.C. Rennie, "Social Psychiatry—A Definition," *International Journal of Social Psychiatry* 1, no. 1 (Summer 1955): 10.

59. See Michael Staub, *Madness Is Civilization: When the Diagnosis Was Social, 1948–1980* (Chicago: University of Chicago Press, 2011).

60. Dr. Joshua Bierer, "Editorial," *International Journal of Social Psychiatry* 1, no. 1 (Summer 1955): 4, emphasis added.

61. Norman V. Bell, Ph.D and John P. Siegel, M.D., "Social Psychiatry: Vagaries of a Term," *Archives of General Psychiatry* 14 (April 1966): 345; Grob, *From Asylum to Community*, 102.

62. See the anthology edited by Arnold M. Rose, *Mental Health and Mental Disorder: a Sociological Approach. Prepared for the Committee of the Society for the Study of Social Problems* (New York: W.W. Norton, 1955); and see *Interrelations Between The Social Environment and Psychiatric Disorders* (New York: Milbank Memorial Fund, 1953).

63. Wertham was, though, a member of the American Psychiatric Association; see "Fredric Wertham," *Current Biography* (1949): 635.

64. The *American Journal of Psychiatry* did, however, publish Wertham's 1962 article "The Scientific Study of Mass Media Effects," *American Journal of Psychiatry* 11 (1962): 306–11.

65. For more on the Group for the Advancement of Psychiatry and efforts to shift psychiatry toward a focus on socioenvironmental factors in the study and treatment of mental disorders see Grob, *From Asylum to Community*, esp. 24–43.

66. Jonathan M. Metzl, *The Protest Psychosis: How Schizophrenia Became a Black Disease* (Boston: Beacon Press, 2011), 81–82.

67. Wertham, "What Is Social Psychiatry?," lecture read at the Brooklyn State Hospital Psychiatric forum on December 5, 1946, box 85, folder 8, Wertham Papers.

68. "The Head Fixers," *Monthly Review*, November 1958, 282.

69. Wertham, "Analytic Psychotherapy," in Wolff, *Contemporary Psychotherapists Examine Themselves*, 36.

70. "Lafargue Clinic Statistics," box 1, folder 9, Lafargue Clinic Records.

71. Ibid. Jonathan Metzl convincingly argues that race and other primary categories of social identity are always already inscribed in the diagnostic criteria for mental disorders, but most especially in the major psychoses, namely schizophrenia and depression, where African Americans in particular are overdiagnosed in the former and underdiagnosed in the latter. See Metzl, *Protest Psychosis*.

72. Patient file 2–20–48, box 3, Lafargue Clinic Records.

73. Patient file 5–3–53, box 3, Lafargue Clinic Records.

74. Patient file 11–7–50, box 3, Lafargue Clinic Records.

75. Norman M. Lobsenz, "Human Salvage in Harlem," *Coronet*, March 1948, 135–36, reprint, box 3, folder 1, Lafarge Clinic Records.

76. One exception to this is Bendiner, "Psychiatry for the Needy," 22.

77. See Jay Garcia's superb exploration of this topic, *Psychology Comes to Harlem: Rethinking the Race Question in Twentieth-Century America* (Baltimore: Johns Hopkins University Press, 2012).

78. Ellison, "Harlem Is Nowhere," 300, 299, emphasis added. Ellison wrote the essay for *Magazine of the Year: '48*, but it wasn't published until 1964, when it was included in his collection of essays, *Shadow and Act*. *Magazine of the Year* had folded, and Ellison had to sue in order gain the rights to publish the piece. See Lawrence Jackson, *Ralph Ellison: Emergence of Genius* (New York: John Wiley & Sons, 2002), 335–36. See also Sharifa Rhodes-Pitts, *Harlem Is Nowhere: A Journey to the Mecca of Black America* (New York: Little, Brown, 2011) and Shelly Eversley, "The Lunatic's Fancy and the Work of Art," *American Literary History* 13, no. 3 (Fall 2001): 445–68

79. See Greenberg, "*Or Does It Explode?*," and Jeanne Theoharis and Komozi Woodard, eds., *Freedom North: Black Freedom Struggles outside the South, 1940–1980* (New York: Palgrave Macmillan, 2003).

80. Hazel Rowley, *Richard Wright: The Life and Times* (New York: Henry Holt and Co., 2001), 348; Constance Webb, *Richard Wright: A Biography* (New York; G. P. Putnam's Sons, 1968),

chap. 20; Florence Hesketh Wertham to Richard Wright, July 30, 1947; Via Radio France Telegram, August 7, 1947, box 108, folder 1677, Wright Papers.

4. Children and the Violence of Racism

1. Constance Curtis, "Mental Hospitals Bar Negroes," April 27, 1946; "Charge 'Favoritism' at Bellevue," May 4, 1946; "Psycho Race Bias Tough," May 11, 1946; "Cure for Alcoholics of Negroes in N.Y. About Non-Existent," May 18, 1946; "Jim Crow School Kids as Mentally Unfit," May 25, 1946; "School Reshapes Courses for Retarded Kids," June 1, 1946; " 'Retarded Kids' Classes Changed following Blast," July 13, 1946: all in *New York Amsterdam News*.

2. "Lost Children," editorial, *New York Amsterdam News*, April 27, 1946.

3. Constance Curtis, "Mental Hygiene Clinic Planned in Harlem Area," *New York Amsterdam News*, May 18, 1946.

4. See Ben Keppel, *The Work of Democracy: Ralph Bunche, Kenneth B. Clark, Lorraine Hansberry, and the Cultural Politics of Race* (Cambridge, MA: Harvard University Press), 1995.

5. "Lafargue Clinic Statistics," March 6, 1956, box 1, folder 9, Lafargue Clinic Records.

6. Bart Beaty, *Fredric Wertham and the Critique of Mass Culture* (Jackson: University Press of Mississippi, 2005), 135–36.

7. Fredric Wertham, "The Comics . . . Very Funny!," *Saturday Review of Literature*, May 29, 1948, 6–7, 27–29.

8. See James Gilbert, *A Cycle of Outrage: America's Reaction to the Juvenile Delinquent in the 1950s* (New York: Oxford University Press, 1986).

9. Wertham, "Comics . . . Very Funny!," 6–7, 27–29. Wertham, "Episodes," Wertham Papers. See also Beaty, *Fredric Wertham*, 118–19; Gilbert, *Cycle of Outrage*, 98–99.

10. The historical literature on Wertham and *Seduction of the Innocent* is vast and growing, as is the critical discussion of his views (notably taking place on the Internet). See Gilbert, *Cycle of Outrage*; Amy Kiste Nyberg, *Seal of Approval: The History of the Comics Code* (Jackson: University Press of Mississippi, 1998); John A. Lent, ed., *Pulp Demons: International Dimensions of the Postwar Anti-Comics Campaign* (Teaneck, NJ: Fairleigh Dickinson University Press, 1999); Bradford W. Wright, *Comic Book Nation: The Transformation of Youth Culture in America* (Baltimore: Johns Hopkins University Press, 2001). Bart Beaty's *Fredric Wertham and the Critique of Mass Culture*, a sympathetic look at Wertham and the context of his arguments about the effects of comic books on children, is a valuable correction to much of the extant anti-Wertham literature, as is Andrea Friedman's *Citizenship in Cold War America: The National Security State and the Possibilities of Dissent* (Amherst: University of Massachusetts Press, 2014). David Hajdu, on the other hand, presents a flagrant caricature of Wertham in his popular history of the midcentury anti–comic book movement *The Ten-Cent Plague: The Great Comic-Book Scare and How It Changed America* (New York: Farrar, Straus and Giroux, 2008).

11. Fredric Wertham, *Seduction of the Innocent* (New York: Rinehart & Co., 1954), 100–105.

12. Ibid.

13. The clinical orientation and evidence used in *Seduction of the Innocent* remain a source of historical debate and analysis. Carol Tilley, "Seducing the Innocent: Fredric Wertham and the Falsifications That Helped Condemn Comics," *Information & Culture* 47, no. 4 (2012): 383–413.

14. Wertham, *Seduction of the Innocent*, 166.

15. Ibid., 157.

16. Invoking his favorite comparison, Wertham argued that "the problem of the effect of crime comic books is like a combined clinical and laboratory problem in infectious diseases. You not only have to study the possibly affected individuals; you have to investigate the potentially injurious agents themselves, their varieties, their lives, their habitat. There is a considerable distance from the pure culture of the bacillus to the clinical case": *Seduction of the Innocent*, 30.

17. Gilbert, *Cycle of Outrage*, 107–8; Fredric Wertham, *A Sign for Cain: An Exploration of Human Violence* (New York: Macmillan Co., 1966), 197.

18. Richard Kluger, *Simple Justice: The History of Brown v. Board of Education and Black America's Struggle for Equality* (New York: Alfred A. Knopf, 1976).

19. See Kluger, *Simple Justice*, 305–14; David Southern, *Gunnar Myrdal and Black White Relations: The Use and Abuse of An American Dilemma, 1944–1969* (Baton Rouge: Louisiana State University Press, 1987); and especially Walter Jackson's exhaustive, exceptional study, *Gunnar Myrdal and America's Conscience: Social Engineering and Racial Liberalism, 1938–1987* (Chapel Hill: University of North Carolina Press, 1990).

20. See Ellen Herman, *The Romance of American Psychology: Political Culture in the Age of Experts* (Berkeley: University of California Press, 1995); Daryl Michael Scott, *Contempt and Pity: Social Policy and the Image of the Damaged Black Psyche, 1880–1996* (Chapel Hill: University of North Carolina Press, 1997); Ruth Feldstein, *Motherhood in Black and White: Race and Sex in American Liberalism, 1930–1965* (Ithaca, NY: Cornell University Press, 2000).

21. See Gerald Markowitz and David Rosner, *Children, Race, and Power: Kenneth and Mamie Clark's Northside Center* (New York: Routledge, 2000); John P. Jackson Jr., *Social Scientists for Social Justice: Making the Case against Segregation* (New York: NYU Press, 2001); Keppel, *Work of Democracy*.

22. Kenneth B. Clark and Mamie P. Clark, "Emotional Factors in Racial Identification and Preference in Negro Children," *Journal of Negro Education* 19 (1950): 341–50, quoted in Herman, *Romance of American Psychology*, 194.

23. Jackson, *Social Scientists for Social Justice*, 82–91.

24. Herbert Hill and Jack Greenberg, *Citizen's Guide to Desegregation: A Study in Social and Legal Change in American Life* (Boston: Beacon Press, 1955), 92.

25. For a comprehensive, critical discussion of this argument see Scott, *Contempt and Pity*.

26. See Hill and Greenberg, *Citizen's Guide to Desegregation*.

27. Kluger, *Simple Justice*, 316; Otto Klineberg quoted in Kenneth B. Clark, *Prejudice and Your Child*, 2nd ed., enlarged (1963; Middletown, CT: Wesleyan University Press, 1988), xviii–xx. For more on Klineberg see Gardner Lindzey, ed., *A History of Psychology in Autobiography*, vol. 6 (New York:Appleton-Century-Crofts, 1976).

28. Clark's report appears in Helen Leland Witmer and Ruth Kotinsky, eds., *Personality in the Making: The Fact-Finding Report of the Midcentury White House Conference on Children and Youth* (New York: Harper & Bros., 1952), 145.

29. Kluger, *Simple Justice*, 320–21; Clark, *Prejudice and Your Child*, xx–xxi; Herman, *Romance of American Psychology*, 195–99; Keppel, *Work of Democracy*, 98–99; Jackson, *Social Scientists for Social Justice*, 110–13.

30. Jackson, *Gunnar Myrdal and America's Conscience*, 279–90. See also Leah Gordon, "The Question of Prejudice: Social Science, Education, and the Struggle to Define the 'Race Problem' in Postwar America, 1940–70" (PhD diss., University of Pennsylvania, 2008).

31. Jackson, *Social Scientists for Social Justice*, 114–24; Clark, *Prejudice and Your Child*, xxi.

32. See John Greenwood, *The Disappearance of the Social in American Social Psychology* (Cambridge: Cambridge University Press, 2004), esp. chap. 8.

33. Brett Gadsden, "'He Said He Wouldn't Help Me Get a Jim Crow Bus': The Shifting Terms of the Challenge to Segregated Public Education, 1950–1954," *Journal of African American History* 90, nos. 1–2 (Winter–Spring 2005): 9–28. And further, Gadsden's *Between North and South: Delaware, Desegregation, and the Myth of American Sectionalism* (Philadelphia: University of Pennsylvania Press, 2012).

34. Peter Irons, *Jim Crow's Children: The Broken Promise of the Brown Decision* (New York: Penguin Press, 2004), 106–7; Jack Greenberg, *Crusaders in the Courts: How a Dedicated Band of Lawyers Fought for the Civil Rights Revolution* (New York: Basic Books, 1994), 143–44; Kluger,

Simple Justice, 425–50; Daniel M. Berman, *It Is So Ordered: The Supreme Court Rules on School Segregation* (New York: W. W. Norton & Co., 1966), 20–22.

35. Kluger, *Simple Justice*, 346–56. On the lasting significance of the "doll tests" see Gwen Bergner, "Black Children, White Preference: *Brown v. Board*, the Doll Tests, and the Politics of Self-Esteem," *American Quarterly* 61, no. 2 (June 2009): 299–332.

36. Excerpts of Clark's testimony appear in Hill and Greenberg, *Citizen's Guide to Desegregation*, 96–98; see also Kluger, *Simple Justice*, 346–56. For a detailed examination of Clark's testimony see Jackson, *Social Scientists for Social Justice*, 135–52.

37. Jack Greenberg to Fredric Wertham, September 17, 1951, and Louis L. Redding to Fredric Wertham, October 15, 1951, box 18, folder 12, Wertham Papers; Kluger, *Simple Justice*, 444; Fredric Wertham, "Psychological Effects of School Segregation," *American Journal of Psychotherapy* 6, no. 1 (January 1952): 95.

38. The best description of Wertham's clinical method comes from Lafargue physician-in-charge Hilde L. Mosse. See Mosse, "Individual and Collective Violence," *American Journal of Psychoanalysis in Groups* 2, no. 3 (1969): 23–30.

39. Dr. Elizabeth Davis Trussell, interview by author, tape recording, New York, January 6, 2006.

40. Rev. Shelton Hale Bishop's daughter Dr. Elizabeth B. Davis became the first director of Harlem Hospital's Department of Psychiatry in 1962, and Dr. June Jackson Christmas, who volunteered at Lafargue while an intern at Queens General Hospital, was appointed New York City commissioner of mental health in the mid-1970s; see *Reaching Out: An Epic of the People of St. Philip's Church* (Tappan, NY: Custombook, 1986), 54.

41. Albert Deutsch, "State Psychiatric Institute Here Bars Negro Patients and Doctors," *PM*, February 10, 1947, 24; "Report of Lafargue Clinic Statistics," March 6, 1956, box 1, folder 9, Lafargue Clinic Records.

42. Wertham, "Psychological Effects of School Segregation," 95; Fredric Wertham, "Nine Men Speak to You: Jim Crow in the North," *Nation*, June 12, 1954, 497–98; Mosse, "Individual and Collective Violence," 24–25.

43. Kluger, *Simple Justice*, 442–43.

44. Wertham, "Nine Men Speak to You," 497.

45. Dr. Walter Barton quoted in Gerald Grob, *From Asylum to Community: Mental Health Policy in Modern America* (Princeton, NJ: Princeton University Press, 1991), 196.

46. "Psychiatrist Tells Court School Segregation Harmful," *News from NAACP*, October 25, 1951, 5–6 (hereafter cited as "Psychiatrist Tells Court"), box 18, Wertham Papers.

47. Wertham, "Psychological Effects of School Segregation," 97; Fredric Wertham, "Psychiatric Observations on Abolition of School Segregation," *Journal of Educational Sociology* 26, no. 7 (March 1953): 334.

48. Greenberg, *Crusaders in the Courts*, 145; For Wertham's discussion of psychiatric testimony in criminal trials see his *The Show of Violence* (Garden City, NY: Doubleday, 1949).

49. Greenberg, *Crusaders in the Court*, 145–47.

50. "Psychiatrist Tells Court," 5–6; Kluger, *Simple Justice*, 440; Greenberg, *Crusaders in the Court*, 145–47.

51. "Psychiatrist Tells Court," 6; "Psychological Effects of School Segregation," 97–98.

52. See W. E. B. Du Bois's classic description of a quite similar process of conflict, repression, and overcompensation that appears in the first pages of "Of Our Spiritual Strivings," in his *The Souls of Black Folk* (Chicago: A. C. McClurg & Co., 1903).

53. "Psychiatrist Tells Court," 8–9. For more on Wertham's arguments about the role of the state in protecting and/or threatening the basic rights and security of its citizens see Friedman, *Citizenship in Cold War America*, 157–91.

54. Ibid., 9–10; Kluger, *Simple Justice*, 444.

55. Fredric Wertham, "Psychiatric Observations on the Abolition of Segregation," *Journal of Educational Sociology* 26 (1953): 334; here he was challenging the mainstream of intergroup relations theory as promulgated by such luminaries as John Dollard of Yale's Institute for Human Relations and Harvard social psychologist Dr. Jerome Bruner, who would follow Wertham on the witness stand the very next day. See "Segregation Held Equal-School Bar," *New York Times*, October 24, 1951, 36. See Daryl Michael Scott's chapter on *Brown v. Board* in *Contempt and Pity*, 119–36.

56. "Psychiatrist Tells Court," 14; Untitled Notes on Examination of Delaware Children, n.d., box 18, folder 12, Wertham Papers.

57. "Psychiatrist Tells Court," 17.

58. Kluger, *Simple Justice*, 445.

59. "Psychiatrist Tells Court," 18.

60. *Belton v. Gebhart* and *Bulah v. Gebhart*, 87 A.2d 862–71, Del. Ch. 1952; Irons, *Jim Crow's Children*, 114–17; Kluger, *Simple Justice*, 447–50; Collins J. Seitz, "Segregation: What Is Past Is Prologue," *Delaware History* 25, no. 4 (Fall–Winter 1991–92): 217–28.

61. Thurgood Marshall to Fredric Wertham, May 25, 1954, box 18, folder 12, Wertham Papers; *Belton v. Gebhart* and *Bulah v. Gebhart*, 87 A.2d, 864; Wertham, "Episodes," 104; see footnote 10 in the opinion of the Court in *Brown v. Board* in Leon Friedman, ed., *Argument: The Oral Argument before the Supreme Court in* Brown v. Board of Education of Topeka*, 1952–1955* (1969; New York: Free Press, 2004), 330.

62. Herman, *Romance of American Psychology*, 197–98; Waldo E. Martin Jr., *Brown v. Board of Education: A Brief History with Documents* (Boston: Bedford / St. Martin's Press, 1998), 173–74.

63. Kluger, *Simple Justice*, 706.

64. Paul L. Rosen, *The Supreme Court and Social Science* (Urbana: University of Illinois Press, 1972), 156–57.

65. I do not have the space to address it here, but during 1951 Wertham was clearly tainted by his participation in the epochally controversial Rosenberg case, testifying in behalf of Ethel Rosenberg, informing the court that she was experiencing a form of prison psychosis and should be allowed to see her two sons and possibly her husband, Julius. See Robert and Michael Meeropol, *We Are Your Sons: The Legacy of Ethel and Julius Rosenberg*, 2nd ed. (Urbana: University of Illinois Press, 1986).

66. Clark, *Prejudice and Your Child*, 172.

67. Jackson, *Social Scientists for Social Justice*, 162.

68. Wertham discussed the distinctive quality of the clinical method in a number of works, but the clearest digest of his argument is found in the essay "The Scientific Study of Mass Media Effects," *American Journal of Psychiatry* 119 (1962): 306–11. Justice Frankfurter's comments are found in Friedman, *Argument*, 172–73.

69. Greenberg, *Crusaders in the Court*, 137; "Psychiatrist Tells Court," 10–11.

70. Beaty, *Fredric Wertham*, 135–36.

71. Fredric Wertham to Jack Greenberg, March 31, 1974, quoted in James Reibman, "Ralph Ellison, Fredric Wertham, M.D., and the Lafargue Clinic: Civil Rights and Psychiatric Services in Harlem," *Oklahoma City University Law Review* (Fall 2001): 1050; Bayard Webster, "Fredric Wertham, 86, Dies; Foe of Violent TV and Comic," *New York Times*, December 1, 1981, D31; Letters to the Editor: "A Key Witness against School Segregation," *New York Times*, December 11, 1981, A34.

Epilogue

1. Ralph Ellison, "Harlem Is Nowhere" (1948), in *Shadow and Act* (New York: Vintage Books, 1953).

2. I am drawing here on philosopher Lewis R. Gordon's definition and discussion of *oppression* as the creation of a context in which extraordinary measures are required of individuals and/

or collectives in order to live an ordinary life; see *Existentia Africana: Understanding Africana Existential Thought* (New York: Routledge, 2000), 86–91.

3. Gerald Grob, *From Asylum to Community: Mental Health Policy in Modern America* (Princeton, NJ: Princeton University Press, 1991).

4. Frantz Fanon, *Black Skin, White Masks*, trans. Charles Lam Markmann (1952; New York: Grove Press, 1967), 11.

5. Wertham, "What Is Social Psychiatry?," lecture read at the Brooklyn State Hospital Psychiatric Forum on December 5, 1946, box 85, folder 8, Wertham Papers.

6. See most especially Cornel West's "A Genealogy of Modern Racism" in *Prophesy Deliverance: An Afro-American Revolutionary Christianity* (Westport, CT: Westminster Press, 1982).

7. Cedric Robinson, *Black Marxism: The Making of the Black Radical Tradition* (1983; Chapel Hill: University of North Carolina Press, 2000).

8. See my discussion of Fredric and Florence Hesketh Wertham's study *The Significance of the Constitution in Mental Disease* (Baltimore: Williams & Wilkins Co., 1926) in chapter 2. See also Dorothy Roberts, *Fatal Invention: How Science, Politics, and Big Business Re-create Race in the Twenty-First Century* (New York: New Press, 2012). The term "normal science" derives from Thomas Kuhn's *The Structure of Scientific Revolutions*, 3rd ed. (1962; Chicago: University of Chicago Press, 1996).

9. Jonathan M. Metzl, *The Protest Psychosis: How Schizophrenia Became a Black Disease* (Boston: Beacon Press, 2009), xi.

10. Department of Health and Human Services, U.S. Public Health Service, *Mental Health: Culture, Race, Ethnicity; A Supplement to Mental Health: A Report to the Surgeon General* (Washington, DC: Government Printing Office, 2004).

11. American Psychiatric Association, "Cultural Competencies for the Clinical Interaction," cited in Metzl, *Protest Psychosis*, 200; see also President's New Freedom Commission on Mental Health, "Policy Options Subcommittee on Cultural Competence," February 6, 2003, available at http://govinfo.library.unt.edu/mentalhealthcommission/subcommittee/ Sub_Chairs.htm.

12. See Susan Hegeman, *Patterns for America: Modernism and the Concept of Culture* (Princeton, NJ: Princeton University Press, 1999).

13. See also Metzl's conclusion to *The Protest Psychosis*, 199–212, and Jonathan M. Metzl and Helena Hansen, "Structural Competency: Theorizing a New Medical Engagement with Stigma and Inequality," *Social Science & Medicine* 103 (2014): 126–33.

14. Grob, *From Asylum to Community*, 171–73; "Memorandum Re: Contracts with the N.Y.C. Community Mental Health Board," September 16, 1955, box 1, Administrative Papers, Lafargue Clinic Records.

15. Dr. Hilde L. Mosse to Dr. Paul H. Hoch, August 20, 1955, box 1, Administrative Papers, Lafargue Clinic Records.

16. "Father Bishop Says NY Negroes Lack Real Adventuresome Spirit," *New York Amsterdam News*, June 8, 1957, 19; "St. Philip's Picks Rev. Moran Weston," *New York Amsterdam News*, May 11, 1957, 2; "St. Philip's Starts New Health Program," *New York Amsterdam News*, June 21, 1958, 23; Fredric Wertham to New York State Department of Mental Hygiene Statistical Services, December 14, 1958, box 52, file 15, Wertham Papers.

Index

Lightning Source UK Ltd.
Milton Keynes UK
UKHW010701130521
383296UK00013B/330